The Lionkeeper of Algiers

How an American Captive Rose to Power in Barbary and Saved His Homeland from War

Des Ekin

 Prometheus Books

Essex, Connecticut

 Prometheus Books

An imprint of Globe Pequot, the trade division of
The Rowman & Littlefield Publishing Group, Inc.
4501 Forbes Boulevard, Suite 200, Lanham, Maryland 20706
www.rowman.com

Distributed by NATIONAL BOOK NETWORK

British Library Cataloguing in Publication Information Available

Library of Congress Cataloging-in-Publication Data

Names: Ekin, Des, author.
Title: The lionkeeper of Algiers : how an American captive rose to power in Barbary and
    saved his homeland from war / Des Ekin.
Description: Lanham, MD : Prometheus, [2022] | Includes bibliographical references.
    | Summary: "This page-turning narrative follows the twists and turns of the life of
    hostage-turned-diplomat James Leander Cathcart upon the international stage of
    diplomacy, trade, and maritime statecraft at a time when America's place in the world
    was hanging in the balance"—Provided by publisher.
Identifiers: LCCN 2022025373 (print) | LCCN 2022025374 (ebook) | ISBN
    9781633888630 (cloth) | ISBN 9781633888647 (epub)
Subjects: LCSH: Cathcart, James L. (James Leander), 1767–1843. | Cathcart, James
    L. (James Leander), 1767–1843—Captivity. | Prisoners of war—Algeria—Algiers—
    Biography. | Diplomats—United States—Biography. | United States—History—
    Tripolitan War, 1801–1805. | United States—Foreign relations—Algeria. | Algeria—
    Foreign relations—United States. | Africa, North—History, Naval—18th century.
Classification: LCC E335 .E45 2022 (print) | LCC E335 (ebook) | DDC 973.47092—
    dc23/eng/20220531
LC record available at https://lccn.loc.gov/2022025373
LC ebook record available at https://lccn.loc.gov/2022025374

Contents

Part III

Part IV

Prologue

$\mathcal{A}$lmost twenty years ago while I was researching another book, I stumbled upon a true story that took my breath away. It goes something like this.

Just a few years after US independence, a young American is kidnapped at sea and carried as a prisoner to the maverick North African statelet of Algiers, where he is held as a political hostage. The corsairs of Algiers have just decided, without any warning, to exploit the vulnerability of the newborn United States by seizing its mariners and holding them for ransom while ruthlessly exploiting their free labor.

Put to work by his captors, the eighteen-year-old prisoner starts off as a lionkeeper, shoveling dung in the cages of the dey's private zoo. But thanks to his flair for languages and his formidable networking skills, he rises steadily up the ranks until he becomes chief clerk at the palace—the most powerful position an outsider can attain.

Although he remains a hostage and a captive, he buys his own merchant vessel and runs his own chain of bars where he becomes a version of Rick from *Casablanca*—cynical, just a bit shady, adept at working the system, forever one step ahead of the law, and always knowing the right people to schmooze and the right palms to grease.

However, beneath the veneer of tough cynicism lies a generous heart. Every day he secretly diverts food from his taverns to his fellow American hostages in a bid to ensure that they never go to bed hungry.

The United States begins peace negotiations and the captures cease. But nearly eleven years into his captivity, when the peace talks suddenly break down and the corsairs return to the offensive, this man must step up and face his destiny as a reluctant hero. He must make a desperate dash home to America through dangerous waters to warn President George Washington that hundreds more US merchant seamen are unwittingly sailing right into the jaws of a trap.

And so, on a fine May day in 1796, James Leander Cathcart stands on the quarterdeck of his own ship and sails out of the city where he has been held captive for more than a decade. He carries a vital letter that will alert his president to the looming crisis. And the most incredible thing is that, even at this stage, he is *still a prisoner of the dey*. Technically, he only has "left with dispatches"—been released on parole to conduct this vital mission to save the peace.

Even more remarkably, his sense of honor compels him to return to the scorpions' nest of Algiers—where he has never formally been freed—to see the peace project through and salvage the treaty.

At times, James Cathcart's dizzy rise from prisoner to palace power broker so closely mirrors the famous biblical tale of Joseph (in another part of North Africa), that it easily could be dismissed as fiction were it not for the supporting testimony of so many witnesses.

Cathcart went on to become a US diplomat and was praised by no less a figure than Thomas Jefferson as "the honestest and ablest consul we have with the Barbary powers: a man of very sound judgement, and fearless." A later president, John Quincy Adams, described his service to his nation as "long, faithful and important."

Today, the name James Leander Cathcart has been all but forgotten by history. And yet he was one of the most remarkable figures in the early story of the fledgling United States.

He was a fearless advocate for the principles expressed in the Declaration of Independence, passionately arguing before the skeptical ruler of Algiers that his nation's ideals were new and different: "In our country we have no religious test, nor enmity against those of your religion," he declared. "You may build mosques, hoist your flag on the tower, chant the symbol of your faith in public, without any person interrupting you. Muslims may enjoy places of honor or trust under the Government, or even become President of the United States."

These are stirring words that still speak to us today. Maybe more so than ever.

James Cathcart saw himself as a peacekeeper. In some ways he was centuries ahead of his time: for instance, he studied the Koran until he was able to out-argue many locals about its teachings (not such a good idea, as we see later). He never made the mistake of confusing Islam as a religion with the brutal Algiers hostage-taking system of which he was a victim.

This book has also been careful to avoid that error. Nowhere here will you find any negative references to Islam or to its adherents. Although in the

1500s and 1600s Algiers had prided itself as the cutting edge of the jihad or holy war, by this stage in the late 1700s religion had little to do with its human trafficking activities. The motive was purely financial. One wise American captive put this succinctly when he wrote home that focusing on religious differences would be a distraction—it was actually "money" that was "the god of Algiers."

While on the subject of disclaimers, it is vitally important to note that this book does not suggest any equivalence between the experiences of American political hostages in Algiers and the brutal treatment that was meted out in the United States to victims of the Africa-to-America chattel slave trade. The latter system was inconceivably worse by any measurement: in America, chattel slavery was lifelong, it was hereditary, and it was based solely on race. The widespread nineteenth-century view that the American experience of captivity in Algiers somehow mitigated, or even cancelled out, the evils of the transatlantic slave trade could not be more erroneous or offensive.

★   ★   ★

The more I studied it, the more I became fascinated with Cathcart's life story: born in Westmeath, Ireland; sent off to sea by his family at age ten; serving as a midshipman in the Revolutionary War in his early teens under the famous naval war hero Seth Harding; captured by the British and held in the notorious prison hulks off New York; freed and then captured again by the corsairs of Algiers off the coast of Portugal. He was, in fact, the first citizen of the free United States to be captured by the Algerines.

Cathcart worked as zookeeper, gardener, quarry worker, docker, carpenter, and coffee maker before being talent-spotted and appointed as a junior functionary in the Ministry of the Marine. He shot upward through the ranks, partly because of a supportive network of friends in the European diplomatic corps, but mostly because his incredibly robust immune system kept him alive during repeated outbreaks of a plague that killed nearly all the staffers around him. At one point he was literally the last man standing.

He did not have things easy. Along the way he was bastinadoed (systematically beaten with sticks on the soles of his feet) three times, so severely that his feet were disfigured. He lived under the constant threat of being beheaded or burned alive: several times he plunged into deep depressions.

But he had such a keen sense of justice that, even when he had saved enough money to bribe his way out of Algiers, he refused to pay his own ransom and leave because he knew that many of his countrymen would die of neglect without the life-saving supply of food from his taverns.

This book tells his story. But the surprises do not end with Cathcart.

At one stage in his captivity there were 119 American hostages in Algiers, all mariners captured at sea. Each had a different story.

For me, the most intriguing US captive was an African American named Scipio Jackson from New York, who had almost certainly been an enslaved person in America under the brutal and racist transatlantic chattel slave system. Somehow, Scipio had gained his freedom from his American masters. As a free man, he joined the merchant navy to serve as a mariner. But by an amazing stroke of ill fortune, he ended up in chains once again, this time in Africa.

Not only was Scipio Jackson forced by his captors to work until he dropped, but he also suffered racist attacks from his white fellow Americans. And he was not alone. There were other African Americans among the 119 US hostages, including a John Thomas from Massachusetts. This was not, as is sometimes supposed, a form of captivity that affected only white people. The rapacious corsairs of Algiers kidnapped people of all ethnicities—Caucasian, African American, central African, Asians—without discrimination.

In this book you also meet Captain Isaac Stephens, whose wife Hannah was plunged into destitution by the capture of her husband. We follow Hannah as she is evicted from her middle-class home in Concord, Massachusetts, and forced to take on menial labor while desperately trying to keep her family together. We join her as her protests prick the consciences of congressmen while she moves heaven and earth in a bid to bring her beloved Isaac back home again.

This is not a biography—James Cathcart's half-century of life after Algiers holds little interest for me and, I suspect, for the general reader. Neither is it an academic work. It is simply a rattling good story of human survival under pressure involving ordinary people who were suddenly uprooted from their normal lives and thrown into an exotic land and an alien culture where all bets were off, where all social applecarts were well and truly upset, and where the last in rank could literally become the first. That was what intrigued me most about this tale.

I had been researching this fascinating story on and off for nearly two decades but never got around to writing it: too many other things got in the way. The 2020–2021 coronavirus lockdowns robbed me of any further excuse to procrastinate, and when I finally started work, the story seemed to surge along under its own pent-up energy. I hope that you share my enthusiasm for these remarkable people and for this astonishing tale.

A Note about the Text

$\mathcal{T}$his is a work of nonfiction. Nothing has been made up or "novelized." Everything is attributable to an identified source—nearly always a direct witness—and listed in my source notes.

No dialogue has been invented. Any words in quotation marks are direct quotes, albeit sometimes edited for space reasons and to modernize spellings. Quotes used without quotation marks signify indirect speech: a faithful reflection of what was said but not necessarily using the original words. Both types of quotes are fully sourced and attributed. However, for clarity, I have edited some quotation marks into Cathcart's palace journal, which reported entire sections of back-and-forth dialogue without any punctuation or paragraphs in a way that readers might otherwise have found confusing.

A Note about the Text

I

• 1 •

The First Captive

The Algerine pirate ship hovered restlessly on the Atlantic horizon, silhouetted against the ocean skyline like some dark and evil bird of prey waiting for its moment to swoop.

James Cathcart, a stocky, bullnecked American seaman only just turned eighteen, was as intrigued as everyone else on board the US merchant ship *Maria*. The mystery vessel appeared to be in no hurry to approach, yet it shadowed their every move. The plodding *Maria*, sailing from Boston toward Cadiz with a cargo of furs, timber, and dried fish, was of no particular interest to anyone. The newborn United States of America had made peace with Britain after its bloody battle for independence and was trying to rebuild its international trade. It didn't even possess a national navy. So why was this sinister-looking vessel stalking the Boston ship so relentlessly?

The old hands aboard the *Maria* identified the ship as a xebec, a light, fast galley used in the Mediterranean. It was low and sleek, built for speed, and its long oars made it ideal for hunting other ships even in calm weather conditions. Most worryingly, it featured an ominously raised bow designed to allow its crew to leap aboard a target vessel at close quarters.

The *Maria*'s captain, thirty-five-year-old Isaac Stephens, had no choice but to maintain his steady course. The *Maria* was just a trudging merchant vessel, slow and cumbersome. Any attempt to outrun a xebec would be sure to end badly.

On the positive side, the *Maria* had almost reached the end of its voyage. They had been sailing for twenty-six days, and Stephens calculated that he was a mere three miles off the coast of Portugal's Cape St. Vincent, the most south-westerly point in continental Europe. Naval warships regularly scoured

3

these waters searching for pirates. Another hour, a fair wind, and he would be safe.

★   ★   ★

On board the xebec, the mood was optimistic. The Algerine pirates were experts at stalking and attack—it was, after all, what they did best—but they knew not to move in until they were sure of a smooth and bloodless operation. Hostile navies had been known to lure pirates into traps by posing as merchant ships and concealing armed troops below decks until the last minute.

However, by this stage, the pirates were sure that the *Maria* was exactly what it seemed to be: a rudimentary trading vessel with a captain, mate, and four crewmen sailing under the unfamiliar flag of the United States of America. They knew little about the United States—it was too new, too far away, and didn't share any of the ancient hatreds and toxic alliances that had locked the nations of Europe and North Africa into a seemingly endless death grapple for nearly three centuries. But they had been briefed about the new state. The Americans, they'd been assured, were "a set of beings without strength or resources" and "contemptible."

The corsair captain, later identified as Yusuf Rais, or Captain Joseph, was a grizzled veteran of this cold war of tit-for-tat hostage taking. In his time, he had been both captor and captive, seized and held at different times by the Spanish and the Genoans. His attitude toward the whole business was fatalistic: the path of your life was already "written on your forehead," as the Algerines believed, and the forces of destiny had already decided whether you would be predator or prey. If you were captured, then fate again would decide whether you would stay that way for life or be redeemed.

Yusuf prepared to move in. He had done this so often that it was almost routine. First you must observe your prey carefully: ensure there are no nasty surprises. Then get close enough to display your overwhelming manpower and firepower. Finally, demand surrender. In this case, his force of twenty-one men outnumbered the Americans by more than three to one. His xebec had fourteen big guns; the Americans would be lucky if they had a few rusted muskets. Any struggle would be pointlessly bloody, the outcome inevitable, and when it was all over, the Algerines would exact a cruel revenge on the survivors. Far simpler for everyone to accept their fate. It was destiny, after all.

★   ★   ★

The wind dropped and both ships were becalmed. It took a full two hours for the xebec to maneuver close to the *Maria*. The captain studied the Boston ship closely before making a final decision. It was "a good prize," he told his crew—fair game in international law.

The crew shouted their approval.

"A good prize!" they roared in unison, and that whoop of joy in an unknown language chilled the Americans to the bone.

The capture of the *Maria* was typical of the North African pirates' attack technique. No waste of firepower or energy, no risk to attackers or victims, simply a show of muscle followed by an almost anticlimactic transfer of power. "To escape was impossible," wrote another American seaman who was captured in similar circumstances. "Weapons of defence, we had none. We must therefore resign ourselves to the mercy of piratical sea-rovers."

★ ★ ★

At this stage, the crew of Cathcart's ship still did not know exactly what was happening. They knew they were being targeted by pirates, but pirates from which country? Of all the *Maria*'s crew, only the eighteen-year-old Cathcart had ever heard of the Barbary States, the ragtag collection of North African slaving nations that had held Europe in terror for hundreds of years.

There were four of these states, Cathcart explained as they waited, and their pirates were known as corsairs. From west to east along the North African coast, you had Morocco, Algiers, Tunis, and then Tripoli. The last three were part of the Turkish Ottoman Empire. Algiers was the most powerful, but its ships rarely ventured out into the Atlantic these days for fear of hostile Spanish naval patrols—and anyway, it was not at war with the United States. Cathcart's best guess, based on recent politics, was that these pirates were from independent Morocco. It was the closest, and it was the only one of the four states that had ports on the Atlantic coast. Besides, Morocco had previous form in targeting American shipping—nine months ago it had captured the US vessel *Betsey* as part of a diplomatic spat, although it later returned the ship intact and freed its crew. So perhaps this was simply a similar misunderstanding.

It was a reasonable assessment, but Cathcart was wrong. What the crew of the *Maria* were about to witness was a major shift in the gears of US history. The dreaded Algerine corsairs had suddenly reappeared in the Atlantic—and they had America very firmly in their sights.

★ ★ ★

At last, the pirates made their move. Most of them remained on the xebec while a few men rowed across in a small boat and brusquely boarded the *Maria*.

Show us your papers, they ordered Captain Stephens in Spanish.

Stephens spoke no Spanish. Cathcart, the only one who did, translated.

The pirates explained that they needed to see a Mediterranean passport—a sailing permit that the Algerines issued to those nations that paid them protection money. Since many corsairs were illiterate, a typical pass consisted of precisely spaced illustrations on parchment. Each Algerine crew had a special stick with notches that exactly matched the size and positions of the drawings. By laying the stick against the document, they could check its validity.

Prior to independence, all merchant ships from America had been covered by British passes. Not anymore. A subsequent plan to get protection from France had failed. These days, American mariners had no cover. They were dangerously exposed and forced to live by their wits.

Some captains forged Algerine passes, meticulously reproducing the spacing on the drawings. According to one writer of the era, this was not difficult even "for the most bungling artist . . . and, by this means, many vessels have been preserved." Others carried false flags and pretended to be English or (especially) Irish, since the similarity between the accents of New England and Ireland would fool most people.

However, Captain Stephens had not forged a passport. Stephens was essentially a straight shooter, an honest mariner without an ounce of guile or deviousness in his entire being. He always said exactly what he thought, a trait that sometimes got him into trouble. He was a career captain from a small village in Massachusetts and an unassuming family man who enjoyed reading magazines and American history in his spare time. He simply did not see why he should have to resort to forgery or denial of his nationality in order to do the job he loved. He had absolutely nothing to show his captors. The *Maria* was a "good prize," indeed.

The corsairs motioned the Americans to get into the boat.

Can we get our belongings from the cabin? they asked.

The pirates smiled at their innocence. Their new captives really had no idea of what lay ahead for them.

While some of the corsairs tore through the ship, enthusiastically rifling through its valuable cargo of fur, the others rowed the six Americans across to the xebec. James Cathcart was the first to board the attack ship and therefore made history as the first citizen of the independent United States to be captured as a hostage by the Algerines.

That step proved to be a major turning point in American history. In that instant, the US dream that it could trade freely in the Mediterranean, relying on nothing more than its infancy, innocence, and idealism, was decisively shattered. Within a decade there would be more than a hundred US hostages in Algiers, and the thirteen newly independent colonies would embark on a road that eventually led to their first foreign war—not in Europe, not in the Americas, but, unexpectedly, in faraway Africa.

★   ★   ★

Once on board, the Americans were forced to walk the length of the xebec's deck to its quarterdeck. On the way they had to run a gauntlet of pirates, who ritually pinched each captive's skin to claim a personal share in the prize.

"Every person had a pull at us as we went along, in order to benefit from our capture," Cathcart later recalled.

The Americans soon realized how naive they'd been in asking for their belongings. They stood helplessly as every item they possessed—right down to shoes, hats, and handkerchiefs—was taken from them. The scorching summer heat made the deck intolerably hot, and the Americans were forced to move from one foot to another in a humiliating dance as their bare feet cooked on the melting pitch. Meantime, their unprotected heads began to redden painfully under the relentless July sun.

One by one, they gave their names and positions.

"Isaac Stephens, captain."

"Alexander Forsyth, mate."

"James Cathcart, seaman."

"Thomas Billings, seaman."

"George Smith, seaman."

"James Harnet, seaman."

They were forced to wait in the heat until eventually the pirate captain, described by Cathcart as "a venerable old Arab," emerged and introduced himself.

Yusuf looked at them, took in their obvious distress, and sighed. "Christians," he intoned calmly, "be consoled! This world is full of vicissitudes [reversals of fortune]. You shall be well used, as I have been a slave myself, and I will treat you much better than I was treated."

He offered them hot drinks and food. "Take some bread and honey and a dish of coffee," he said, "and God will redeem you from captivity as he has done me twice."

★   ★   ★

Cathcart and his shipmates soon discovered that they were not the only victims. The busy Yusuf Rais had already captured a variety of Portuguese craft, ranging from fishing boats to "two pretty large vessels," and there were already thirty-six men and a woman aboard.

The Americans were ordered to join the Portuguese men in the sail storage area, a cramped and airless hold. The "horror" was indescribable, Cathcart later recalled: "Forty-two men shut up in a dark room in the hold, filthy in the extreme, destitute of every nourishment and nearly suffocated with heat."

Another American seaman later suffered the same experience: "We were obliged to creep in, hands and knees, and stow ourselves upon the sails." Sleep was impossible. "[There were] vermin such as lice, bugs and fleas . . . in such quantities that it seemed as if we were entirely covered." Besides, "our minds were filled with horror and dreadful apprehensions of the fate we might experience [in] Algiers."

At mealtimes, the captives were given coarse bread, overripe black olives, rancid oil, and filthy water. "We were literally obliged to strain it through our teeth and to stop our noses," Cathcart recalled.

Sometimes the diet was varied with bulgur wheat, which the Americans found impossible to swallow. However, a few of their captors smuggled them some fresh fruit and vegetables—onions, oranges, raisins, and figs—from their own personal supplies.

The *Maria*'s crew tried to make the best of their situation, but for five of them, the horrendous combination of captivity, confinement, and claustrophobia proved hard. For Cathcart, though, it was all strangely familiar.

Because he had been a prisoner before.

The Twelve-Year-Old Midshipman

*J*ames Leander Cathcart was born in County Westmeath, Ireland, on June 1, 1767. His family were prosperous landowners who'd come over from Scotland in the 1600s.

Little James, the second son of Malcolm Hamilton Cathcart and Elizabeth Humphreys, had been only eight years old when his father decided to send him to sea under the care of his uncle, Captain John Cathcart. James was a natural seaman and learned quickly. He ended up in America in 1775, just in time for the revolution, and after a spell as a cabin boy aboard a privateer ship, he was enlisted as a midshipman on the thirty-six-gun US frigate *The Confederacy* under the command of the famous adventurer and naval hero Captain Seth Harding. Aged only twelve, he was reportedly the youngest midshipman to serve during the war.

Harding, forty-four, from Massachusetts, had already built a reputation for capturing British ships along the American coast. A former privateer, he was commissioned as an officer in the US Continental navy, and during 1778 and 1779 he sailed around the American seaboard engaging British frigates and seizing three enemy prizes. His young midshipman must have witnessed some heated action.

Cathcart was by nature insatiably curious, swooping from deck to deck like a seagull hungrily seizing any morsel of education that was flung in his general direction. "He was taught sailing by a Portuguese helmsman from whom he learned his language," one family historian recalled. "From the Spanish navigator he learned celestial navigation, mathematics and a strong command of Spanish."

According to one account, James Cathcart was among the crew of his uncle's ship *Tyrannicide* ("tyrant killer") during the horrific naval debacle known as the Penobscot Expedition in 1779. The fourteen-gun sloop, which John Cathcart had just taken over as captain, was among a fleet of more than forty revolutionary ships that sailed into Penobscot Bay in Maine with the aim of taking over a British fort there. The British had been hopelessly out-numbered and were ready to surrender, but the attacking Americans dithered for nearly three weeks until they were trapped in the bay by a Royal Navy relief fleet. The desperate Americans burned and scuttled their ships at Bangor, Maine, and then footslogged across rough countryside to Boston. If young James were among them, he certainly would have endured hunger and hard-ship on that tough march.

And worse was to come. Two years later, according to his daughter and biographer J. B. Newkirk, James was back aboard Seth Harding's ship *The Confederacy* when it was captured. "[He was] taken prisoner by the British . . . and carried into New York," she wrote. According to Newkirk, her father had ended up on one of the notorious prison ships at Wallabout Bay.

At that time the British regarded the insurgent colonists as traitors rather than honorable military opponents and treated them with contempt. On the *Good Hope* and the other ships occupying the bay—most notably the infamous *Jersey*—hundreds of men were confined belowdecks without even the most basic washing facilities. In summer the heat was suffocating, and in winter the men either froze or tried to sleep as rain poured down on them through the deck timbers. One prisoner said he was "almost suffocated with the heat and stench." Another wrote: "The heat was so intense that [the 350 prisoners] were all naked. . . . Their sickly countenances and ghastly looks were truly horrible, some swearing and blaspheming, some crying, praying, and wring-ing their hands and stalking about like ghosts. . . . Boys were not missed till they had been dead ten days." Since water for cooking was taken from the same part of the river into which waste was emptied, it was not surprising that dysentery, smallpox, and fever were rampant and that the death toll continued to mount every day.

Yet James rose above it all. "[He] learned how to survive under horrible conditions, and acquired French from fellow prisoners," recorded another Cathcart descendant.

The British guards were cruel and cynical but also corruptible. "Attempts to escape from the prison ships were frequent and not uncommonly success-ful," writes naval historian Gardner Weld Allen. "By eluding the vigilance of these guards, or perhaps bribing a sentry, it was sometimes possible to get away from the ship in a boat or by swimming."

According to J. B. Newkirk, Cathcart was among those fugitives. "With a fellow prisoner," she writes, "he made his escape." Frustratingly, she gives no details of what must have been a dramatic getaway. As Gardner Weld Allen points out, the swim toward shore through the stinking water was only the first part of a long, difficult journey to freedom that involved fighting their way through the hostile, pro-British territory of Long Island.

However, another version of family history says that he was simply "liberated at the end of the war."

Either way, James emerged remarkably unscathed from a traumatized adolescence that would have emotionally scarred many a youngster for life. By 1785, three years after the end of hostilities and nearly two years after the Treaty of Paris recognized US independence, he stood dockside in Boston, signing on to the *Maria* and ready to go back to sea as a basic merchant-navy seaman.

In later years he often talked about his time as a US midshipman and his spell in the prison ships that ended when he obtained his freedom around 1782. What he never talked about, as we find out later in a surprise twist to the story, was what he actually did during those three years in between.

★   ★   ★

As the xebec continued to plough through the Atlantic swell, the atmosphere relaxed and the Algerines allowed their captives a greater degree of freedom. Cathcart and his shipmates were allowed to stay on deck unless the ship was under threat. Recapture by friendly European ships was always a tantalizing possibility, but despite some close encounters, the *Maria* crew was out of luck.

Although he was only a teenager, Cathcart spoke more languages than his countrymen, and he had a natural ability to make friends. Putting his formidable social skills to work, he soon found himself chatting amiably in Spanish to the ship's steward. He offered to help at the helm and was rewarded by a pipe of tobacco. Cathcart didn't smoke, but instinctively recognizing the camaraderie among smokers, he soon learned and used this to his advantage. (Years later in Algiers, when he was able to gather a small amount of money, he would seek out the same man and repay him for his kindness.)

Unexpectedly, Cathcart also found female company. The sole female hostage—Spanish by birth but captured aboard a Portuguese ship—proved to be cheerfully philosophical. She was naturally "facetious," he recalled, and "seemed perfectly reconciled to her situation, and endeavored to reconcile everyone to theirs." Yet this attitude seemed to rankle Cathcart rather than to comfort him. He had no intention of accepting his fate as a captive.

For Captain Isaac Stephens, the experience of captivity was especially bitter. He was the only man aboard the *Maria* who had left a wife and children at home, and as the Algerines continued to sail toward the rising sun, with every sea mile taking Stephens closer to a life of captivity, he must have wondered whether he would ever see his much-loved wife Hannah again.

* * *

Four weeks earlier, Isaac had said goodbye to Hannah and their three children when he left their family home in Concord, Massachusetts.

As a mariner's wife, Hannah was used to farewells. The couple had married in Braintree, just ten miles south of Boston, on a hot August day in 1770. Isaac was twenty. Hannah Hunt was slightly older. Isaac was a native of Braintree—best known at that early stage as the hometown of the lawyer and revolutionary activist John Adams, who later figures in this story. Hannah was from the nearby village of Hingham. Four years later they were blessed with their first child, a girl. Two other children followed, and as Isaac started to earn good money as a sea captain, they moved north to the pleasant riverside town of Concord, where they bought a house and a bit of land to grow their own crops.

In New England, sea captains were not only well paid, but highly respected. "The shipmaster's calling has always been of high repute in Massachusetts," wrote one observer. "Only the clergy, the magistracy, and the ship-owning merchants (most of whom were retired mariners) enjoyed a higher standing." In Concord, Captain and Mrs. Stephens would have ranked as upper middle class, on par with the local church minister and the schoolteacher. Hannah would have accompanied Isaac on the social rounds of Concord and occupied a prominent pew in the church on Sundays.

Isaac was not a conventionally educated man. He wrote the way he talked, mixing singulars and plurals in the old-style New England manner ("The people is . . .") and making basic misspellings ("hear" for "here"), but he was a formidable commander and well liked. Whether he was speaking or writing, he was honest and direct to a fault. His earnings were substantial: a ship's master would earn around $35 a month, one month in advance, which meant more than $100 for a typical voyage.

Isaac and Hannah still faced mortgage payments on their Concord home, but with this sort of wage they would have expected to be free and clear within a few more years. Both probably hoped that Isaac's career would follow the normal trajectory for sea captains; that is, retirement from sea in his forties followed by a lucrative second career as a well-connected maritime merchant. The Stephenses were not only happily married but genuinely devoted to one another, and life had been looking good for them.

Like most people during the postwar period, however, the couple had been hit hard financially by the conflict. "By misfortunes in the war," Isaac was to explain later, "I did not leave [my family] in so agreeable a situation to live without my help as I could wish them to do."

Isaac's absences were always a stressful time for Hannah. Besides the obvious dangers due to weather—the sudden storms, the freak waves, the abrupt drops in temperature that could leave entire crews frozen to death—there were many other hazards. A ship could be blown so far off course that its crew might starve while waiting for a fair wind. A fire at sea could kill the crewmen within minutes, or its stealthy fumes might slowly asphyxiate them. Disease might rip through the vessel after a stop in a foreign port. The crewmen might be seized by privateers or wrongfully press-ganged into the Royal Navy. And then there were the baffling cases of the ships that were simply "lost at sea" or spotted drifting, empty and crewless, with no explanation at all.

These possibilities must have haunted Hannah as she lay awake at night, her worst fears churning around and around her head in the early hours. She must have realized how many widows there were in ports like Boston (twelve hundred in the mid-1700s). In 1750, for instance, nearby Salem had no fewer than 205 widows among a female population of 1,710.

As she hugged Isaac goodbye, however, despite all her worries, she would never have imagined in her wildest dreams that her husband would end up as a hostage in North Africa—and that nearly a dozen years would pass before they could be reunited.

★   ★   ★

In contrast, the teenaged James Cathcart had no wife or mother in Boston to wave him farewell as he sailed from the quayside on June 24, 1785. But that is not to say that his last few days in the seaport had been lonely. Boston was a sociable sort of place, and he was a man who made friends easily. Taverns like the Crown, the Ship, and the King's Head were popular spots, and the city was famous for its coterie of merry widows who enjoyed socializing.

Cathcart would have had a bit of money in his pocket. As a basic seaman on a merchant ship, he would be paid around $10 a month, with a month's pay upfront. Yet to his fellow seamen, he must have been a bit of an enigma. Well educated, multilingual, and descended from a family of gentry, he must have stood out among the other seamen who, according to one historian, were "mainly from the lowest ranks of society, from the children of laborers, farmhands, [and] seamen themselves" or from those who could get no other work elsewhere. However, Cathcart was highly ambitious and already skilled in advanced navigation. Probably he saw his time aboard the *Maria* as just a prelude to a steady rise in fortune to the point at which, one day, he might command his own ship.

During his time in port, in a chance meeting that later proved to be serendipitous, Cathcart became friendly with two affable Italians. Giovanni de la Cruz and Angelo d'Andreis were both from the freeport of Leghorn, or modern-day Livorno. Angelo Bartholomew d'Andreis was a celebrated writer who was working as a supercargo—a commercial agent who sailed alongside a crew to oversee the safe delivery of goods. Angelo had everything to look forward to: in four months' time, he was due to marry Sarah Moody, the twenty-six-year-old daughter of a Massachusetts shipping magnate. Cathcart joshed the proud Leghornese that the match would make him 50 percent American, and it became a running joke between the two.

His fellow Italian, Giovanni de la Cruz, was a professional ship's officer currently working as chief mate aboard a large Leghornese ship. The three men had hit it off while they relaxed between stints of work at the busy international port. The merchant navy was a small world, and when they finally split up to go their separate ways, they probably suspected that they would meet again at some port or other. They would never have imagined that the port would be the pirate nest of Algiers and that when all three of them would meet again, it would be as captives in Africa.

· 3 ·

"The Crazy Capital"

A few days later the captives had their first view of the "well-guarded city" of Algiers—the nightmare destination for all captured Europeans and, now, Americans. Seafarers would look at the map and compare Algiers, with its curved coastline angled toward France and Spain, as a drawn bow with its arrow aimed at the heart of Europe.

Yet as the xebec drew close, James Cathcart found himself enchanted. "At the distance of two miles," he wrote later, "Algiers, with its marine fortifications, vessels in the mole and bay, its minarets and beautiful country seats, forms one of the most beautiful prospects in the world."

A contemporary writer agreed: "The town appears beautiful from a distance when approaching from the water," he said. "It stands on a bay of the Mediterranean. . . . The houses rise gradually from the seashore up the ascent of a mountain, in the form of an amphitheater. The mosques, castles and other public buildings have a striking effect."

To another American captive, it was surreal to see the blinding whiteness of Algiers emerge from the heat haze like a northern snowscape: "At a great distance, it appears like a snow bank," he wrote, "which is occasioned by all the houses being whitewashed." It was so steep that "when you are at sea, you may see almost every house in it."

A traveler who sailed into Algiers a few decades later compared it to a giant creation of white marble, "contrasting beautifully with the dark masses of the surrounding country. . . . The monotony of the Moorish houses, flat roofed and glaring with whitewash, is somewhat broken by . . . the domes and towers of the mosques, and by the graceful forms of the cypress and palm."

However, on closer approach, its fortifications and its cannon revealed a darker picture—one of a belligerent city, permanently crouched, ready to

15

attack, and constantly bracing itself for defense. "The mole, stretching from the shore in the shape of a T, and dense with cannon, forms with its southern arm a secure harbor, still further defended by the triple tiers of the batteries of the mainland," wrote the same traveler. "From the shore the buildings rise terrace above terrace to the summit of the city, where the Kasbah, the ancient palace and citadel of the Deys, forms the apex of the triangle."

Another fortress, the Fort of the Emperor, commanded a ridge to the south. "The hills, gently sloping to the sea, are studded with country houses and gardens; and in the extreme distance are seen the lofty range of the lesser Atlas, whose highest summits [are] still capped with snow."

A few years later, a visiting American diplomat found himself wondering, like many others, how such an enchanting place could cause so much human suffering. "With the exception of the climate, the fruit, and the natural beauty of the vicinity . . . it is the most detestable place one can imagine."

For all returning corsair ships, there was a ritual to observe. On approach, the vessel traditionally fired its guns to alert the captain of the port. They would fly the national flags of their captives (in this case, the United States and Portugal) upside down, and the number of gunshots revealed how successful they'd been. "Demonstrations of joy ensue according to the number of [captures] they have made and the value of the prizes," Cathcart later explained. "When they are unfortunate, no guns are fired, no shouts of joy are heard, everyone seems dejected, and the captains are frequently degraded and even bastinadoed [beaten with staves], imprisoned or dismissed."

In this case, the xebec had performed relatively well for its size, with the twenty-one corsairs returning with two captives apiece. The gunshot would have been enthusiastic and greeted with proportionate shouts of delight from shore. The ululating shrieks of the city's womenfolk provided an eerie soundtrack to their final approach to this strange and alien city.

Since this was the moment when terrified captives often panicked and made a last-minute break for freedom, the corsairs took no chances. They anchored their returning ships far out in the roads and then lay their prisoners facedown in open boats before ferrying them in.

On this last leg of the journey, they passed a series of giant cannons, defense forts, and static gunships, while all the time two patrol boats, each carrying twenty-one harbor police, kept them under continual observation. This was their welcome to Algiers.

It wasn't called "the well-guarded city" for nothing.

★ ★ ★

There were two types of pirate ships—the huge state-owned ships whose captives belonged to the Regency of Algiers and the ships that were owned by licensed entrepreneurs and syndicates. On state-owned ships, captives were sent directly to the dey's palace. But these forty-two prisoners had been captured by a freelance captain and were thus private property—although the dey always had first option on them.

Once ashore, the sole female captive was separated from the menfolk and led off toward a hospital run by Spanish monks, where she would remain until her appearance before the dey a few days later. Meanwhile, Cathcart and his five crewmates were stripped of their shipboard clothes and provided with secondhand gear—in his case, a dirty old shirt, brown trousers, and a brimless hat, all "swarming with vermin."

After being inspected by the ship's owner, they walked unsteadily toward the Admiralty office at the marine. Parched in the summer heat, they were grateful to find a marble fountain flowing with plentiful fresh water "clear as crystal." In comparison to the gritty water on board ship, this water seemed like nectar, and they drank their fill. This basic experience was so blissful that it left a lifelong impression on the young man. "I shall remember the Fountain of the Kiosk of the Marine of Algiers to the latest hour of my existence."

Following inspection by the city's leading businessmen who had invested in the voyage, they were shepherded back to a private house, their owner's home. They hadn't eaten for more than a day, and they were starving. But because it was Ramadan, the period of fasting, they were told that no one could bring them food until nightfall. However, a group of Europeans heard of their plight, took a risk, and sneaked them some bread and fruit.

That night, after being served camel meat and bulgur, the new captives stretched themselves out on the bare bricks of a ground-floor room and endured a sleepless night "tormented by vermin and mosquitoes."

The following day, they were taken back to the dock to unload their ship. For security reasons, after each trip, ships would be almost completely disassembled, right down to their ballast of sand and rocks, which was painstakingly shoveled out and stored in heaps until the next cruise demanded the same task done in reverse. It was a backbreaking, Sisyphean job that could be feasible only in a port that ran on the unpaid labor of hostages. Finally, even the rudders were removed and the empty shells of vessels tightly moored stem to stern in the inner harbor.

On their second full day in Algiers, the captives were lined up for the traditional parade around the city in which cheering citizens had a chance to view the new arrivals. This procession was billed as an extra-special event—the first to feature exotic creatures from the New World of the Americas. As they turned each corner, Cathcart and his shipmates saw the faces of the citizens light up with expectation, only to dull with disappointment as they discovered that the newcomers were not Native Americans dressed in buckskin and eagle feathers.

They look just like Englishmen, the residents complained.

Newly arrived captives were always overwhelmed by the noise, smells, and sheer baffling impenetrability of the city that one US diplomat, Joel Barlow, would later describe as "the crazy capital." To describe Algiers as a labyrinth would be inaccurate, since labyrinths are designed to be confusing. Algiers was just madly chaotic. "Properly speaking, there are no streets, but little dark alleys which run crosswise and zig-zag among an enormous heap of houses, thrown together without order and without number," Barlow reported. "It needs a long residence before being able to walk a hundred steps without losing oneself."

The winding steps and alleyways—some so narrow that two people could not pass each other comfortably—were usually choked with a tide of humans and animals. Many residents avoided the chaos by hopping like starlings from rooftop to rooftop via connecting arches. "The roofs are flat," one American writer observed in the 1790s, "so that people can visit each other, at a considerable distance, without going into the streets."

Among the braying donkeys, the water sellers, and the shouting traders carrying cages of chickens and rabbits, the prisoners would have had seen a bleak preview of their own future, with the sight of grim-faced, sweating European captives toting massive barrels of wine and sugar suspended from poles on their shoulders.

Having seriously disappointed their audience, the captives were marched to the house of the British consul, Charles Logie, who had agreed to put them up for two nights. After that, they would be offered to wealthy private citizens who would pay to take advantage of their unpaid labor until such times—if ever—that their ransom was paid in full by their family, their friends, or their country. If that never happened, they would remain their unpaid servants, perhaps for life.

If the captives expected to find an ally in the consul, they were soon disabused. Logie delighted in gloating at their plight: "We were made sensible of our situation," Cathcart wrote despondently, "and exposed to a new series of indignities which we did not expect." The consul had a bad reputation. Another Englishman in Algiers at that time dismissed him as "a drunkard," and one modern historian has described him as a man "of such unsavoury reputation that none of the other consuls would associate with him."

★ ★ ★

It was only later that the captives learned that Logie had been partly to blame for their capture. When he had arrived in April that year, he had met the dey of Algiers, Baba Mahmood ben-Osman Pasha, and had informed him that Britain no longer controlled the thirteen North American colonies. But he had gone much further than that. He had explained that American ships would make easy pickings for the corsairs, since the country had no navy and no protection. They would be "good prizes." Abandoning any pretense of neutrality or even human decency, Logie had "wished them success in their attempts to capture those who had refused allegiance to his Master [King George III]."

Many Americans of the era believed that it was British policy to weaponize the Algiers corsairs "as the African emissaries of England" against the United States. Or as one writer put it, "to turn loose the Algerines, that these execrable ruffians might plunder our property" and capture as many American citizens as possible. This was not a far-fetched notion. Two years earlier, an English peer named Lord Sheffield had said it was very much in Britain's interests to take advantage of America's vulnerability: "The Americans cannot protect themselves from the Barbary States," he crowed. "They cannot pretend to a navy."

Logie must have known that his action would condemn countless American seamen to a life of horrendous suffering. It speaks volumes about the toxic state of British-US relations—not to mention Logie's personal character—that he knew exactly what he was doing and did it anyway.

And so, as a direct result of that conversation, the dey unleashed his sea hounds with orders to identify and capture as many Americans as possible. What he may not have realized was that he was starting a cold war that would rumble on for decades.

★   ★   ★

The next stage in the captives' purgatorial journey was the notorious Badistan market. The Badistan was an open square in the heart of town, part of the main thoroughfare of Grand Market Street that slashed across the city. Here, captives were forced to stand for hours without shade, food, or water from dawn until midafternoon while they were inspected by potential buyers.

"[It] is a square built of stones with seats around it," wrote a captive from an earlier era. "The ground was paved with stones which appeared shiny [because] each day they were washed. . . . [We] were brought to the marketplace in two groups. . . . [They] guarded each group in front and behind, and counted us at every corner because the inhabitants will steal such captives given the opportunity."

In this stifling cauldron of commerce, men were treated exactly like livestock: buyers' hands would be forced into their mouths to check their teeth, and they would be made to run around the square to evaluate their fitness and stamina. Then the questioning began. Did they have any special skills? Did they have wealthy families back home? Would their friends ransom them for a fortune or abandon them to their fate?

Eventually, after many hours, the auction began. "The crier proclaims their rank, profession and circumstances, and the price set upon each of them," one contemporary American writer explained. Another witness wrote that the bidding took place "with the people sitting in a circle, and the auctioneer moving about in the centre . . . announcing how much has been bid last."

Cathcart's own experience was humiliating: "We remained from daylight till half past three without any refreshments, and we were treated thus for three days successively."

By the end of it all, only five of the older Portuguese men had been purchased, probably at bargain prices because they were unfit for heavy manual work. It was pointless bidding for the prime captives at that point, since the ruler of Algiers had first choice. Buyers then would get a second chance to buy the ones he rejected.

The hostages were rounded up and moved on. The next step of their long journey into purgatory was the palace of the dey.

· 4 ·

Cast into the Den of Lions

The palace of Dey Baba Mahmood ben-Osman Pasha sat on an acre of gardens in the very center of Algiers. Over the centuries, each of the various rulers of the regency had added new buildings, extensions, terraces, and connecting galleries to create a jumble of edifices of different styles, according to fashion or whim.

Hundreds of cats, pampered and allowed to breed freely, sashayed haughtily through the arcades and preened themselves on top of the marble walls. They were quite literally set among the pigeons—a legacy from an earlier dey—which were equally uncontrolled in numbers as they clattered noisily back and forth from an ornate pigeon loft. In the background, the cats' bigger cousins, the lions, roared and grumbled from their cages in the private zoo.

The Americans, herded through the ornate gate, glanced hungrily at the enormous bunches of grapes that covered every vertical surface of the entrance square. They would not find out until later why these particular grapes remained forever untouched by locals. This dismal square was the center of punishment and execution for foreign hostages who had somehow offended the dey. The roots of these vines were fertilized by the blood of decapitated and amputated captives. There were times when the ground was covered by heaps of heads and ears, until the dey eventually tired of the stench and ordered them to be removed.

Beheading of locals was carried out in private, but decapitations of captives were always public events. Joel Barlow, the US envoy, later recorded matter-of-factly that a Spanish captive "was beheaded before the palace of the Dey for having killed two of his companions in prison."

Another witness described the beheading process: "The criminal is made to kneel down. [One executioner] then touches him on the back part of the head, and as he turns around to see what was the cause, the other with a sharp sword, at the same instant, severs his head from his shoulders. After the execution, the blood is washed through the ground."

If Cathcart shivered as he walked through the square, it may have been a premonition. Several times during his eleven-year captivity in Algiers he would come terrifyingly close to suffering the same brutal form of execution.

Once through the gate, the Americans found themselves in an open reception area where prominent officials circulated and talked business. In the center, a marble fountain gurgled and gushed. They were herded to the left into a courtyard paved with cool marble slabs. At the far end was a raised dais with an arch under which the dey would sit.

"It was composed of pillows covered with embroidered velvet," Cathcart wrote, "placed on a niche on which was a kind of bed composed of sheep skins, with a fine red blanket and a carpet, and in summer an upper covering of silk which served him both to sit and take a nap upon when he pleased."

The captives waited and waited until, at length, a man in his late seventies appeared from a narrow and darkened stairway. Cathcart wondered why the country's most powerful man should choose this route instead of making a grand entrance down one of the magnificent marble stairways. The truth was that all deys lived in perpetual terror of uprisings and assassinations. If the palace were to be stormed by revolutionaries, "few people could get up [the stairway] at a time, and the Dey would be able to defend himself for longer."

As Dey Mahmood seated himself on his silken throne, he must have felt reasonably free from such concerns. By the usual standards of the Barbary States, his tenure on the throne was a model of boring stability. Like most rulers of that era, Mahmood was Turkish by birth. As a child in Anatolia, he had been conscripted into the elite fighting unit known as the Janissary militia. He had been trained in the arts of war and later posted to Algiers, where he eventually rose through the ranks to this pinnacle of power. At this stage, Mahmood was almost two decades into a reign that would last a quarter century, which was already recognized as a golden age of wealth and prosperity for the city.

Historically, Algiers had been ruled by governors who were first known as "pashas"—an honorary title similar to a British peerage—and later as "deys" (a Turkish term for "uncle") as the Regency began to achieve greater autonomy. A hundred years ago, the statelet had been at constant risk of attack from its ancient enemies Spain and France, not to mention the burgeoning naval power that was Britain. Algiers captured their citizens by sea and land and ransomed them until one or more of these nations finally capitulated and paid for peace. The problem was that deys never reigned for long, so each new ruler simply ripped up his predecessor's treaty and went back on the attack. Mahmood's long reign had offered a rare stability. This meant that Algiers had become more of a traditional tributary state that would offer European nations long-term immunity from attack in exchange for yearly payments of protection money. Spain, France, and Britain had all agreed to this arrangement, which had also enabled Algiers to build up its trade in a normal way. However, the system would rapidly collapse if warlike Algiers did not continue to take hostages from *some* nation to show it still had teeth: now it was America's turn to suffer.

The double influx of wealth from tributes and trade had made the pirate state rich beyond the wildest dreams of the original predatory Barbary corsairs: according to one estimate, Algiers had $15 million in gold reserves alone; its total reserves were worth up to $54 million.

The treasury, guarded by fearsome Janissary troops, held so much coin that it was divided into wooden bins, "one for gold, another for silver, foreign and native coin: when money was to be paid in, the amount was thrown in uncounted into the appropriate bin." The speed and carelessness of the exercise was revealed by the marks left on the plaster walls by coins hurled in the general direction of the bins.

The treasury door could be opened only by a team of three officials, each with a separate key. This system had been introduced just a few years prior, after a captive who'd worked as palace cleaner had obtained the sole key, duplicated it, and smuggled out golden coins hidden under the rubbish in the panniers of his mule. One day, however, he became too greedy: "The great weight of the gold burst through the bottom of the baskets, and the money fell down upon the marble pavement with such a noise that it resounded through the palace," went one account, "[while he] stood petrified with astonishment." The man lost his head, and from that point on, the treasury was as well guarded as the city itself.

★ ★ ★

Dey Mahmood cast his eye contemptuously over his sorry band of Portuguese and American captives. He had been mildly interested in the Americans until he'd found out that they looked as boringly normal as his previous victims. His interest piqued, however, when the guards brought out the Spanish woman who'd been their companion aboard the xebec. "She was purchased by the Regency," Cathcart reported, meaning that the woman now belonged to the state of Algiers—effectively, she was the property of the dey himself.

If Cathcart ever found out what happened to his cheerfully optimistic female shipmate, he never recorded it. The most likely outcome was that she was taken directly to the palace harem, a square of apartments and arcades built around a private garden and hidden from the world. "Although scarcely larger than a room, and surrounded by lofty walls, [the garden] was the only place where the inmates [of the harem] were permitted to breathe the fresh air of heaven," one later visitor wrote. "Visits to the baths and to the graves of relatives, allowed to other women, [were] denied them."

What did happen to her in the end? It's possible that she was liberated under a later peace deal, but it was notoriously difficult for a harem odalisque to return home and merge back into society during that era. Interestingly, the dey who succeeded Mahmood six years later would break with centuries of tradition by refusing to keep concubines. Did this chirpy survivor manage to last that long? If so, was she kept on as a servant at the palace? Or was she gifted to some grandee as a wife or concubine? We will never know.

As the dey turned his attention to the men, the *Maria*'s captain, Isaac Stephens, was also asked to step aside from the ranks of captives. The Algerines were acutely aware of nuances of rank. Captains, although still unfree, were entitled to a privileged status. They were known in the Spanish-Italian creole language of Algiers as *Paga Lunas*—"moon payers" who paid a special fee at each new lunar cycle. Provided Stephens could find someone to sponsor him for this monthly payment, he would be spared the worst hardships of the work gangs and the notorious prisons. He would be a captive and a hostage but not a prisoner.

The English consul, Charles Logie, volunteered to sponsor Stephens and requested that Stephens be sent to his private house to work as a domestic servant. No doubt the symbolism appealed to Logie: an American who had struggled for freedom from Britain was now reduced once more to serving the British in the even more demeaning position of a household dogsbody. And in view of Logie's key role in organizing the capture of the Americans, it was a request that the dey could hardly refuse.

The ruler then decided to take all five of the remaining Americans and eight of the thirty remaining Portuguese as palace servants. The others were dispatched to the state bagnio, or special prison, for hard labor at the docks.

He chose the two most presentable Americans for his personal apartments. A young man named George Smith was chosen as his page, and a second seaman, probably Thomas Billings, was made a cook. The first mate, Alexander Forsyth, later joined Captain Stephens as a *Paga Luna*. That left only Cathcart and another crewman, James Harnet, who were sent to work in the palace gardens.

By this stage the prisoners would have made a sorry sight: their hair matted, their faces and bodies black with dirt, their borrowed clothes crawling with lice. "We were taken to the hot bath," Cathcart recalled, "and cleansed from the filth of the cruiser. Our old rags were changed for a large pair of cotton trousers, a pair of shoes, and a red cap, all made in Turkish fashion."

Afterward, they were taken in a group to the workers' quarters, where they enjoyed their first good night's sleep since their capture. In the morning, "much refreshed," they were sent to their duties.

Cathcart was just one of sixty-eight prisoners who'd been put to work at the palace. Their roles varied dramatically. Some, like Smith, wore uniforms adorned with gold braid and acted as personal attendants to the dey. Others were janitors who cleaned up after the soldiers who guarded the treasury. Still others were cooks and kitchen staff. But there were also slaughterhouse workers, smithy workers, and manure shovelers. "Besides the Dey's horses [there are] mules and asses for labor, which creates a great deal of dirt." There was actually a palace official, a "head scavenger," who managed manure removal. Since he could sell it for profit, the position was much coveted.

Cathcart and Harnet joined a squad of twelve other gardeners aged ten years old to sixty. Working under a head gardener—a captive from Malta—their job was to tidy the enclosed palace garden, prune the vines, and look after the animals in the dey's private zoo.

The zoo held two antelopes, two tigers, and two feisty young lions. Cathcart was put in charge of the lions, a daunting responsibility for a teenager. His job involved feeding them chunks of beef and mutton from the palace abattoir, making sure they were well supplied with water, and gingerly shepherding them into their holding cages before cleaning their enclosures. The cage walls had to be regularly inspected and strengthened, since the animals regularly tried to shimmy over, dig their way under, or slam their way through the perimeter.

Since the entire palace grounds occupied only an acre, we can assume conditions were cramped and that the lions didn't enjoy the spacious fifty to seventy square yards that is recommended for a pair of big cats in today's zoos. This lack of space, combined with a lack of stimulation, probably resulted in the lions exhibiting the classic symptoms of stress—neurotic pacing back and forth, repetitive actions, and tail chewing—which would have made them more prone to attack a keeper. Cathcart could have been excused a certain nervousness as the three-hundred-plus-pound predators grumbled and growled at him through their bars. Yet these lions were enjoying better conditions than they would later in life. When they grew too big for comfort, they would be shifted to more secure lodgings—crammed into dark internal cells in one of the hostage prisons.

During the daylight hours, when his nocturnal charges were sleeping or dozing, Cathcart also helped out with general gardening tasks. The gardens, which were quite small, were located in the middle of the palace complex. Grapes grew abundantly over the walls that surrounded the groves of lemons, oranges, and pomegranates.

On almost every surface, housecats dozed and stretched in the sun. There were dozens, all supposedly descended from a single breeding pair. It was considered bad luck to interfere with them. The gardeners also had to be careful to avoid tripping over the pigeons that constantly infested the area, pecking seeds from the ground and flying upward in a petulant clatter of wings when disturbed.

At first, the rules governing their lives seemed simple: no alcohol, no smoking (Dey Mahmood hated tobacco), and no eating the produce. "I have known several of my brother sufferers bastinadoed for eating an orange or a small bunch of grapes," Cathcart recalled.

Perpetually hungry, they could only watch enviously as the lions and tigers devoured their haunches of meat. Between the fourteen of them, they had to subsist on bulgur, meat, bread, and yogurt—enough in total, they calculated, to feed no more than four people. They sometimes secretly made a salad from vine leaves, which were not specifically banned, and occasionally the kitchen staff might take a huge risk and smuggle them leftovers.

From time to time, their lust for meat made them look up with starving eyes at the rickety—and very high—pigeon loft. "Not infrequently," Cathcart recalled, "we committed depredations on the Dey's pigeon house, at the risk of breaking our necks, [not to mention] a severe bastinadoing if detected." No doubt the gamy pigeon meat tasted like sweet revenge for the extra path-cleaning work that the birds produced for the gardeners every day.

Compared to the rigors of life at sea, the work was undemanding. "In the palace garden . . . we had not a great deal to do," Cathcart recalled. "The taking care of the [animals] excepted, the work might very well have been done by four." However, this was not at all typical of the life of a captive in Algiers, as Cathcart himself was to find out all too soon. Looking back on it, he would regard his time in the garden as a gentle introduction to life as a hostage: "Alas, I had seen the best part only. I had as yet experienced but few of the bitters." Had he actually known what lay ahead for him, "I should have sunk beneath the weight of such accumulated woe."

Although the work itself was tolerable, the psychological torture was nerve-racking. The captives were under the direct control of the palace chamberlains, led by the Chief Chamberlain Sidi Ali. ("Sidi" was a simple term of respect.) These officials enjoyed psyching out the powerless workers, changing the rules from day to day, lashing out at random, and inflicting beatings on a whim. This was part of the general palace culture, reflecting the behavior of the dey himself.

Mahmood believed in keeping people constantly on their toes and forcing them to guess his mood. The most innocuous phrase could either make the dey laugh with pleasure or result in a savage beating. It was pure capriciousness on the ruler's part, and there was never any appeal.

For instance, one ransomed captive from Genoa paid a terrible price for both misjudging the dey's mood and assuming that he had a sense of justice. The man had been diligent and dutiful during his ten years as a palace worker. After his ransom was paid, he made a courtesy call to the palace to bid farewell to the ruler. Bowing to kiss the dey's hand, he smiled and said: "Thank God, I have been your servant ten years and never received the bastinado once."

"Did you not?" the dey asked sweetly. Turning to his guards, he said: "Give him one hundred blows to the soles of his feet, that he may not have so great a miracle to tell his countrymen when he returns home."

Stunned, the man correctly pointed out that he was now a free man. Besides, the penalty defied logic. "Surely your Excellency will not punish me for not having committed a fault?" he appealed.

"Give him two hundred blows," the dey shot back, adding that if he said another word in protest, his freedom would be revoked. "I will keep him till he dies for his insolence."

The beating was administered in full.

This culture of fear and constant unpredictability filtered down through the palace hierarchy. The captives could not keep to the rules, because the rules kept changing from moment to moment. Cathcart said that the psychological pressures "make a person of any sensibility even more miserable than he would be at hard labor."

One evening Cathcart heard yells of pain coming from the garden. Thinking one of his workmates had suffered an accident, he ran to the scene to find a Portuguese colleague being beaten on the soles of his feet by two chamberlains, each wielding a stick.

Cathcart asked what had happened. "I was seized by four stout Moors who threw me down, pinioned my legs and arms, and the same game was played on the soles of my feet to the tune of twenty-eight hard blows, which produced the most excruciating pain and left me with four toenails less."

The chamberlains administered the same beating to all fourteen garden workers, including sixty-year-old men and a child aged ten. It turned out that some fruit had gone missing. Unable to identify the culprit, the chancellors had decided to punish everyone.

Cathcart suffered similar beatings by bastinado on two other occasions during his time in the palace garden: once when he was caught writing his journal and once when he spoke to a palace worker without permission. A Garden of Eden, this place was not.

His shipmate James Harnet, who may have had an intellectual disability, could not cope with the psychological pressure and began to suffer traumatic stress. "[He was] so much terrified that it had a sensible effect on his mind," Cathcart recalled, "and I am sure it was the first step that caused him to lose his reason."

The two most sadistic chamberlains, Sidi Ali and Sidi Mohamed, were not Algerines but converts from Greece. Cathcart theorized that they felt they had to administer an extra degree of cruelty in order to convince their superiors that they were not halfhearted in their religious commitment. The zeal of the convert, indeed.

Cathcart coped by falling back on his well-practiced survival strategy: he learned new skills. In his spare time, he worked on his language fluency and brushed up on his navigation to the point where he could instruct his fellow captives. Perpetually curious, he studied Arabic and Turkish and began to read the Koran—not because he had any intention of converting, but simply because he wished to understand this unfamiliar religion and draw upon its wisdom. This was definitely not what his captors had expected. They dubbed him "the False Priest."

Chamberlain Sidi Mohamed became convinced that Cathcart was an alchemist who knew how to turn base metals into gold and tried to cajole him into revealing the secret. To his credit, Cathcart rejected this golden opportunity to play along and turn the situation to his own advantage. But denying his alchemical skills only made things worse, and the two chamberlains became Cathcart's "most inveterate enemies." They took petty revenge by confiscating his books and ordering him never to read or write again.

Deprived of his only solace, the young seaman lapsed into a debilitating depression. He gives no details in his journal other than to say: "I became a victim to melancholy reflections. My spirits were so much depressed that I fainted several times in a day." At times he found it physically impossible to move.

The chamberlains accused him of faking sickness, but fortunately for him a Spanish surgeon intervened and convinced them that the American was genuinely ill. "He rendered me assistance, and with the help of a good constitution, I soon recovered."

Meanwhile, the other Americans were having their own problems inside the palace. They were "often bastinadoed for mere trifles, such as speaking loud, procrastinating . . . and a thousand other pretenses," Cathcart wrote.

Throughout it all, the Americans remained hopeful. After all, they reasoned, there were only six of them. The $50,000 or so that it would cost to ransom them would hardly break the national treasury. "Being confident that our country would immediately redeem us," Cathcart wrote, "I resolved to bear my captivity with as good a grace as possible."

And then, overnight, their numbers doubled and their problems did, too.

• 5 •

"Our Sufferings Is beyond Your Conception"

JULY 30, 1785, FIVE DAYS AFTER THE CAPTURE OF THE *MARIA*

*C*aptain Richard O'Brien, a tall, rangy seafarer in his late twenties, took one glance at the corsair ship and knew right away that his days as a free man were over. Bearing down on them was an Algerian State galley bristling with thirty-four guns and a crew of 450 soldiers and marines.

O'Brien's ship, the *Dauphin* of Philadelphia, was on its way home from Portugal with a full cargo. It had embarked two days earlier from St. Ubes (modern day Setúbal, just south of Lisbon) and had sailed about 240 miles to the northwest when the pirates closed in.

No doubt he would have turned to his first mate, Andrew Montgomery, and cursed his luck with some appropriate seafaring metaphor: they were up a creek without a paddle, perhaps, or caught in a hard gale with no rudder or sails. O'Brien always peppered his sentences with maritime imagery, even when he was dealing with everyday problems on dry land. Trouble of any sort was "a squall ahead." Serious trouble was "a hard gale with bare poles." A proposal could be either "hove to" or "hove away."

Although he was only twenty-seven, O'Brien loved to play the role of the crusty old sea dog, and his accent—somewhere between Nantucket and Irish—gave him the appropriate broad vowels. "I am without a compass," he would growl when anything confused him, "and forced to sail by the North Star."

More than one acquaintance joked that O'Brien was a duplicate of the reprobate seafarer Commodore Trunnion, a comic creation of the then-popular author Tobias Smollett. He didn't have Trunnion's eyepatch and wooden leg, but otherwise he looked and behaved the same. Whether the imitation was conscious or coincidental, O'Brien thoroughly enjoyed

29

hamming it up. In our own era we might think of Long John Silver or of Robert Shaw as the half-crazed sea captain from *Jaws*, and we'd have O'Brien's character nailed.

"He was an exact copy of Smollett's novel sailors," John Quincy Adams, the future president and son of John Adams of Braintree, would later write. "His discourse was patched up entirely of sea phrases." Cathcart made exactly the same comparison when he met him.

Adams described O'Brien as "an Irishman" and he played up to that role, too, although he was actually born in the Kennebec Valley of Maine in 1758. His father William was an immigrant from Mallow in County Cork, Ireland. He had married Richard's mother, a Kennebec native named Rebecca Crane, in 1757. William died when Richard was just four, and the child was raised in Ireland.

As he watched the corsair galley close in, O'Brien must have wondered whether he would ever see either country again. There were only fifteen men aboard the *Dauphin*: O'Brien, his mate Andrew Montgomery, eleven seamen, and two passengers. The principal passenger was one Captain Zacheus Coffin, a well-connected mariner whose frail body was constantly racked by the pitiable cough of advanced tuberculosis: all he wanted was to get back home to his family. The other passenger was a French boy named Jacob Tessanaer.

The seamen were all based in America, although several would later claim, without success, to be British in a bid to gain their freedom. One seaman, Philip Sloan, testified that he was just a hitchhiker trying to get home to England by helping out on board the *Dauphin*. Another very young boy, a carpenter's apprentice named Charles Colvill, had a Scottish accent and a stronger case: although based in Philadelphia, he had been born in Scotland and his family still had a strong network of support there.

Right now, there wasn't much the crewmen could do. Large Algerine cruisers like this contained, on average, around five hundred men. "One third of the crews are Turks," O'Brien would observe later. "The remainder [are] Algerine Moors."

The "Turks" he was referring to were the elite troops of the Janissary militia, originally Turkish Christians conscripted from Anatolia. Although occasionally they had to go into full-blown battle wielding their muskets and distinctive curved yataghan scimitars, their role at sea these days was usually intimidatory. Approaching a target ship, they stayed out of view until the last minute then suddenly rose in unison with an ear-shattering cacophony of shouting and beating of weapons. That in itself usually did the job.

The takeover process generally mirrored the experience of the *Maria* crew. "[They were] used nearly in the same manner as we had," Cathcart was to write later.

As they mingled with their captors, they found out that the galley's crew comprised a third soldiers, a third working seamen, and a third conscripts. The seamen went on duty only during the sailing season: during winter, they held down everyday jobs as tailors, shoemakers, barbers, and so on. As for the resentful conscripts, they all had been swept up from the streets at the last minute. "When all the cruisers are fitted out," Cathcart explained later, "[they] are driven down to the mole by the hangman and his deputies like a flock of sheep, and have nothing with them but what they have on."

The *Dauphin* crew did not reach Algiers until August 12. Unlike the men from the *Maria*, they were allowed to keep their own civilian clothes. "When washed and cleaned," Cathcart wrote, "they made a much better figure than we did."

When the two captured crews were introduced, Cathcart came face-to-face with O'Brien for the first time. Although O'Brien was nine years his senior, it was the younger man whose reassuring presence dominated the meeting.

The worst fear of the newcomers was that they would be chained to a galley oar, but Cathcart was able to set their minds at ease. In the 1500s and 1600s, men had indeed been dispatched to this hellish fate, shackled to the benches and forced to haul oars, in some cases until they dropped dead from exhaustion. But these days the oar-driven Barbary galleys of yesteryear no longer dominated the Mediterranean.

As Cathcart and O'Brien talked together, they realized that they were similar in many ways and yet opposite in personality. Both had Irish roots, although O'Brien had spent much of his childhood in Ireland, whereas Cathcart had grown up in America. Both had fought in the American Revolution. O'Brien had served as first lieutenant on the American privateer ship *Congress*, which captured the British warship *Savage* and its 120-strong crew after "a very obstinate engagement" off the coast of South Carolina. (O'Brien was later praised for his "intrepidity and good conduct" in the battle.)

Both men were pragmatists. With Gaelic roots, their blood coursed with the DNA of an ancient culture of horse traders. They were natural wheeler-dealers. The culture of the Algerine pirates was not a million miles away from the culture of the old Gaelic cattle kings, and both men would use this to their advantage.

However, in other ways, the two men could not have been more different. Physically, Cathcart was thickset and bullish, O'Brien tall and gangly. Their approaches to captivity would turn out to be completely different. O'Brien, as a career officer, believed in the system and the hierarchy: if he kept his head down and wrote enough reports and letters home, he believed, his superiors would listen, justice would prevail, and he ultimately would be rewarded.

Cathcart was more of a maverick. As a grunt worker—as opposed to an elite "moon payer"—he had to live by his wits from day to day, even second to second. He knew that it was not enough simply to *survive* captivity in Algiers—his spirit would be crushed. Like a salmon surging up a waterfall, he needed to fight his way upward or die: making the best of whatever skills he had, forging new friendships, and building a network of contacts until he himself became a powerful force in this unfamiliar culture.

James Cathcart and Richard O'Brien's fates were to be closely linked for the next two decades: first as friends, then as rivals, and finally as bitter enemies.

★   ★   ★

Next morning the *Dauphin* crew was paraded before the dey. (As state-owned prisoners, they were spared the humiliation of the Badistan market.) Philip Sloan, the seaman who claimed he had merely hitched a ride on the *Dauphin*, was chosen by the dey as a palace sweeper. The other seamen were less fortunate. They were sent "to hard labor" at the bagnio, or special prison.

British consul Charles Logie stepped forward and once again offered to sponsor the two captains, O'Brien and Coffin, and First Mate Andrew Montgomery for five guineas under the trusted prisoner or moon payer system. O'Brien's relief was almost pathetic. "Seeing our distressed situation, [the British consul] has taken us three masters of vessels out of the workhouses and given security for us to the Dey of Algiers, King of Cruelties," he wrote. He was less impressed when he later discovered that Charles Logie saw him not so much as his houseguest as his houseboy.

(Decades later, a story circulated in America that O'Brien had been "relieved of the chain and ball" by the dey in gratitude for some act of heroism in which he saved the ruler's daughter. There's no evidence that O'Brien himself invented this myth, but he did nothing to correct it.)

Once all three American captains—Stephens, O'Brien, and Coffin—had settled in together, they wrote an impassioned letter addressed to the American consul in London. It landed on the desk of John Adams, the Founding Father who had become US minister at the British court. Both Stephens and Adams were natives of the small town of Braintree, near Boston, and were acquaintances but not personal friends. (Nearly a dozen years later, Adams was able to pick Stephens out on a crowded street.) However, the letter gives no hint of the connection, and it's possible that Stephens did not realize whom he was writing to.

The three officers didn't hold back. They had "been taken by the cruisers of Algiers" and put into captivity, "the severity of which is beyond your imagination." They had been "stripped and left destitute of everything" and if they did not get some sort of subsistence from their own government, their seamen would die. They pleaded for an allowance of $2 or $3 a month.

"Otherwise my people will perish," the letter added, "for I assure you it is impossible they can live on what they are allowed . . . [with] the winter approaching and they being entirely bare of clothes, they will be in a poor, miserable situation." It was urgent that Congress "fall on some plan for our speedy redemption."

Captain O'Brien also sent his own heartfelt letter to Thomas Jefferson, then US minister to Paris: "Our sufferings is beyond our expressing or your conception . . . being stripped of all our clothes and nothing to exist on but two small cakes of bread per day, without any necessities of life . . . my crew certainly will starve if there is not some immediate relief."

Jefferson was first to reply, in September, with a terse three-line letter promising to "exert myself for you." He added: "Say nothing to anybody except what may be necessary to comfort your companions. I add no more because the fate of this letter is uncertain." Adams's reply seven days later was equally cryptic. "I most sincerely condole with you under your misfortune," he wrote, promising to send an envoy "to relieve you . . . [and] to promote peace."

★ ★ ★

Workers at the palace didn't get paid, but they did get a bizarre fringe benefit: "coffee money." Powerful figures who met the dey were always served coffee and, afterward, they left a tip in the empty cup. Twice a year, these tips were divided among the palace staff, freemen and captives alike.

Cathcart decided to use his money to help out his "brother sufferers at hard labor in the nauseous prisons" who had no such income. Taking advantage of a religious feast day when captive workers at the palace were traditionally given a little extra leeway, he and a colleague received permission to visit the prisons and to drop in on the three captains at the English consul's house three miles outside the city.

Entering Logie's garden, he witnessed a sight that filled him with distress. "We found Captain O'Brien with a hoe digging a hole to plant a tree," he said. "Stephens, with the capote [hooded coat] given him by the Regency tied around his middle with a straw rope, driving a mule loaded with manure, and Coffin, who was consumptive, feeding the hogs and poultry.

"We could not refrain from tears at viewing their humiliating situation," he wrote. He expected more humane treatment from Logie, who "was of the same religion and spoke the same language."

Now why should Cathcart have been reduced to genuine tears of pity to see the three men doing a bit of medium-grade gardening, while the other American seamen were at hard labor at the docks and quarries, and he himself was suffering sadistic beatings? His overreaction was a reflection not only of Cathcart's generous character, but also of the rigid class system of the era. Officers were gentlemen and were never supposed to do manual work.

Having said that, Charles Logie did seem to take a spiteful pleasure in humiliating his US servants. He delighted in entertaining foreign consuls and pointing out that their food was being served by captured Americans. As a way of taking revenge for the bitter loss of Britain's thirteen colonies, it was unsubtle but very effective.

Cathcart chatted with the three officers and gave them their share of his coffee money. Then he visited "the poor fellows" at the bagnio prison and dispensed the rest of the money, along with a little extra that he had borrowed. Their plight was far more distressing than the scenes he had witnessed at Logie's house. "We returned to the palace," he confessed, "with a heavy heart."

The officers appreciated the extra money, but it did little to ease their constant anguish about the fate of their relatives at home. "I have an aged mother, brother and sisters: their whole dependence and subsistence are on me," O'Brien wrote. "Captain Stephens and Captain Coffin have families, unknown how provided for."

Back home in America, Hannah Stephens still had no idea that her husband had been captured. But she was about to find out.

· 6 ·

"A Black Eye, a Broken Leg, and Credentials from Congress"

*F*all had set New England ablaze with color, and the oak and maple woods that surrounded the town of Concord had transformed themselves into a burning furnace of red, orange, yellow, and ochre when Hannah Stephens discovered the truth.

Up until now, she had felt no particular concern for Isaac's welfare. A voyage to Europe and back usually took four months, but bad weather could add a long time to the journey. It was not unknown for ships heading home to clear port and remain stuck there for days or even weeks, within sight of the same harbor, waiting for a change of wind.

In the meantime, Hannah had plenty to be getting on with. While her three children were at school, she had endless chores to do: cleaning house, washing clothes, stitching and sewing, harvesting and preserving fruit and vegetables. Like most householders in Concord, she would have grown more than she needed and would have bartered these for other food and services to help augment her income and pay for essential maintenance work.

Her house would have needed constant attention. If it had been a typical middle-class home in central Concord, it would have been a clay brick construction with two rooms, one above the other, a central stone chimney, and a "linter" or lean-to at the back for a kitchen. The adjoining sheds stored firewood and gave dry passage to the outside privy.

Generally, Concord was a fine place to live. "Few places are more healthy, or exhibit a higher average term of human life," wrote one local historian. Forests covered the horizon, although they were getting smaller each year and the game within them was vanishing. Nearby, Walden Pond—which would later become an icon of American literature—provided a fine retreat for anyone who wanted to find harmony in nature. But it was the Concord

River, a confluence of two streams, that dominated the townscape. Since it spread out to a width of three hundred feet every winter, the expansive flood-plain gave a pleasant sense of openness and space. For the original farmers, this had been a wonderful gift: the floods fertilized the meadows with rich river minerals; the grass provided fine hay for the cattle; the cattle in turn fertilized the fields for plentiful crops of Indian corn and rye. Farmers set up holdings of around sixty acres and helped all their sons to set up identical farms nearby, and so the circle continued.

But lately things had begun to change. The land that seemed nearly in-finite had almost run out, and younger sons were forced to leave their home-town and community to make a living. Meanwhile, the earth was becoming exhausted, and farmers complained it took seven times as much work to grow the same harvest. Farms were secretly amassing huge debts that became evi-dent only after a father died and left his sons a toxic legacy. As the descendants of the original settlers steadily were being forced away from Concord, it would have been no surprise if there had been simmering local resentment against outsiders like Isaac and Hannah, who breezed into town and bought property with such airy ease.

Despite the peaceable aspiration in the town's name (pronounced, inci-dentally, like *conquered*), Concord was not a place of harmony in 1785. Ten years before, its North Bridge famously witnessed the first clash in the Revo-lutionary War: "the shot heard around the world." Even after independence, there were violent street demonstrations. And at the church, an inordinate amount of time was spent arguing over who had the right to sit where.

Apart from the communal worship and after events on Sundays, there were not many occasions to which a lone woman was invited in a New England town. The exception was the annual "husking bee" every autumn, when communal husking of corn became a party. As one poet described it, the husking bee was a time "when ladies joined the social band, nor once affected fear," making it clear that in this Puritan society, women were not welcome at social activities at other times.

This isolation felt worse during the winter, when temperatures in Con-cord could fall well below freezing and the dark nights seemed to last for-ever. Even in the shelter of her home, Hannah would have found daily life a struggle, with basins of warm water rapidly turning to ice and inefficient open fires that roasted you on one side but left you freezing on the other.

Yet winter was still a few weeks away, and Hannah was probably feel-ing reasonably content during those October days as she walked around the town on her round of activities, passing the meeting house with its tall bell-tower, the old manse, the courthouse, the bakery at Wright's Tavern, and the Middlesex Hotel on Lexington Road where the gentlemen—those fortunate gentlemen!—gathered in the communal warmth to learn the latest news over a cup of hot toddy or strong local cider.

But on this day, the newspaper that was being passed from hand to hand was the *Salem Gazette*. It told how Algerine corsairs were once again active in the Atlantic. A Captain McComb, who had himself survived an attack by the pirates, had come home with news from Cadiz that two American ships had been seized and taken to Algiers where their crews had been "sold at auction." One ship was from Boston, the other from an unknown port. McComb had risked his own safety to get the news back to New England as quickly as possible.

Shipowners along the coast didn't take long to connect the dots: the *Maria* had not been heard of since it left Boston, and the *Dauphin* should have returned to Philadelphia long ago. It would take another month to officially confirm the news, but right then in Concord, everyone knew that one of the captured men must have been their neighbor—that sociable sea captain, Isaac Stephens. And the first question on everyone's lips must have been: who's going to tell his wife?

★   ★   ★

Autumn became early winter, and as the first frost began to whiten the rooftops of Philadelphia, politicians at last learned the fate of the twenty-one American citizens who had been thrown into captivity in Algiers.

A copy of O'Brien's letter arrived in November, sixteen or seventeen weeks after capture. The news spread rapidly.

"On the 25th of July, 1785, the schooner *Maria*, captain, Stephens, belonging to Mr. Foster of Boston, was taken off Cape St. Vincent by an Algerine cruiser," one contemporary report read. "Five days afterwards, the ship *Dolphin*, [sic] captain, O'Brien, belonging to Messrs. Irvines [sic] of Philadelphia was taken by another, fifty leagues westward of Lisbon. These vessels with their cargoes and crews, twenty-one in number, were carried into Algiers."

The revelation did not create the sort of reaction that might have been expected, partly because many people just did not believe it (there were false reports of three other captures), and partly because the politicians had other serious things on their minds, such as desperately trying to keep their new nation together with a workable Constitution.

The owners of the two ships were understandably upset. The *Dauphin*'s co-owner, Mathew Irwin, lamented that the Algerines had cost him almost as much as the British navy had during the war. However, he was philosophical, conceding that "poor O'Brien" and his crew were in captivity while "I have my liberty."

Once the news was verified, few people in the United States could understand why their shipping had been targeted by pirates from that tinpot state—and almost nobody could fathom why they should be expected to join the browbeaten Europeans in paying annual tribute to them.

Despite this, Congress had much earlier allocated $80,000 toward peace treaties with all the Barbary States. It was a hopelessly low sum, but the formidable trio of John Adams, Thomas Jefferson, and Benjamin Franklin had been appointed to kick-start negotiations. They already had laid the foundations for a treaty with Morocco. However, the kidnapping of the twenty-one Americans now made things in Algiers much, much more complicated.

It didn't help that the three men were at loggerheads on strategy. When the two ships were captured, Adams couldn't resist an "I told you so." In October, he wrote: "As long ago as 1778 I engaged earnestly in treating with the Barbary Powers: but Dr. Franklin's opinion always was that the freedom of the navigation of the Mediterranean was not worthy of the presents [tribute money], and everything always withered that Dr. Franklin blasted."

The dilemma was starkly simple. America had lost Britain's protection and had not acquired alternative cover from another European nation. There had been only three options open to them: to avoid the Mediterranean altogether, to negotiate a deal, or to go to war.

Thomas Jefferson, the US minister plenipotentiary in Paris, was inclined toward the war option. Jefferson, a tall, sandy-haired Virginian who had been the prime author of the Declaration of Independence, had read all about the depressing history of this ancient and intractable problem.

Nearly three centuries before, Spain had driven the forces of Islam from the Iberian Peninsula and had followed up by expelling large populations of Spanish Muslims. These displaced peoples settled in places like Algiers, where they put down roots while nursing an understandable grudge against Europeans in general and the Spanish in particular. Things came to a head when Spain occupied the island off Algiers. Two freelance pirates, the Barbarossa brothers, unexpectedly managed to oust them and assume control of Algiers city. The Ottoman sultan then cut a pragmatic deal allowing these "corsairs" and their successors to effectively run the city jointly with his own representatives, the Janissary militia. The tense partnership between them had worked surprisingly well, although by the later 1700s, it was the regent or dey who held the real power.

The conflict had now chilled into a background war—the "politics of plunder"—in which the corsairs of Barbary captured European ships and raided coastal villages for hostages, while European pirates in centers like Naples and Malta did the same to citizens of Barbary. By this stage the whole sorry business had settled down into an established protection racket, with even the mightiest European nations gritting their teeth and paying tribute to the dey of Algiers. And now it seemed to be America's turn to pay up.

Jefferson hated the idea of that happening on his watch. "I very early thought it would be best to effect a peace through the medium of war," he wrote to London minister John Adams. "Justice is in favor of this opinion. Honor favors it."

Stirring words but unfortunately, as both men knew, the United States did not have a national navy (and would not have one until the late 1790s). Jefferson toyed with other options, such as entering an alliance with other nations, but in the end, he had to accept his government's orders. "Our instructions relative to the Barbary States... [are] to proceed by way of negotiation to obtain their peace," he told Adams in July 1786. "Whatever might be our private opinions, they were to be suppressed."

Jefferson and Adams were set to proceed with their mission when they got word from home to hold everything. A new whiz kid was coming to Europe. They knew nothing about the new man except his name.

John Lamb.

★   ★   ★

In London, Abigail Adams was in a state of shock. She had just had her first encounter with Captain John Lamb and was still trying to recover. As she sat, pen in hand, at her writing desk in Grosvenor Square in the fall of 1785, she lamented her government's poor choice of envoy. "Mr. Lamb [is] an utter stranger," she wrote primly, "and his appearance [is] not much to his favor."

Abigail, forty-one, was John Adams's most trusted adviser as well as his beloved wife. She was a shrewd judge of personality, and her misgivings about Captain Lamb proved to be not only perceptive but prophetic.

Lamb—not to be confused with the Revolutionary War general of the same name—sailed on from England to France, and when he arrived in Paris, it was Thomas Jefferson's turn to be shocked. The refined statesman was having a civilized cup of tea with a guest when Lamb suddenly burst in, looking exactly like a caricature of a disheveled, half-crazed sea captain, "with one black eye, a leg broken in a gale off the Isle of Wight, a pair of tarnished black stockings hanging about his heels . . . [with] a long beard, hair uncombed, coat, waistcoat and breeches full of dirt . . . one part of the flap of his breeches unbuttoned, a great, coarse hat . . . and credentials in his hands from Congress."

Captain John Lamb, a tough-talking, hard-drinking mariner from the town of Norwich in Connecticut, had landed a job for which he was spectacularly unsuited. Admittedly he had some experience in Morocco, but he had never been to Algiers. He didn't speak French, the court language of the city, and even his English was sprinkled liberally with swear words. Cathcart later described him contemptuously as "a degenerate American."

Jefferson was astonished but reassured himself that Lamb *must* have been competent, otherwise he would never have been given the job—a circular argument that has deceived even the wisest of politicians on other occasions. (In fact, as Jefferson was later to discover, Lamb had never been formally appointed as a diplomat.) "I have not seen enough of him to judge his abilities," he wrote hesitantly to Adams. "He seems not deficient, as far as I can see . . . as to his integrity, we must rely on the recommendation he brings."

Meanwhile, John Lamb was sampling the delights of Paris and viewing the city through the bottom of a glass. One night a drinking buddy had to carry him to bed "drunk as a lord."

When Lamb finally set off for Algiers, the official cover story was that he was making a long-scheduled visit that had nothing to do with the ship seizures. However, Jefferson and Adams were worried that the American captives might soon be sold individually and "dispersed through the interior," so they privately instructed him to negotiate for the ransoms within a strict budget.

★   ★   ★

When Lamb was on his way to Algiers, Adams received a letter from Isaac Stephens. "Some of us has been at death's door," the captain wrote. "Myself has been two months under [medical] care for a bilious disorder, but thank God I am better. . . .

"If you can give us any intelligence concerning our redemption, I should be exceeding glad. . . . If you would be so good as to extend your charity a little in sending me 'The History of America,' if old, no matter, and some late magazines . . . as we have no books."

He added caustically that he expected to die a captive in Algiers "as the sum is so great an object to our country."

Adams wrote back to assure the Americans that help was on its way: "Mr. Lamb . . . will do for you all in his power, as well as for all the other unhappy captives in Algiers."

• 7 •

The Undiplomatic Diplomat

𝒥t was March, and Lamb went in like a lion. He sailed into Algiers on a Spanish brig and immediately stormed around the city like a force of nature. Lamb—an argument against the theory of nominative determinism if there ever was one—appears to have swaggered aggressively from tavern to tavern, rubbing everyone the wrong way.

As a diplomat, John Lamb suffered a major disadvantage: he was undiplomatic. He was "illiterate and vulgar" according to Cathcart, who as a seaman was not easily shocked. O'Brien agreed, calling him "ungentlemanlike."

Wild haired and full bearded, hat crumpled and dirty trousers often unbuttoned, he shocked the diplomatic circuit, abusing any French and Spanish he met in "the most vulgar language." Over dinner, he loudly discussed confidential American policy, wrongly assuming the Algerines couldn't understand English. His words were rapidly conveyed to the Spanish legation. As Richard O'Brien reported home, other consuls found it unbelievable that the US Congress "would have sent such a man to negotiate so important an affair."

Lamb met the American captives and breezily assured them that he would have them freed "within a few days." Then he promptly chose the British consul Charles Logie, another heavy drinker, as his new companion and confidante. "Mr. Logie received me as an old friend," he reported gratefully, adding with pathetic naivete: "[He] declared to me that he had no orders from his court to counteract my mission."

The horrified Richard O'Brien could only watch with mounting dread as Lamb made "a bosom friend" of "America's most inveterate enemy."

Logie went into full saboteur mode. He privately informed the dey that Lamb had arrived with a mountain of cash to pay the ransom—untrue, of

41

course—but warned Mahmood that the American would plead poverty in a bid to cheat him. The seeds of bad faith were sown right from the start.

The dey reacted coldly to Lamb's advances, forcing the envoy to cool his heels for a few days while Mahmood decided whether to see him at all. At last, he agreed to meet, but only to discuss ransom payments.

Privately, the ruler anticipated a cash bonanza. "[Lamb's behavior] had become such town talk," said O'Brien, "that the Dey hardly knew what sum to ask."

★   ★   ★

First, a quick word about the financial side of such negotiations. The ransom of the captive hostages and the creation of a future peace deal were usually two separate transactions. There could be no talk of a treaty until the ransoms were agreed.

Whatever sum they settled on, there were the inevitable taxes, presents, backhanders, tips, and bankers' commissions. Also, the Algerines insisted on being paid in the local currency—the Algerine sequin—which foreigners would be forced to buy at crazily inflated rates.

At the time, a basic seaman's ransom was around $2,000, a captain's around $3,000, and a mate's somewhere in between. With a general ransom, however, there would be discounts. No nation had ransomed its captives in bulk for an average of less than $1,217 per head. O'Brien guessed the twenty-one captives would cost $1,800 each. Logie estimated $2,137 per man.

So, what exactly was Lamb's budget?

The figure was depressing. "We do not expect to redeem our captives for less than a hundred dollars a head," Adams had instructed him, "and we should be fearful to go beyond double that sum."

★   ★   ★

Lamb arrived at the palace courtyard, removing his crumpled hat before entering the grand hall. He entered the dey's private staircase—the narrow, twisting stone stairway that was specifically constructed to repel invaders. The dey himself, who was pushing eighty, was usually carried by servants, but for everyone else it was an exhausting journey to negotiate the five bewildering, mazelike flights. For the ruler, there was the added advantage that any visitor would arrive panting, perspiring, and at a disadvantage to the coolly composed ruler relaxing on his velvet cushion.

Once the opening pleasantries were over, the dey made an unexpected request. He told Lamb that he was "familiar with the exploits of General

George Washington, [but] never expected to set eyes on this hero of free-dom." Could Congress send him a full-length portrait of the revolutionary leader to display in his palace?

Having finished his lofty musings on liberty, the master kidnapper of Algiers got down to business and demanded nearly $60,000 (an average of $2,833 each) to free his US captives. Lamb countered with an offer of $4,200, which was $200 per head. As the negotiations warmed up, Mahmood waited for Lamb to dip into his hoard of cash. He was disgusted when he finally real-ized that $200 per head really *was* all Lamb had to offer.

When it became clear that they were in completely different financial universes, there was no point in talking further. Lamb went home and packed his bags.

★ ★ ★

Or so runs the standard narrative in modern histories. However, Cathcart and O'Brien had a different version of events: they claimed that Lamb returned for several more meetings and finally agreed to a ransom sum that worked out, after extras, to $48,300, or an average of $2,300 per man. The US envoy promised that the sum would be paid within four months.

Cathcart's version is so rich in detail, with exact dates of meetings and precise sums that it suggests he got his information from the dey's archives dur-ing a period when he had unlimited access to the records. O'Brien, for his part, claims to have received an eyewitness account from the palace chamberlain.

If all this is true, what was going on? Did Lamb go rogue and take a solo run at the negotiations? Or was he obeying secret orders from US government officials and acting in some official but deniable capacity?

Cathcart was as confused as anyone else by the episode. "I was not in-formed at this time by whom Mr. Lamb was empowered to negotiate, or whether he was empowered at all." One thing, however, he was sure of: "That he made the agreement and that the Government of the United States never ratified it." The result, he said, was eleven more years in captivity.

Writing separately four years later, O'Brien broadly confirms this ver-sion. "Mr. Lamb had five audiences . . . and agreed for the ransom of the Americans. . . . He promised to return with the money in four months, but he broke his word."

Reacting to these reports, Jefferson flatly denied them. "We cannot be-lieve this fact to be true," he wrote, "and even if it were, we disavow it totally, as far beyond his powers."

★ ★ ★

Before he left, Lamb organized another meeting with the American captives. He left them $400 to cover some basic needs and told them that they could expect some news within four months.

The Americans were at first crestfallen by the whole affair—"it was badly planned and worse executed" complained O'Brien—but eagerly seized on the hope of freedom. They were "reanimated," Cathcart wrote, "and resolved to bear the remaining four months of their captivity with patience and fortitude."

Meanwhile, Lamb had been secretly visiting a highly influential figure who was reported to be pro-American. Ali Hassan El Amia, the minister for the marine, was the third most powerful man in Algiers after the ruler and the prime minister and known as "a man of uncommon abilities." They had a series of clandestine meetings in Hassan's garden.

Hassan advised Lamb not to be deterred by "the little putoffs by the Dey." Lamb should leave Algiers and await developments. He also gave him sound advice: America should not waste time dealing directly with the sultan of the Ottoman Empire, since Algiers "had an entire right to make peace or war without the voice of the Grand Signor."

He made Lamb swear to keep their dealings secret. Otherwise, Hassan "might lose his life," Lamb wrote, "and when I returned, I might expect the same."

Hassan left Lamb with a word of encouragement. "I myself am well disposed towards the United States," he whispered. "It is my greatest desire that peace might be made between us. For my part, I will use my utmost endeavors."

It was a pledge that America would remember five years later when Ali Hassan succeeded Mahmood as the all-powerful dey of Algiers.

★ ★ ★

John Lamb left Algiers and never returned. He went to Madrid, where he reported home: "[The dey] would not speak of peace, [and demanded] a most exorbitant price, far beyond my limits."

Back in Algiers, time dragged unbearably while the captives awaited news on each arriving ship. Four months passed, and in September a letter arrived from Lamb saying he had been too ill to go to America but had dispatched his report by sea. The following year, Lamb wrote again with the bad news that the US government would not agree on a sum for their redemption.

As far as Jefferson was concerned, the whole enterprise had simply petered out. As Lamb had "never settled the accounts of his mission, no further information has been received," he wrote.

Lamb's fruitless trip did not go down well in the United States—especially after he submitted an expenses bill in London for £3,212, or more than $14,000, enough to have redeemed a third of the twenty-one Americans.

"You and I were not censurable," Adams reassured Jefferson. "We found him ready appointed to our hands. . . . [He is] as indifferent to me as a Mohawk Indian." It turned out, however, that nobody in America had ever formally appointed Lamb as an envoy. Recommended by the governor of Massachusetts, the captain had simply ricocheted from America to Europe to Africa, bouncing off other people's assumptions. "But as he came from Congress with their dispatches of such importance," bewailed John Adams, "I suppose it was expected we should appoint him. There is no harm done."

The captives in Algiers would have begged to differ with the last sentence. "It led the Dey to believe that the Government of the United States was trifling with them," Cathcart complained. Good faith, the fundamental plank of any negotiation, had been destroyed. Also, it gave the Americans "false hope of obtaining their liberty soon."

Years later, John Lamb himself summed up the whole fiasco in three words: "Unhappy mess, indeed."

And on that, at least, everyone was in agreement.

★　★　★

"For God's sake, and for the love of man, assist us."

Captain Isaac Stephens's next letter to John Adams in April 1786 was an anguished plea from the heart. The captives' situation, he said, was now "desperate."

He acknowledged that the ransom sum demanded was enormous, but the captives were not responsible for that. "It is of so great a consequence to me, especially, that has a family, and a great mortification to me, for the [ransom] sum must be paid if ever we are redeemed from this desert place," he wrote. "The [Americans] are carrying rocks and timber on their backs for nine miles out of the country over sharp rocks and mountains, which raises great lumps on their shoulders as big as one's fist."

Yet they were powerless to do anything about it. "We are the property of the King [i.e., the dey] as much as his horse." As they walked around the city, he said, they had to endure the taunts of locals.

Knowing that his wife Hannah would probably receive a copy of his letter, he tried to reassure her. "Blessed be to God, I am middling well . . . and keep my spirits up as well as can be expected with an iron around my leg, and bearing all the insults from the Moors."

Perceptively, Stephens warned Adams that it would be counterproductive to try to cheat or hoodwink the dey. "Mr Lamb . . . told the King that he would be here in four months, and this King never puts any confidence in a nation that deceives him once."

*   ★   ★

James Cathcart had been a hostage in Algiers for exactly one year and four days when his life was upended a second time. He was, literally, cast out of the garden and hurled into an even more frightening and uncertain future.

It happened, like most things in this craziest of cities, by the whim of the dey. A new batch of captives had arrived and Mahmood had decided he wanted to see new faces around the palace.

Cathcart had no inkling about the change until the evening of July 29, 1786, when a palace official visited the garden and selected eight of the workers to be sent to the notorious prison of the Bagnio Belique. He pointed to two Portuguese, four Spaniards, and the two Americans—Cathcart and his "unfortunate companion" James Harnet.

Gather your possessions, he told them. You leave immediately.

Cathcart does not reveal whether he was given a chance to say a last farewell to the two young lions that he had cared for during the last twelve months or whether the prospect of parting from them filled him with sadness or relief. But if he thought he was done with lions in Algiers, he was badly mistaken—as we find out later.

It didn't take long to pack. Cathcart's sole possessions were a small basket of clothes, two blankets, some books and papers that he'd managed to hide away, and his savings from the coffee money—$4 and two Algerine sequins. He had heard enough about the Bagnio Belique to know that he would need every penny of this money, not for luxuries or extras, but for bribes to ensure his basic survival.

Although he had heard the horror stories about life in the bagnio, a part of him was keen for a change. "I resolved to bear the hardest labor accompanied with hunger, nakedness and all their miseries," he wrote. It would be better than the dread of daily life at the palace, which had created the psychological problems he called his "sentimental afflictions." He was also keen to put his language skills to better use. Knowledge was power, and at the bagnio he could become "the means of alleviating the sufferings of my unfortunate fellow citizens."

In that, at least, he would be proved correct. But in thinking that life in the bagnio would be better than life in the palace, he could not have been more mistaken. Looking back on it, he admitted: "We were ignorant of the situation we were destined for, but we were soon undeceived." He would find "a great deal of difference between the Bagnio Belique [with its] hard labor at the public works, and the palace garden with all its evils." People, he mused, were "never sensible of the blessings they enjoy until they are deprived of them."

He had suffered much from the two chamberlains. "But we were now exposed to the more ferocious Ibram Rais, the Guardian Bashaw . . . the most cruel, unrelenting guardian that had ever been in Algiers."

· 8 ·

The Threshold of Pain

*C*lutching their meager bundles, the eight former palace workers presented themselves at the massive gateway to the Bagnio Belique. In the distant past, this grim three-story building had been a public bath, and the name had stuck. But where once the prevailing sound had been pleasant splashing and the soft buzz of conversation, there was now only the clanking of chains, the moaning of inmates, and the barking of orders by prison guards.

Cathcart's keen eye took it all in: a rectangular structure measuring about fifty yards by twenty and around fifty feet high. It was built around a court-yard, with arched arcades leading to a communal area where prisoners and freemen could mingle during the day.

To gain access to the prison, a newcomer had to pass through a macabre vestibule equipped like a torture chamber: a literal threshold of pain. "The walls of the porch were decorated with clubs, halters, chains, shackles and handcuffs," Cathcart recalled, "forming the most dejecting *coup de oeil* [sic] that imagination can possibly achieve."

Above them in the shadows swung a gallows noose, which emphasized the ultimate deterrent. In its shadow sat the prison warden or guardian bashaw, Ibram Rais. He was flanked by prison guards wielding sticks, thick ropes, and other weapons. Nearby stood Janissary troops armed with muskets and their distinctive yataghan scimitars. For the new arrivals, the message could not have been clearer.

Even worse, it turned out that Ibram was a man who carried a giant chip on his shoulder—and not without reason. He himself had been held for years as a captive on the island of Malta, a corsair enclave that was in many ways a mirror image of Algiers but run by the Christian Knights of St. John. The Knights seized ships from the Barbary States and treated their captives just as cruelly as their own people were treated in Algiers. The Barbary corsairs would then take their revenge on their next haul of European captives and the Maltese would do likewise with theirs, each upping the ante in a self-stoking cycle of bitterness and retribution.

If there was ever an embodiment of this process in Algiers, it was Ibram Rais. "He had remained in captivity for fourteen years," Cathcart wrote, "and having been cruelly treated himself on board the Maltese Galleys, he was determined to retaliate."

The guardian surveyed his latest acquisitions with a cold eye.

"Well, gentlemen," he said ominously, "so you were not content with your situation in the palace, and have preferred my acquaintance." He said they were all far too healthy and well-dressed, and he aimed to change that. It was time they learned how inmates at the bagnio were treated. "You shall have something to divert you tomorrow. . . . I will show you there how I was treated at Malta."

He turned to the guards. "Put stout rings on these gentlemen's legs, and let them be awakened and brought to me tomorrow at the Marine Gate."

But as the other prisoners cowered and moved to kiss the guardian's hand, Cathcart impulsively spoke out in protest.

I come from a country six thousand miles from Malta, he told the guardian. We have no history of enmity toward Islam and have never been at war with any Islamic nation. It would be harsh indeed to make us suffer for the injuries you received from the Maltese.

Ibram curled his whiskers thoughtfully. "True," he said, "but [that] was not for the want of will, but for want of power. If you should chance to take any of our cruisers, how would you treat our people?"

"That will entirely depend," Cathcart countered, "on how you treat those of my nation."

"You are too loquacious for a young man," Ibram shot back. "Be silent and obey."

Cathcart continued to protest, but the guards intervened. The interview was over.

What had motivated Cathcart to speak out so courageously when he could easily have been sentenced to a beating? Perhaps it was sheer frustration, a howl from a man at the end of his tether. Perhaps it was exactly what it seemed to be, a proud citizen of an independent nation declaring his refusal to be browbeaten. From a tactical viewpoint, however, he had scored an important victory. He had placed himself in a different category than the other prison inmates. He was laying down a marker. He was making it clear that, whatever they did to his body, his spirit would always soar free.

In the meantime, however, he was a prisoner like any other. With well-practiced hands, the guards shackled their ankles with iron rings weighing twenty to thirty ounces—around the same weight as a modern smoothing iron. They were told that the weight could be exchanged for a lighter iron ring if they each paid one Algerine sequin—about $2—to Ibram and a smaller sum "for his trouble" to the guard who'd have to undo it.

As he wandered around his new "home" looking for some corner to lay his head, Cathcart's morale must have hit a new low. And then, out of the blue, a guardian angel came to his rescue.

★   ★   ★

Angelo d'Andreis, dapper and well groomed, strode through the milling throng of prisoners, looking as out of place as a Bible student at a Hells Angels convention. When at last he spotted his old friend James Cathcart, he shouted a warm welcome.

You may recall that Cathcart and the Italian writer had become friends in Boston, where d'Andreis had worked as a commercial agent. Cathcart had dubbed him "half American" because of his upcoming marriage to a Boston woman. D'Andreis had indeed married his society belle Sarah Moody in October 1785 but—like Isaac Stephens—had become separated from his beloved wife through captivity. The Italian had been taken prisoner at sea by the Algerines a year after Cathcart, and had ended up as a hostage in Barbary. Perhaps because of his writerly reputation, d'Andreis had been appointed as the dey's chief Christian clerk, the highest position attainable by any non-Muslim in Algiers. (He was to keep the job for six years until he was succeeded in 1792—by James Cathcart.)

D'Andreis had been unable to intervene when his old friend was moved into the city's grimmest prison. But he knew that most new prisoners were forced to sleep outdoors, in all weather, until they could bribe their way to a bunk inside, and he wanted Cathcart to avoid that humiliation. Fortunately, the position of chief Christian clerk carried with it the privilege of a private apartment inside the prison.

You can stay in my apartment for a few days, he said. Sleep on the sofa until you have time to provide for yourself.

The offer was strictly temporary but welcome nonetheless, and Cathcart "thankfully accepted." D'Andreis led him into a forbidden stairway that led up the prison's three stories to the top terrace. The American gazed around open-mouthed at the luxury of the apartment, with its two large rooms, private kitchen, and sea view. Through four open windows, soft Mediterranean breezes wafted away the "insufferable stench" of the prison below.

Yet Cathcart recalled later, "[I] could not enjoy his civilities. My imagination was wound up to such a degree that I was nearly insane. I retired to rest on his sofa but slept but little, and awaited the approach of day in anxious expectation of knowing my fate."

★　★　★

At exactly 3:00 a.m., the sleepless Cathcart was startled by a thunderous bass voice that boomed and echoed through the arcades and corridors of the Bagnio Belique. "Arise, all those who sleep! The day approaches!"

As he rolled off the sofa and fumbled in the darkness for his shoes, the same voice bellowed out again.

"Depart, sleepers!" the guard roared. "Each one to his daily labor!"

Hundreds of workers thronged into the prison courtyard, where they were herded like cattle into the narrow street that led to the Marine Gate.

"The dreadful clanking of the chains was the most terrible noise I had ever heard," wrote John Foss, an American captive who was to join Cathcart at the Marine a few years later. "Never during my whole captivity did I feel such horrors of mind, as on this dreadful morning."

At the same time, all the city gates were thrown open, and immediately the marching workers were inundated by a tsunami of people and animals, all headed in the opposite direction. "The influx of camels, mules, asses and laborers was so great we could hardly pass," Cathcart recalled.

The beasts were all laden with provisions for the city market, and amid the chaos, the starving prisoners seized the opportunity to filch as much food as they could. The chaos was indescribable. The furious merchants tried to fight off the thieves: "Infidel without faith, I will have you bastinadoed to death!" But trying to catch the offenders was as pointless as trying to focus on one bird amid a wheeling flock. The starving men were skilled at distraction and pilfering, and food thieving was almost built into the system.

Eventually a side street allowed the captives to escape the incoming tide of traders. It led to the main harbor gate, where they were expertly formed into rows. After waiting for fifteen minutes, the minister for the marine appeared, flanked by his head guards. Some of the captives were paraded off to their various duties at the docks, which most agreed was the most arduous work they'd ever experienced in a lifetime of hard labor at sea.

Once again, Angelo d'Andreis came to Cathcart's rescue. "[He] took us to the Guardian Bashaw, who presented us to the General of the Marine," Cathcart wrote.

This was Ali Hassan, the same man whom John Lamb had met for clandestine peace talks.

Hassan pointed to the new arrivals from the palace. Tell me about these men, he said.

D'Andreis was lavish in his praise of their exceptional abilities. "After receiving a favorable account of us from the clerk," Cathcart recalled, "we were ordered to our respective destinations."

The captives filed out, leaving the officials alone. We can assume that Ibram Rais, the warden, would have told Hassan about Cathcart's outburst in the prison reception area the previous night. Hassan was probably intrigued and perhaps even a little impressed. Whether it was at that point or later, the future leader of Algiers marked down Cathcart as a possible asset—and as someone who could be trusted not to back down on his principles under pressure.

Cathcart and his shipmate Harnet were both dispatched to the woodworking joinery, part of a complex of dockside workshops where more than sixty "coopers, carpenters, shipbuilders, pail makers and blacksmiths" all noisily plied their trade. Algiers was a great leveler: "I have seen merchants, doctors, priests and actors, blowing their bellows there together," Cathcart reports, "and bewailing their misfortunes in concert."

Whether by good luck or through d'Andreis's intervention, Cathcart was made apprentice to a craftsman who was prized as "the best house carpenter in Algiers." This "genteel looking" soldier from Barcelona had earlier been banished from Spain to its garrison at Oran, the notorious posting-from-hell to the west of Algiers. He had made a break for freedom across the desert, only to be caught by a wandering band of Arabs and presented as a tribute to Dey Mahmood.

Since he'd been a deserter, he had been rejected for ransom in the Spanish peace deal of 1785. Bereft of all hope, he had resolved to learn carpentry and had become such a master of his craft that his services were sought by the most prominent citizens in Algiers.

This meant he was allowed to travel freely around the city with his latest young apprentice in tow. Cathcart made full use of the opportunity, building up his language skills, chatting to everyone he met, and learning as much as he could about the geography and customs of this alien city. Because his Spanish mentor was "very much in favor," he avoided the usual displays of contempt, insults, and random violence that marred daily life for most of his comrades. Forever watching, ever learning, he began to understand the unique rhythm and cadences of communication in Algiers: the old-world formality and respect, the dark sense of humor, the culture of fatalism, and above all, the social boundaries.

He learned, for instance, that in any dispute between an outsider and a local, the local was always seen as right; justice had nothing to do with it.

And that, however provoked, a captive should never raise so much as a finger in anger toward a citizen on pain of death. Self-defense was no justification. Janissary militiamen were the worst threat. Arrogant, bored, bristling for a fight, they swaggered down narrow alleyways daring anyone to get in their way. These were tough rules, but they were the hard reality of life in this corsair city.

He also learned who was who. Algiers was a class-based society, with social strata defined by ethnic background and religion.

The Turks were at the very top. Around twelve thousand strong, these were either natives of Turkey or their descendants: they were colonist administrators and Janissary officers.

The Moors were descendants of Islamic North Africans who had lived in southern Spain—mostly Andalusia—during the era of rule by the caliphs and who'd been expelled during the Christian Reconquista. These displaced refugees had moved to North Africa, where they survived for many generations by dint of their skills and work ethic. Even though they had been the most productive of citizens—they had designed and built the aqueducts that supplied Algiers with crystal clear water from the mountains—the ruling Turks still treated them with contempt.

The *kuluglis* were a mix of the two. Although the top-level Turks were supposed to remain racially pure (the Janissaries, for instance, were meant to live as chastely as monks), they had intermarried and interbred with the Moors so enthusiastically that their offspring had created a whole new layer—the *kuluglis*. Being half-Turkish, they outranked the Moors in importance.

The renegadoes were either European pirates who had converted to Islam or former hostages who had done likewise and afterward gained their freedom. Some of them were the dregs of Algiers. Others became rich and prosperous.

Toward the lower levels were the original indigenous people of Algiers, and at rock bottom were the workers from Europe, Asia, America, and sub-Saharan Africa, who kept the whole place running with their forced labor: in the mid-1780s, there were three thousand of them.

This was not to say that these castes were clear and distinguishable. Centuries of mingling and social mobility had blurred the layers to the point that they were often hard to tell apart.

Cathcart absorbed all this information as he roamed far and wide with his master carpenter. On most working days, his life was tolerable. "Had our duties been confined to the carpenters' shop alone, there would have been no reason to complain of hard usage," Cathcart recalled with a sigh. "But that was not the case."

★ ★ ★

Fridays were the worst. Every Friday, as the good citizens of Algiers observed their sabbath, nearly all the workers at the Marine were whisked away from their usual jobs and sent to hard labor at the quarries and building sites. Cathcart was called in to join the others as they were marched a mile out of town to work on the construction of a new fort that was intended to store the city's gunboats during the off-season.

"No rest was allowed on Friday," he recalled. "[It] was worse than the labor of the whole week.

"Figure to yourself: above a thousand poor wretches, many of them half naked without hat and shoes, at work in the heat of the sun all day till four and sometimes till five or six o'clock on a summer day, carrying earth in a basket to the top of a high building, exposed to the heat and often blistered with the sun, chafed and scalded with the weight of their load, the perspiration flowing from them.

"Add to this, that they only received two small loaves of black bread of seven ounces each in all the day, and a very small proportion of horse-beans."

Health and safety precautions were, of course, nonexistent. Captives carrying heavy loads would have to stagger across planks stretching from the top of one high wall to another. As they tottered over the yawning gaps, taskmasters followed, prodding them with sharp cattle goads.

The new fort was so badly designed that it regularly collapsed under its own weight, and every time this happened, all the captive workers in the Marine had to help clear the rubble. (When the fort was eventually finished, the city authorities finally realized a truth that should have been obvious from the beginning: that hauling heavy gunboats a mile inland was not the most efficient practice in the world, no matter how many workers you put to the task. The idea was quietly shelved.) At other times during the week, apprentices like Cathcart also were required to abandon their skilled jobs to work at the docks "whenever hard loads were to be carried." This included the regular dismantling of returning cruisers, the shoveling of ballast, and the hauling of guns and ammunition.

But the most backbreaking work of all was harbor maintenance: dredging the water of mud and stones and endlessly replenishing the five-hundred-yard breakwater known as the mole. This artificial causeway connected the mainland to the island and sheltered the harbor. "[We had] to bring heavy stones to throw to the back of the mole to prevent the sea from breaking over in stormy weather," Cathcart said. It was a grinding, thankless task made all the more frustrating by the fact that one single gale could suck out all the rocks and undo a year's work overnight.

Adding to their woes were the taskmasters, who operated their own penny-ante protection racket. As the sweating captives concentrated on hauling and pushing the boulders, the guards would randomly lash out at them with twisted rattan whips, often drawing blood. The aim was not to make them work harder, but to "oblige us to purchase our peace with them." By paying the guards thirty or forty cents, the captives could avoid the lash. It was admittedly a small enough sum, but "for those who had it not to give, it might as well have been a million."

For the majority of the American seamen, this heavy labor formed a normal daily routine. Captain Richard O'Brien recorded that eleven of the sixteen ordinary sailors were forced to do this sort of work at the docks, suffering all the severities that it was possible to endure. In letters home, he complained about "the lamentable situation of my crew in the Marine, where they are employed on the most laborious work. . . . [They are] exhausted."

Isaac Stephens of the *Maria* painted the same grim picture. As we've seen, he wrote home that his seamen were forced to carry loads of boulders and timber for nearly ten miles across mountainous terrain, developing giant lumps on their shoulders as a result.

Conditions were so bad that one captive wrote home: "Death would be a great relief and more welcome."

• 9 •

"If There Were No Algiers,
I Would Have to Build One"

$\mathcal{D}$eath did not need a second invitation. By 1787, the first American seaman had indeed passed away, as the combination of relentless labor, savage corporal punishment, poor diet, and close confinement in unhygienic conditions had begun taking its inevitable toll. "One of my crew is dead," O'Brien wrote home, referring to Peter Smith of the *Dauphin*. He added that another man had miraculously recovered from plague after fourteen days during which he had developed the classic buboes, or skin swellings, of bubonic plague. Others would not be so lucky. Over the next three years, six seamen from the *Dauphin* would die. (The eventual death toll of this crew would be eight—more than half the fifteen captured.)

It was starting to become painfully obvious to the captives that inaction by the US government was actually solving the problem by default: if the Americans continued to drop dead at this rate, there would be nobody left to worry about. It was left to Captain Richard O'Brien to prick their consciences and suggest practical solutions.

O'Brien had remained as a servant at the British consul's house until a new Spanish envoy, Count d'Expilly, had arrived in town. The count's aristocratic nose had wrinkled in disgust when he learned that a group of officers and gentlemen were being treated as serfs in the house of his British counterpart. Using his considerable political leverage, he had arranged for the American officers to be moved to the house of a French expatriate. "He does everything in his power to make our situation agreeable," O'Brien admitted.

The Spanish consul also arranged for a small allowance—seven and a half cents—to be paid daily to the ordinary American seamen. It was purportedly provided by a Spanish charity operating in Algiers, but the bills were sent to the American government.

This allowed the crewmen to pay bribes to ease their situation as they toiled daily at the docks and construction sites. Although the *Paga Luna* officers were occasionally called to service at the marine—usually to work at the sail loft—they were more usually left to do whatever they wanted.

Stephens wanted to read history books. But what O'Brien wanted to do most was write reports. The Algerines did not object to captives writing letters home—in fact, they actively encouraged the practice. They hoped it would arouse the sympathies of friends and relatives and make them dig deep in their purses. Over the next few years, O'Brien's extensive and detailed dispatches would be the American government's only source of information about what was actually happening in Algiers.

Richard O'Brien was not an educated man: his reports were meandering, ungrammatical, and full of basic spelling errors. But he was well informed, and his agile mind continually searched for imaginative solutions to the impasse.

★　★　★

The way O'Brien saw it, the best option was to make a deal, and the sooner the better. He didn't object to warfare, but the politicians in Philadelphia should threaten war only if they really meant it. Empty threats did more harm than good.

"It is bad policy to use any threats or make any parade with cruisers if we intend suing for a peace," he wrote.

The option of war, as advocated by Thomas Jefferson from Paris, seemed attractive but was fraught with hidden dangers. This would be no ordinary conflict, O'Brien explained.

With any normal conflict, the United States could create a powerful navy and defeat the Algerines in a decisive sea battle.

But Algiers was not normal. America could build up a big enough fleet to outnumber and outgun the Algerines' nine fighting xebecs, but the epic battle would never happen. The Algerine corsairs never sailed in packs. They were "lone wolves." Besides, their intel was superb. Fed information by friendly nations, they simply would avoid confrontation until the threat had subsided.

With any normal conflict, the United States could send gunboats to Algiers, either to blockade the port or to use heavy firepower to reduce the corsair capital to rubble.

But Algiers was not normal. Militarily, everything was invested in the defense of their city. Besides their seagoing xebecs, they had fifty-five gunboats that never left port, augmenting the heavy artillery at the hillside forts. Other nations had tried to assault Algiers from sea and failed. One military expert said bombarding the city had proved to be as useless and expensive as "breaking glass windows with guineas." (Later, a bombardment would indeed bring Algiers to its knees, but it would require truly epic firepower.) The Algerines had also survived extensive blockades. France had tried that tactic and had ended up paying for peace just like everyone else.

With any normal conflict, the United States could capture the Algerines' merchant ships and cut off their trade.

But Algiers was not normal. "The Algerines have no merchant ships . . . except for a few coasting craft," O'Brien wrote. Anything more valuable was carried by French ships.

With any normal conflict, the United States could form an unbeatable alliance with other countries and end the corsair menace forever.

But Algiers was not normal. The main players in Europe preferred to exploit the corsairs in a bid to get the better of their trading rivals and ensure, as one critical US diplomat put it, "rivals chained, yourselves ignobly free." Or as the former French king Louis XIV famously explained: "If there were no Algiers, I would have to build one."

With any normal conflict, the United States could capture Algerine prisoners and trade them for the American captives held in Algiers.

But Algiers was not normal. Two-thirds of seamen captured aboard Algerine ships would be Moors. "The Dey cares not about his people, particularly the Moors," wrote O'Brien. "The Turks he sets a little store by." If a ruler ever agreed to trade prisoners, it would never be on an equal basis: two for one was the norm, but there were times when offers of six for one were refused.

O'Brien pointed out that there was no point threatening war, because Algiers, by its very nature, always needed to be at war with somebody. "A war with the Algerines would be a very expensive war. . . . The United States should use every means to obtain a peace," he wrote.

But he also pointed out that the Americans enjoyed certain advantages. The Algerines harbored no particular animosity to a newborn nation in a new world. Second, America was so far away that there was very little risk of suffering the sort of vengeful coastal raids that the corsairs had inflicted on Spain, Italy, and Britain.

O'Brien suggested some imaginative solutions to the impasse. If America chose war, it would need super-fast ships to outrun the corsairs. But if America chose peace, it didn't have to pay in hard cash. Algiers always *wanted* money, he pointed out, but it *needed* the sort of supplies that could come only from modern industrial nations. Instead of cash, America could offer "naval stores, masts, yards, planks, tar, pitch and turpentine," which could be bargained at far more than they cost to produce. It was a practical solution and, in the end, the one that the United States was later to adopt.

★ ★ ★

While O'Brien was busy writing his reports, the American hostages were trying every trick in the book to extricate themselves from a seemingly endless life of enforced drudgery. One such trick was to play the "foreign citizenship" card.

The United States was still so young that many of its citizens had been born in other countries or had immigrant parents. It was part of the new nation's patchwork of diversity. None of this mattered to the Algerines, whose laws held that the flag of a captured ship dictated the nationality of anyone working aboard. However, for desperate men, this technicality could be used in a bid to persuade the governments of other countries to intervene in their favor. The ruse was quite cynical. If a country friendly to Algiers could claim you as a citizen and put enough pressure on the dey, he could accept you as a special case and set you free. Once safe in Europe, you could plead duress and resume your American nationality. These pleas rarely worked, but they were worth trying.

A year or so after their captures, several men from the *Maria* and the *Dauphin* began to petition the British government on the basis that they had been born in Scotland or Ireland. Among the applicants was James Cathcart, whose birthplace in County Westmeath had entitled him to British citizenship.

The ruse didn't work. The British simply ignored the petitions, and all the applicants remained in captivity.

But by sending his petition to King George III, Cathcart had to expose a secret that he probably would much rather have kept hidden. It had been a difficult choice: he could either conceal his past history or bring it out into the light and thereby gain a shot at freedom. He chose the latter.

The truth was that, in his teens, James Cathcart had not always fought for the American Revolution. After his escape from the hellish prison ships in New York, he had ended up serving briefly as a seaman in the British Royal Navy.

You may recall that back in 1781, the British had captured the American warship *The Confederacy* and thrown Cathcart into the bowels of the infamous prison ships where filthy drinking water and unburied corpses caused raging dysentery. According to family historians, he managed to escape in March 1782, after which he had to fight his way back to safety through the intensely loyalist territory of Long Island.

He obviously didn't make it. Eight months later, he is recorded as a basic seaman on the crew of the Royal Navy ship *Enterprize*. And seven months after that, he appears as a seaman on another British warship, *Leander*.

Exactly how he got there is obscure, not least because Cathcart later wished the episode to remain obscure. But the facts are indisputable. What remains intriguingly indefinable is his motive. Was he captured after weeks on the run and forced into the British navy? Did he get an ultimatum: serve under the British flag or go back to the hell ships of New York? Or was the entire escape story a myth?

Whatever the reason, the revelation—made only recently by modern historians—is a severe blow to anyone who wants life to be black and white, hero versus villain. However, it makes Cathcart a more interesting and nuanced person. For a start, we cannot automatically assume that this was a voluntary choice. Once the navy recruiters discovered that Cathcart had been born in Ireland (and thus regarded by them as a subject of King George), he probably had no say in the matter. And even if the choice were voluntary, who can say what any of us would have done if we had been faced with a choice between an early death from dysentery among the rotting corpses in a prison ship or a lifeline to freedom?

Another point to consider is that when Cathcart joined the *Enterprize* in November 1782, the war had effectively ended: the British Parliament had voted to end the conflict in February, and the first peace treaty was ready to be signed.

Whether our views on the matter are instinctively sympathetic, condemnatory, or neutral, we must above all bear in mind one enormously powerful mitigating factor: when all this happened, the poor kid was only fifteen.

★   ★   ★

On Wednesday, January 10, 1787, a tall figure walked purposely through the streets of Paris toward the Rue de Mathurins. Making sure that he was not being observed, he stole into the entrance of the Church of Saint-Mathurin and prepared himself for one of the most unorthodox and top-secret meetings of his remarkable career.

Thomas Jefferson, the minister plenipotentiary for the United States in France, was about to ask a favor from a man who was his polar opposite. Thomas Jefferson, passionate advocate of the separation of powers of church and state, was about to ask for help from the head of a powerful religious order whose very raison d'être was meddling in politics. Thomas Jefferson, the religious nonconformist who famously rejected the doctrine of the Holy Trinity, was about to seek support from the head of the Order of the Most Holy Trinity. Rarely has any meeting had such an inauspicious start.

Yet Jefferson was determined to make this meeting work. He knew all about the history of the Trinitarians, who'd been founded six centuries earlier with the aim of ransoming Christians who'd been captured during the Crusades. Six hundred years and many wars later, they were still doing much the same job.

Together with another order known as the Mercedarians, they worked tirelessly and courageously in the belly of the pirate capitals, dispensing charity to European captives and manning hospitals to heal the sick. Jefferson had heard that the Trinitarians—known as Les Mathurins after their founder St. John of Matha—had recently used charitable funds to redeem three hundred captives from Algiers at around $200 per man. The US government had not been able to get anything like the same deal for its captured citizens.

Jefferson's secret meeting with Father Francois Maurice Pichault, head of the Trinitarians in Paris, had an ambitious aim. If he could persuade the order to redeem the captives of the *Maria* and the *Dauphin* of its own volition, as a charitable venture, without any apparent involvement by American politicians, the price would be kept low. The money could be secretly backchanneled to the Trinitarians. The United States could remain aloof and principled and would not be regarded as a soft touch.

As the cold January light filtered through the windows, playing on the pictures of the saints and martyrs on the church walls, Jefferson went straight to the point of his visit. Although he had recently dislocated his wrist and was in constant pain, he forced himself to concentrate.

I should be grateful if you would lend your agency toward the redemption of our captive citizens, he told Father Pichault. At the expense of the United States, naturally.

You are welcome to all the services we can render, the churchman replied generously. We have agents on the spot, constantly seeking out and redeeming captives. They will act for your nation exactly as they do for ours.

Jefferson asked what service the United States could provide in return.

Nothing, Father Pichault replied simply. This is why our order exists. However, we must be realistic. The last redemption of our citizens cost 2,500 livres a man [around $460] by the time all expenses were paid. And we are unlikely to get the same deal again. The Algerines regard your people as special, and they are hoping to earn a higher amount for them. Still, I am hopeful the price won't be much higher.

Jefferson thanked him and walked into the streets of the city with a happier and brisker stride. He immediately mailed a letter to his counterpart John Adams in London. "The Mathurins . . . [can] redeem at a lower price than any other people can," he wrote. "I have had interviews with them . . . and they offer their services with all the benignity and cordiality possible . . . on the best terms possible."

Adams's reply was polite but discouraging. The Mathurins "deserve our kindest thanks," he wrote, but handing over cash to them would set a dangerous precedent. He had already been burned by the expenses involved in the

John Lamb fiasco, and he thought it would be best to hold off until "further orders of Congress"—a process that would inevitably take a few more months.

Jefferson didn't give up. He sent his proposal to US Foreign Secretary John Jay in February. Then he set off to Aix-en-Provence to take the waters. This turned into a three-month grand tour of Provence and northern Italy (life was so much more relaxed in those days). He returned in June, just as Jay was putting Jefferson's proposal to Congress.

It wasn't the only document on the subject to be put to Congress that month. The representatives also received a heartbreaking petition from an obscure woman in Concord, Massachusetts. Her name was Hannah Stephens.

Hannah and Isaac

How long the lovesick maid, unheeded rove
The sounding shore, and call her absent love?

—poet-diplomat David Humphreys on the plight of the
families of American hostages in Algiers, 1793

$\mathscr{B}$ack in Concord, the vultures had already begun circling around the Stephens household. It was only a matter of time before the bankers and lawyers fixed their greedy eyes upon her family home.

They told Hannah that the mortgage payment was overdue. Hannah explained the situation and told them she hoped her captive husband, Captain Isaac Stephens, would soon be freed to earn again. That didn't impress the men waving the court writs. They wanted her out.

No doubt Hannah thought at that point that she would still have some financial reserves: even if her house had to be sold, she would keep the money that the couple had originally invested in it. The bankers reacted with a grim shake of the head. The sale had been constructed in such a way that if a single payment were missed, then everything would be forfeit—house, equity, everything.

"[My husband] paid part of the purchase money," Hannah explained later. "But by means of his great misfortune in being made a prisoner, he has been unable to complete the purchase, and the money that has been paid has been lost by reason of the failure of the payment of the remainder; therefore I have been turned out of doors."

And so, one bleak day, Hannah and her three children were evicted, homeless, by the side of the road, without a penny to their name. "[I am] destitute and forsaken," she wrote.

Because there was no modern-style system of welfare, Hannah would have been reliant upon the charity of her neighbors in Concord. With a population of 1,320 in the 1780s, the town had always had a fund for "maintenance of the poor," paid first by subscription and then by a "poor rate." A small almshouse had also been built. Hannah probably had to avail herself of both. There were also church subscriptions, and sometimes a group of well-off locals agreed to sponsor an individual in rotation. According to a local historian, "the people of Concord have ever been ready to bestow their aid with generosity."

However, times were hard in postwar New England, and townspeople naturally tended to give priority to their own kinsfolk. Was Hannah, as a recent arrival, placed at the end of the queue? It's difficult to tell, but we do know that she had to pack away any pretense to middle-class status and roll up her sleeves for some tough domestic work just to get by.

"[I have been] driven to the cruel necessity of doing the lowest duties of a servant to prevent myself and my children from suffering hunger and nakedness," she testified later. At the time, a housemaid could expect to earn around $7 a month, which would not have gone very far. It was certainly not enough, because very soon Hannah was forced to put all three of her children to work. When Isaac, far away in Algiers, learned of this development, it broke his heart that his wife had been "obliged to put our children out for their living, and herself obliged to work hard for our bread."

However, the staple food in the Concord area, Indian cornmeal, was usually relatively cheap, and firewood was available to gather if she walked far enough, so she knew that she wouldn't starve or freeze. Some of the meaner-spirited townsfolk in Concord might not have been completely displeased to see the privileged captain's wife reduced to sweeping floors and hanging out other people's washing, but they would have been a minority. Most of her neighbors would have been deeply sympathetic and helpful as she shouldered what she called her "accumulated load of human woe."

Hannah's only hope was to get Isaac back home again—and she resolved to do everything in her power to do just that. Summoning all her courage, in 1787 she sent the first of several heartfelt petitions to Congress "praying that [her] husband be redeemed from captivity at Algiers."

★ ★ ★

Back in the pirate city, Captain Isaac Stephens was beside himself with worry over Hannah and his children. The captives had just received a letter from John Lamb claiming that John Adams, personally, had refused to pay their ransoms. Stephens had been unwell with stomach problems for some time, and he took this news as yet another blow to the gut. He obviously knew nothing at this stage about Jefferson's negotiations with the Mathurins, and his chronic illness combined with his sense of betrayal led this straight-talking seaman to write words he would later regret.

"I must think you to be the greatest enemy that I have in the world and not a friend to liberty," Stephens wrote to Adams, his former neighbor in Braintree. "It did lie in your power to hasten our redemption."

He demanded that the politician help "my distressed family" and added ominously: "If you don't, make your peace with God before you get a peace with the Dey of Algiers."

He appealed to Adams, as another family man, to put himself in Stephens's situation. "You are not so old but you may have as great calamities as mine before you die," he told Adams. "Look on your children and pray no judgement might fall on them."

Much later, when he tried to mend fences with Adams, Stephens maintained that Richard O'Brien had stoked him up and provoked him into adopting such a caustic tone. That sounds plausible: we can well imagine O'Brien restricting his own correspondence to informative reports and positive suggestions, with a view to his own future career, while manipulating the simpler and more trusting Stephens into playing bad cop to his good cop.

Whatever the truth, Stephens ended his diatribe against Adams by stressing their common roots in Massachusetts. "I shall look on you not to be a friend to mankind and liberty until you give me better proofs of it in your next letter, Sir, to a gentleman [you were] once acquainted with."

★ ★ ★

Hannah's courageous petition actually succeeded in getting things moving. Secretary of Foreign Affairs John Jay wrote to Congress that summer, drawing their attention to "a petition from Hannah Stephens praying that her husband be redeemed" and deliberately tying it in with Jefferson's plan "that a certain order of priests be employed for such purposes."

Prodded into action by Hannah's plea, Congress officially gave Jefferson the green light to proceed with his Mathurins plan. This time Jefferson went directly to the order's top man, General Pére Chauvier, who warned him that secrecy was of the essence. If news leaked out, it could push up ransom prices for everyone—not just the Americans.

The general had another problem. His agents in Algiers had told him that the Americans were receiving a daily allowance from a Spanish charity. This had annoyed some French prisoners who were reliant on much smaller contributions from his own order. On principle, the Mathurins could not help until this inequity ended.

It was an unexpected twist, but Jefferson had no choice but to agree. As both men knew, the Spanish payments were not genuine charity aid: they were actually US government money laundered through Spain. Not only would this miserable pittance be cut and replaced with a much smaller amount paid through the Mathurins, but the American captives could not even be told the reason for this drastic change.

"[We had to let] the captives and their friends believe for a while that no attention was paid to them, no notice taken of their letters," Jefferson lamented three years later. "They are still under this impression. It would have been unsafe to trust them with a secret . . . which might forever prevent their redemption . . . [but it] drew from them the most afflicting reproaches."

And those reproaches were indeed heartbreaking. One letter home lamented: "We were for some time supplied with such sums of money . . . to alleviate in some degree the rigor of our captivity, but those supplies have ceased for a considerable time. . . . We have been reduced to the utmost distress . . . [and] depend on the charity of transient people."

Cathcart was also in the dark. "We were allowed seven and a half cents a day for some time from our own country," he complained, "but that allowance was soon withdrawn from us, and for some years no more notice was taken of us. . . . Our situation could not be worse."

Leaving that aspect aside, Jefferson's plan was a brilliant example of lateral thinking and provided a golden opportunity for the US government. A mere $500 (or so) for the price of a citizen's freedom was a relative pittance, and the nation could still claim that it had refused to surrender to blackmail.

Yet, incredibly, the US government did not act in time. It took a full year for the money to be lodged in Paris, and by that time the effects of the plague in Algiers (combined with ransoms by other nations) had reduced the population of foreign captives in the city to around a quarter of its 1785 figure, creating a shortage. That year, there had been 3,000 captives, the following year, 2,200; by 1789, there would be only 655, barely enough to provide the city's essential labor. For the first time in decades, captive hostages had become more important as actual workers than as pawns for ransom. They "had become scarce, and would hardly be sold at any price," Jefferson reported.

Even though there were fewer Americans alive to rescue, the government set the ceiling at a niggardly $550 a man. However, the general of the Mathurins remained optimistic, and the plan swung into action in late 1788.

But the United States had acted too late. A few months later, an angry crowd stormed the Bastille, and a new National Assembly took control in what became known as the French Revolution. The rich and powerful church was among its first targets, and before long, all clerical lands and assets had been seized. The Mathurins were no exception. "[This] seems to have suspended the proceedings of the Mathurins in the purposes of their institution," Jefferson reported dolefully.

One of the most carefully constructed hostage extraction schemes in American history had collapsed, completely and irretrievably. "It is time," Jefferson wrote, "to look for something more promising."

It was an unfortunate choice of adjective, because for the next six years, "promising" was just about all the politicians did.

★　★　★

Now here's a curious thing. In Paris, Jefferson spent hours each day working with this humanitarian organization in a bid to free the Americans held captive in Algiers. Then each night he returned home to his apartment in the Hotel de Langeac on the Champs-Élysées to enjoy the cuisine of his personal slave, James Hemings, an African American cook whom he'd brought from the States.

James was soon joined by another enslaved person, his sister Sally. At some point during Jefferson's stay in Paris—or very shortly afterward—the widowed statesman began sleeping with Sally Hemings, and this secret master-concubine relationship continued for many years. It's now widely accepted through modern DNA evidence that Jefferson was the father of five or six of Sally's children. Yet she lived and died as an enslaved woman.

During the last few months of her stay in Paris, Sally could have walked out at any time: under French law, she was a free woman. Aware of that, Jefferson negotiated a special contract with her, ensuring that she would "voluntarily" return to America with him and continue to serve as his slave in return for special privileges for their future children. (She may have been pregnant at that time with a child who did not survive.)

This is an example of what modern historians tactfully call "the paradox" of Thomas Jefferson. Which is that the man who personally wrote the most electrifying phrase in the US Declaration of Independence was himself a slave owner. "All men are created equal," he famously thundered. Yet during his lifetime he owned an estimated six hundred slaves.

Until quite recently, this inconsistency has been explained away by the specious argument that he was some sort of benevolent employer maintaining a rural community of contented workers on a well-run Virginia farm. Jefferson felt they were better off staying with him, albeit as slaves, than being liberated into a hostile world where others would mistreat them.

But recent research has shattered the myth that his motives were selfless. Jefferson was actually a wholehearted supporter of slave ownership for financial gain, enthusing to friends that his human portfolio of slaves increased in value by 4 percent per year before they did a single stroke of work. His lavish standard of living and his stratospherically high household expenses were made possible only by putting young boys to work at an industrial nail factory, where "the small ones" were whipped for idleness or truancy. When one of his adult slaves ran off, Jefferson hired slave trackers to haul him back and recorded that he had him "severely flogged in the presence of his old companions."

Sally Hemings outlived Jefferson, dying in her sixties without ever having been formally emancipated. Even though Jefferson had the option of setting her free in his will—if only as a simple act of appreciation for long service—he declined to do so.

· 11 ·

Lions and Tigers and Rats

$\mathcal{B}$ack in Algiers, unaware of Jefferson's diplomatic maneuverings, James Cathcart continued his grim existence as a working hostage. On weekdays he worked as a carpenter's apprentice, on Fridays as a grunt laborer at the docks and construction sites. The months dragged on, and every day began much the same way. First the dreaded bass roar of the guard at 3:00 a.m., the assembly in the yard, and the miserable procession down to the *squiffa*, or portal to the Marine, where the mouth-watering smell of fresh bread from the port bakery mingled with the tang of salt and seaweed and the stench of fumes from the nearby pitch house, where tar was kept constantly boiling to caulk the ships. Under the disdainful stare of the minister for the marine, the workers lined up to receive their food ration.

This ritual was in itself a calculated display of deference and humility. "With profound submission, their caps in their hands if they have any, [they] receive each time a small loaf and then move off in regular file before their taskmasters, silent as mutes," Cathcart wrote. It was a harrowing sight that could have come straight from the pages of Dante.

After their eleven- or twelve-hour shifts, the workers shuffled back to the bagnio—not to rest, but to use the remaining hours before lockdown to earn some pin money. The system encouraged private enterprise. Anyone who could mend old shoes, repair tools, fashion children's toys, busk music, or write letters for illiterate clients could use these late afternoon hours to make a few pennies that would make his life a bit more tolerable.

"In all the prisons in the evenings may be seen different tradesmen at work," Cathcart wrote. "Shoemakers, tailors, carpenters, coopers, sawyers, and some hucksters are those who [have] the most constant employment and

71

make the most money." Less talented workers collected garbage from local homes.

Most of this money went toward bribes to corrupt officials, earning the workers such basic benefits as a sleeping spot indoors or dispensation from the dreaded rattan whip. The most successful entrepreneurs were allowed to save money toward buying their own freedom. The Algerines wanted ransom cash and didn't care where it came from—if a prisoner could pay it himself through years of moonlight working, so much the better.

Less scrupulous captives used this free time to steal. They became experts at pickpocketing, shoplifting, and petty burglary, roaming the alleyways of the city and distracting harassed traders on one side of their stalls as their partners expertly filched food or saleable items from the other. In theory, there were heavy penalties for those caught thieving, but in reality, the ruling Turks laughed it off since the victims were usually Moors. Besides, the practice allowed the authorities to scrimp on food rations without the risk of starving their workers to death. In effect, the traders were subsidizing the government: every stolen loaf of bread meant less cost to the state.

During the day, the bagnio was open to freemen as well as inmates. And it was where the action was. Its central courtyard buzzed with the multilingual hubbub of wheelers and dealers hammering out deals—both legal and illegal, since the bagnio operated in practice as a sort of freeport wherein the normal rules were suspended. So long as public order was maintained and the guards had their palms well-greased, nobody cared much whether that tobacco you were selling had been lawfully acquired or had fallen off the back of a wagon.

In a city where alcohol was supposedly banned, the bagnios also provided an outlet for locals to enjoy a forbidden cup of wine or even to sample the shocking taste of pork sausages. In fact, the entire ground floor of the bagnio consisted of taverns run by well-off Christian captives who could afford to pay huge bribes on top of the basic rental.

To preserve a certain decorum, the taverns were all tucked out of sight, with not so much as a window or vent to release the dense, suffocating atmosphere of liquor, human sweat, and tobacco smoke. "They are perfectly dark and in the day are illuminated with lamps, and [are] full of drunken Turks, Moors, Arabs, Christians and now and then a Jew or two," Cathcart recalled.

In such a small area, the cacophony of shouted conversation was deafening, especially since everyone had to raise their voices against the background noise of hopeful buskers playing guitars, fiddles, and tabors. "Each [was] singing or rather shouting in different languages, without the least connection. The place [was] filled with the smoke of tobacco which renders objects nearly impervious to the view. Some [were] wrangling with the tavern keepers for more liquor and refusing to pay for it . . . on the whole it must resemble the infernal regions more than any other place in the known world."

The noise would reach a crescendo each evening when a thunderous basso profundo voice roared: "We are closing the gates! We are closing the gates! We are closing the gates!" As the prison guardians prepared to seal the entrance, drinkers desperately scrambled to get themselves out of the bagnio.

"[There] emerged from the taverns a motley crew . . . all intoxicated, some half naked, having sold or pawned their clothes for liquor," Cathcart recalled, "others singing or shouting, some with drawn swords swearing that they would kill the first person who offended them." Others reeled unsteadily homeward, and the off-duty Janissary troops grudgingly returned to their barracks. No one wanted to be caught inside the bagnio once it reverted to its darker role as a penal complex. "The gates of the prison were then shut for the night, and a heavy chain was drawn across the inside of the outer gate, and the inner one was bolted and locked."

Each night, that doleful metallic grinding and clattering underlined the change in atmosphere. All the drinking and moonlighting and wheeling and dealing was over; this was now a prison, and the only people left inside were inmates and their guards. The prisoners were now at the mercy of the *Carneros*.

The *Carneros* were the night guards and, according to Cathcart, they were notorious as "the most hardened villains in the Regency." They were prisoners themselves, mostly from Spain, and they were unique among the inmates because they had actually volunteered for captivity. They had all been criminals in their previous lives and had been sentenced to serve as soldiers in the infamous Spanish garrison at Oran, a 250-mile trek from Algiers. Conditions there had been so dire that starving soldiers had deserted in large numbers and footslogged overland, reasoning that life as a captive in Algiers could not be any worse than their hellish existence at Oran. Hence, they were dubbed *Carneros*—sheep who had offered themselves for slaughter.

Their reasoning was sound, however. Their military experience, criminal mindset, and sheer sadism made them perfect candidates for night guards in a bagnio. In return for their service, the *Carneros* were allowed to run one of the taverns. If they saw that an inmate had saved a bit of money from his off-duty work, they would insist that he spent it in their bar. Those who didn't frequent their tavern "are continually persecuted by them," said Cathcart, "as the prisoners at night are entirely under their command, and an unfavorable report in the morning from one of these miscreants will [result in] a severe bastinadoing and several weeks in chains besides."

Cathcart had quickly learned to keep on good terms with the *Carneros* because they had the power to recommend that certain prisoners be sent to the "hardest and most disagreeable work."

The criminal *Carneros* also fenced stolen goods. If they were caught in the act, they lied with practiced ease and blamed a completely innocent prisoner: one more reason to keep them well supplied with backhanders.

Every night, fresh consignments of stolen goods would appear in the bagnio for disposal by the *Carneros*. Most of the plunder had been spirited away from the docks while supervisors had looked the other way: it included sails, planks, iron nails, and even whole barrels of gunpowder. "I have known whole cables of large dimension disposed of in the middle of daylight," Cathcart reported.

The workers were supposedly searched when they left the harbor each night, but these checks were obviously halfhearted. Still, there would be the occasional crackdown. John Foss, another captured American, witnessed one man being bastinadoed for trying to remove three nails.

The bagnio doubled as a jail for conventional criminals. The *Carneros* would often chain one of these jailbirds and leave him fettered for days or even weeks. "Sometimes forty or fifty are here chained two and two together for months, nay, some for years, for different crimes," Cathcart recalled. "The jingling of chains adds horror to this dismal dungeon . . . which with the stench and unnatural imprecations and blasphemy of some of its miserable inhabitants, makes it a perfect pandemonium."

As we saw earlier, new arrivals often slept outside in all weather until they could afford monthly rental for a bunk inside. "On the evening after the moon changes, the keeper of the Bagnio calls out for all hands to pay for their rooms," recalled John Foss. "If anyone . . . cannot pay it down, his hands are put into irons behind him, and his legs chained to a pillar every night until the money is paid." He said that those who couldn't raise the cash "are obliged to sleep every night upon the cold stones, with nothing but the heavens to cover them."

Cathcart had been unable to stay with his friend d'Andreis for more than a couple of nights. However, he'd gathered enough money from his tips at the palace to pay for a bunk inside. The inmates slept on the second and third stories of the jail, in long, narrow, airless rooms where their hammocks were hung in frames over each other, four deep. "They repose as well as miserable wretches can be supposed to do, who are swarming with vermin of all sorts, many nearly naked, and few with anything more than an old tattered blanket to cover them in the depth of winter," Cathcart wrote drily.

Others paid to sleep on tables in the empty taverns or in specially constructed "rooms"—small timber boxes that lined the galleries.

There were times when the prison was so overcrowded that beds were not available at any price. Men were obliged to lie on the floor "or wherever they could find shelter from the inclemency of the weather."

After a grim spell at the Bagnio Belique, Cathcart became desperate to leave. He had tired of the multilingual babble and yearned for the comforting sound of American accents. Most of the Americans had been allocated to a different bagnio, the Bagnio Gallera, and Cathcart longed to join them. The move wouldn't be much of a step upward. Although his present prison was universally regarded as "the most miserable," the Gallera had its own particular disadvantages. Cathcart still had a few dollars left, and he had developed a good working relationship with the *Cameros*, so he cautiously sounded them out about a possible move. They said they could arrange it for a small consideration of $2. It would turn out to be the wisest two dollars he ever spent.

★   ★   ★

The Bagnio Gallera had once housed the captives who crewed the galley ships, hence the name. Although smaller than the Belique with only two stories, its layout was exactly the same. However, there was less pressure regarding accommodation. Americans who had enough money were able to stay together in their own room.

Whereas the Belique had a distinctly criminal air about it, the Gallera was reputed to hold "the more respectable prisoners" and "the better sort," as Cathcart put it a little sniffily. He obviously saw it as his first tentative step up the social ladder, and he was right.

Clutching a basket containing a blanket and his few meager possessions, Cathcart arrived at the Gallera on a soupy, airless night without the slightest breeze to offset the stomach-turning stench that hit him as soon as he walked through the door. It was an overpowering, musky smell that the former zookeeper immediately recognized, and which he'd probably hoped that he would never have to deal with again.

Lions.

Every so often, a muffled growl or a full-throated roar emanated from the bowels of the bagnio. As Cathcart gingerly explored his new home, he found out why. Lodged inside dark prison cells in the very heart of the building were the older lions and tigers that had outgrown their welcome at the dey's palace.

No one knew what to do with the unfortunate animals. Responsibility for their welfare had been dumped on the tavern keepers, who resented this extra role and didn't devote much care to it. The huge beasts were kept chained in the semidarkness. Their cells were rarely cleaned, and every day a terrified inmate tossed in a few heads of bullocks or sheep to keep the creatures alive.

"I have known twenty-seven animals of this description to be kept at once in this prison," Cathcart explained. American hostage John Foss later confirmed that a "great number of animals of prey" were kept shackled in the Gallera's cells.

The big cats, half-crazed by their confinement, regularly tore free of their chains and ran amok around the prison. Nobody was allowed to touch them without express permission from the dey; during every breakout, a messenger had to run to the palace to ask for an armed guard to come and shoot the snarling, rampaging beasts before they savaged too many prisoners.

"They frequently break loose and have killed several," Cathcart testified matter-of-factly. The prisoners "dare not destroy them even in their own defense."

Meanwhile, the animals' manure not only produced "an insufferable stench" that was almost unbearable in the summer heat, but also hosted an infestation of rats: "an enormous number," wrote Cathcart, "the largest I ever saw."

For anyone who was hungry enough, these giant rats proved an irresistible temptation. Cathcart once saw a French captive walking away with a large rat and naively asked what he was going to do with it.

The Frenchman shrugged as only Frenchmen can and replied in his own language: "A man's gotta eat."

Rat infestation was unpleasant enough in itself, but it also carried a major health risk. Rats carried fleas, and the fleas carried bubonic plague—although nobody knew that at the time. It was no coincidence that the Bagnio Gallera suffered more plague deaths than any other prison.

If Cathcart had harbored high hopes of an easier life in the Bagnio Gallera, he was soon disillusioned. He'd assumed that his $2 transfer fee would smooth his passage into the new prison, but no—as soon as he arrived, his new guards immediately hit him with the old shackle shakedown. "A large ring of iron . . . was put on my leg," he recalled, and he had to pay another bribe to have it switched for a lighter one.

He had hoped that he could join the other American prisoners in their separate room, but they told him there was no space: it was already crowded to capacity. He went to the tavern seeking to rent a tabletop to sleep on. But by the time he arrived, all the available spots had been taken.

Cathcart looked around the room and found what he thought was an ideal sleeping spot: a cozy gap on the floor between a large wine cask and the wall. "I was obliged to spread my blanket [there]," he wrote, "with my basket containing all my worldly possessions under my head, to serve for a pillow and prevent the contents from being stolen."

The heat and stinking airlessness were soporific, but as soon as he drifted off to sleep, he found out why nobody else had chosen this cozy spot. It was a rat run, and the fearless giant rodents scampered over him "continuously" throughout the night. Voracious fleas hopped off the tavern floor and bit every inch of his flesh, while mosquitos and other biting insects "attacked on all sides." It was such an excruciating night that, when the bass voice of the guard boomed around the prison summoning the workers to rise, Cathcart actually felt happy to hear it.

That night signified the rock bottom of James Cathcart's career. Deprived of his liberty at eighteen, he had moved steadily downward from a worker's berth in a garden, a hammock in the bleak Bagnio Belique, to the hard floor of this filthy, stinking, rat-infested den. Cold-shouldered by his shipmates, seemingly abandoned by his government, and isolated in this strange new prison, he had just spent a sleepless night being overrun by rats and devoured by fleas before being summoned at three in the morning to work, unpaid, for twelve or thirteen hours, thousands of miles away from his homeland.

But things were about to change. Cathcart's indominable spirit had remained unbroken. From this low point in the stifling darkness of prison, his fortune was about to soar upward like a rocket's red glare.

II

· 12 ·

The Man Who Made a Million

$\mathcal{F}$or an Irish American like Cathcart, it was apt that the turning point in his life came on Saint Patrick's Day. On that auspicious date in 1787, a frigate from Naples glided sedately into Algiers Bay, sailing under a flag of truce and laden with gold and silver coins to ransom its citizens.

For locals, this was a momentous event. The Neapolitans were among the Algerines' deadliest opponents. Like the Genoese and the Maltese, they had spent centuries locked in a bitter existential grapple with the Barbary corsairs.

In 1787, the king of Naples decided that enough was enough. He agreed to pay a predetermined sum to free the three hundred Neapolitans held as hostages in Algiers. The money was handed over, and the Italian captives sailed happily off to freedom. Many had been in captivity for decades.

By coincidence, the long-running dispute between Algiers and Spain was settled around the same time. A peace treaty negotiated two years before was finalized, and four hundred newly freed Spanish seamen sailed off to Minorca.

This deal did not include those Spanish who had deserted from Oran. "When the ship sailed, she was followed by the eyes of those poor captives," Cathcart recalled, "and when she disappeared in the horizon, a universal groan was heard . . . declaring that their last hope had vanished."

As the Algerines counted their money, they realized they had a problem. The mass evacuations had left some gaping holes in their management structure. Over the decades, the Spanish captives, in particular, had worked themselves up into key positions in the state bureaucracy. Administrators, accountants, managers—all had vanished, together with their invaluable years

81

of experience. The Turkish governors needed to train some more hostages as bureaucrats and quickly.

Where would they find them? Certainly not in the disreputable Bagnio Belique, with its crooked *Carneros* and its jailbirds and its stink of criminality. No, they went straight to the Bagnio Gallera, where "the most respectable prisoners" were confined. Cathcart had made his move in the timeliest manner. For once, he was in exactly the right place at the right time.

Until that point, Cathcart had been continuing his arduous schedule as before. Merely reading his list of jobs leaves the reader exhausted: "I [was] working in the carpenter shop in the daytime, occasionally sent to carry heavy loads to disarm the cruisers, load vessels with wheat, carry ballast on board the cruisers, and, on Friday, either sent to work at the Magazine [construction site] or to the Ponte Piscado to load the pontoon with heavy stone to throw at the back of the mole . . . in short, every sort of labor."

When the Neapolitans left, Cathcart and his fellow American James Harnet had been told to report to the offices of Sidi Ali Hassan, the minister for the marine (and the man whom John Lamb had secretly sought out for advice). They were to join the crew of half a dozen men who worked as servants at the ministry office. Their duties were to serve meals and coffee to Hassan and his high-profile guests, to monitor the stores, carry the keys, and—in a remarkable reversal of roles—to dispense the rations to the other captives each morning.

It got better. When the Spanish sailed off a few days later, two positions were left vacant in the same office: that of Hassan's righthand man, the clerk of the marine, and that of the *coffeegie* or chief coffee server. Cathcart was elevated to coffee server, a role that was much more important than the title suggests. He was charged with supervising the other staff and ensuring their good behavior.

The benefits included coffee-cup tips, just as in the palace, but on a much more lavish scale. Hassan was regarded as a major player in Algiers. Into his office came "Beys, Caliphs, Alcaides, Ambassadors and Christian consuls" who all followed custom by dropping coins into their empty cups as they left. They could not scrimp, because a niggardly tip was regarded as an insult to their host. Each Thursday night, the money was divided among the office staff.

These captives were also given decent clothes, a good diet, and Fridays off. Best of all, Hassan's personal staff were answerable only to him. "They are not subject to the Guardians [of the bagnio] nor to the orders of anyone else."

Cathcart scarcely had time to get used to his dramatic change of fortune when he had a third stroke of good luck. The man appointed to the office's top job, that of clerk to the marine, was Giovanni de la Cruz—Cathcart's *other* friend from Boston. The Italian seafarer had been captured a year after

Cathcart, and now fate had thrown them together again. De la Cruz was so delighted that he invited the American to share his private room.

Perhaps we should pause for a moment to consider the phenomenon of Cathcart's luck. Throughout his life, he enjoyed a series of serendipitous meetings and coincidental reunions that would change his life. Yet it wasn't *just* luck. He had natural skills that we would now describe as soft power: emotional intelligence and adept social networking. He was very much a social animal: multilingual, well read, and a relaxed conversationalist with a deadpan sense of humor. But he also left a lasting positive impression, which is not at all the same thing. Although he wasn't universally loved—far from it—Cathcart made friends easily, and those friends stayed loyal to him. Years after a typical encounter, his acquaintances would remember him fondly and somehow feel compelled to help him. To that extent, he made his own luck.

Whatever the reason, Giovanni de la Cruz became Cathcart's new guardian angel. He encouraged the coffee server to shadow him as he carried out his duties as chief clerk. As always, the young American learned quickly, assimilating information with a natural ease.

Which was exactly what his young shipmate from the *Maria*, James Harnet, was sadly incapable of doing. Harnet had accompanied Cathcart at every stage of his journey, but this promotion was a step too far for him. "He was sent out for incapacity," Cathcart wrote sadly, "as he was a simple, ignorant lad, and could not learn the duties exacted from him." Cathcart could do nothing to prevent his removal but continued to help him as Harnet began his downward spiral into insanity.

Meanwhile, Cathcart's daily routine started as early as ever. He had to get up at the same time as the captives in the prison—three in the morning—and "go to the Marine as soon as the gate was opened, in order to have [Hassan's] seat made and coffee ready for him on his arrival."

Each morning the minister for the marine sat under an arch on a nest of velvet pillows on a sheepskin sofa. A silken parasol protected him from the sun, and a red carpet lay underneath. After supervising the assembly and dispersal of the captive workers each morning, he received favored visitors. Cathcart served the coffee—Turkish style, of course—and later lit a pipe of tobacco for those who smoked. At mealtimes, Cathcart and his team prepared the dining area. Honored guests sat cross-legged around a finely inlaid table about eighteen inches high. A curtain was drawn, and they would eat soup followed by fowl or lamb, then fish with couscous or rice pilaf, and finally fruit and sherbet. After coffee, the diners would "rise according to rank, kiss [his] hand, and retire."

★   ★   ★

Hassan was a muscular man in his fifties but looked much younger. "[He has] a long black beard," wrote one American. "He is a man of venerable aspect and of a majestic person, being about six feet high, but inclining to leanness. He speaks in a very imperious and authoritative tone. He goes bare-legged, but with slippers on his feet."

According to John Foss, who encountered him a few years later, Hassan was "a thick, well-built man with a white beard covering his breast. He is of a very light complexion [and] does not appear to be much decayed by the weight of years, which have rolled over his head."

Originally from Smyrna (present day Izmir) in Anatolia, he began his career as a common soldier and worked his way through the ranks of the Janissary militia to become an official in the dey's palace in Algiers.

He was an internationally respected diplomat: "a man of uncommon abilities and a wise politician," according to Robert Montgomery, the US agent at Alicante in Spain, who added that he displayed "great wisdom and talents" in his role as marine minister.

The crowning point of his career had been the historic peace treaty with Spain—Algiers's oldest and most bitter enemy. Having delivered the deal, he made sure he received a major slice of the action. "[He] made himself vastly rich, particularly by the Spanish peace," wrote Joel Barlow, the American diplomat. "[It] was the richest treaty they ever made. . . . I am told that it cost about five million dollars, of which this man received one million."

He had pulled off this diplomatic coup by turning a personal catastrophe to his advantage. Fifteen years earlier, he had been captured by the Spanish—still at that stage the enemies of Algiers—and thrown into prison in Cartagena. However, the Spanish had messed up: Hassan had been sailing on a French ship at the time and thus under French protection. A major diplomatic row erupted between the two European giants. He was freed from prison but "detained for some time" in Cartagena, during which time he cultivated some high-level contacts and tested the waters for a peace deal. When he was allowed to return to Algiers, he resumed talks with these contacts and eventually finalized the treaty.

Finding himself a millionaire—quite an achievement in the 1780s—Hassan invested a large chunk of his cash into secret bribes to everyone who mattered in Algiers, in return for guarantees that he would be next in line to the throne when the aging Dey Mahmood died. But this was Algiers, and in Algiers nothing was certain.

Wise and talented though he may have been as a diplomat, Hassan was also notorious for his mercurial temperament. Calm and good-humored at one moment, he could suddenly fly into irrational rages the next. Anyone unfortunate enough to be around him at the time could suffer the consequences as he "commanded deeds of inhumanity, of which he repents afterwards," according to Foss.

On this point, everyone agreed. "A man of a most ungovernable temper, passionate, changeable, and unjust to such a degree that there is no calculating his policy from one moment to another," wrote American diplomat Joel Barlow. One biographer referred to Hassan as "as full of whims and fancies as a sick child, as difficult to amuse . . . as a cross bear."

So it appears there were many versions of Hassan, depending on context. To his fellow diplomats, he was sagacious, shrewd, and patient. Among the courtiers of Algiers, he was notorious for his corruption and terrifyingly single-minded ambition. To the people who worked for him, he was a nightmare—fickle, capricious, impulsive, and often violent. And as we see later, he was a faithful husband and a doting father, and yet he was capable of ordering cold-blooded hits on family members if he thought they stood in the way of his career. Hassan contained multitudes.

★   ★   ★

That year, a plague-infected ship arrived in Algiers from the Levant, and the contagion swept through the narrow streets and alleyways of Algiers like a raging, uncontrollable fire. It found a perfect breeding ground among the tightly packed captives in the prisons. In January 1787, as we've seen, the plague claimed its first American victim: seaman Peter Smith of the *Dauphin*.

Smith had been in the Bagnio Gallera, long acknowledged to be a hotspot for the disease. No one in that era knew exactly how the plague spread, so the prison's seething population of rats remained uncontrolled. Cathcart theorized that the Gallera was a plague magnet because it shared a sewer with the adjacent hospital—and that certainly didn't help. Whatever the reason, the door that connected the two buildings was constantly busy as victims were carried through from prison to hospital. "In less than twelve hours, several were carried to their graves," Cathcart noted grimly.

The disease did not differentiate between captives and citizens. On one single day—April 28—the plague claimed the lives of 215 people, prisoners and freepersons alike.

Once again, Cathcart's timing had been perfect: he had moved out of the Gallera in March, just before the plague reached its peak there. In the well-ventilated, scrupulously clean surroundings of Hassan's office at the marine, he and Giovanni had a much better chance of escaping infection. "With the exception of people dying with the plague all around us," Cathcart recalled drily, "our situation was very tolerable."

That May, 114 captives of all nations died of plague, and in June the figure rose to 155. That same month, Giovanni told Cathcart he was feeling ill. He took to his bed, and the American did his best to nurse him through the illness. "I rendered him all the service in my power, but to no effect," Cathcart lamented. "He lingered a few days, and [in] June, departed this life, regretted by all who knew him. He was a most amiable young man."

The plague had finally entered the marine administration building, and it tore through its corridors with a vengeance. All through that summer, staffers were carried out sick, never to return. As the disease raged on, nearly every single captive there died and was replaced by another person who later died, until the process was repeated three times and the only two people still above ground in the marine office were James Cathcart and Sidi Hassan himself. Both must have had constitutions like oxen.

Cathcart took over temporary responsibility for Giovanni's work, and the transfer was so smooth that Hassan, clearly impressed, officially appointed him as clerk of the marine.

And so, the nineteen-year-old ordinary seaman who had been sweeping out lion cages at the zoo a year before was catapulted, almost overnight, into one of the most powerful and influential positions in the Algiers bureaucracy.

Several factors had lined up perfectly, like friendly harbor lights, to guide him into this elevated role. As we've seen, his timing was incredibly lucky, and he was fortunate that his contacts were there for him at the right place and the right time, but the main factor was his impressively healthy immune system, which had made him (almost) the last man standing amid the devastation of a plague. It has been said that 80 percent of success is simply showing up. In Cathcart's case, it was simply a matter of showing that he could stay upright.

· *13* ·

The Hassan Whisperer

Cathcart rapidly mastered his new role as clerk of the marine and—more importantly—the art of dealing with the mercurial and explosively vindictive Sidi Hassan. Cathcart himself described his boss as "a man fully governed by his passions."

Fortunately, the new clerk had developed an almost preternatural ability to read his boss's micro-expressions and predict these mood swings before they erupted into destructive rage. Modern card players might say that he could read the "tells." Cathcart put it more simply: "I have been in the habit of reading his countenance."

For instance, when Hassan was secretly pleased by a development, his face showed a brief flicker, "a latent spark of satisfaction," which he immediately disguised with a poker face. But when he was about to explode in fury, his long mustachios curled slightly upward as the corners of his mouth twisted into an almost imperceptible snarl of displeasure. Cathcart learned how to observe these harbingers of danger and act swiftly to forestall them. It was a skill that would later save his life, over and over again.

Cathcart developed his own unique technique for Hassan whispering. He had learned from his rounds with the Spanish carpenter the formal tones and cadences that signified respect in Algiers. To these he added the zest of his own personality: a keen wit, an ability to challenge a statement without appearing discourteous, and a quirky sense of humor that—he'd learned by experience—could surprise Hassan into a chuckle instead of a roar of anger. Above all, he was politely direct in his speech: Hassan despised toadying.

Best to give an example. At one stage during his time at the marine, Hassan made Cathcart a generous offer that sounded suspiciously like a secret test of character.

Years later, Hassan would repeat the story as proof of his young protégé's integrity: "I offered him full pay if he would [convert to Islam]," Hassan recalled, "and the command of my largest cruiser . . . and a wife and a house and garden, and likewise to take care of his fortunes in future. . . .

"[He] thanked me for the good opinion I entertained of him, and that he would endeavor to retain it, but [answered] that he would deserve contempt if he should become an apostate [i.e., a convert] merely to promote his worldly interests."

The reply impressed Hassan, but there was also a zinger of a punch line to his story. The cruiser that he'd offered the American was shortly afterward caught in a sea battle with a Russian warship, and its commander was fatally wounded. If Cathcart had taken the offer, he would have been dead within months.

★   ★   ★

In early 1788, Captain Isaac Stephens wrote another heartfelt plea to Congress in which he pointed out the stark reality that the crews of the *Maria* and the *Dauphin* would probably all soon be dead. "O Lord! Hear our petitions and prayers," he begged. "Only one cargo of tobacco would redeem us all, or a small lottery in each State." He pointed to his own helpless situation as a captive with "a starving family" and added sadly: "Nobody is disposed to charity until we are no more, and then they will say they are sorry: '*The poor man is dead, God be merciful to his soul.*'"

★   ★   ★

In April that same year, Cathcart's integrity was put to another test—one that could have ended very badly for him if he hadn't already earned the minister's trust.

His duties included keeping the account books at his former prison, the disreputable Bagnio Belique. Equipment from the stores had been steadily disappearing, and suspicion had fallen on the prison's guardian bashaw, a former member of the Janissary militia who was "not over honest." But Cathcart—as an outsider and a captive—could never accuse a member of the ruling Turkish caste. "My position was then rendered very unpleasant," he wrote.

The matter reached a crisis when Cathcart noticed a large discrepancy in the prison's accounts. He pointed this out to the guardian bashaw, who tried to shrug it off.

You must have made some mistake in your accounting, he said dismissively.

There is no mistake, Cathcart replied politely. Look here and here.

The guardian changed tack and his tone became wheedling.

You could change the figures without making any fuss, he suggested.

I can't do that, Cathcart replied firmly. It's very clear. Here are the amounts you received, and here are the amounts you paid out.

The guardian saw he was getting nowhere and tried to throw the blame elsewhere.

You're right, he said. The money *is* short. Someone in the prison must have taken the cash from my drawer.

Cathcart wasn't buying that story either.

The cash drawer is always kept locked, he reminded the guardian. And only one person has the key.

The guardian exploded with rage and stormed out. He went straight to Sidi Hassan and complained that a captive had accused him of embezzlement. Either he goes or I go, he threatened the minister.

It was a tense moment. By the usual standards of law, any dispute between a Turk and a captive would always be resolved in favor of the former, and the captive would usually receive a severe beating for his impertinence.

Hassan couldn't break this rule, but he trusted Cathcart's judgment. He solved the issue by removing the American from his duties and putting him under house arrest. He declared, noisily and for the record, that he would never appoint another captive as his clerk. Quietly, however, he made sure that Cathcart did not suffer. Meanwhile, he investigated the accounts and confirmed his clerk's suspicions. When all the fuss was over, the embezzler was quietly fired.

The former guardian had to resort to fishing to feed himself. From time to time, Cathcart would occasionally bump into him as he shuffled back with his basket and his few miserable fish. The encounters were, to say the least, awkward.

★   ★   ★

The plague raged on relentlessly, claiming the lives of four more Americans, all from the crew of O'Brien's *Dauphin*. In 1787, seamen Robert McGinnis and John Doran followed their comrade Peter Smith into the captives' graveyard outside Babel Oued, the city's northern gate. Edward O'Reilly and William Harding joined them in 1788, and the sadly but appropriately named Captain Zacheus Coffin from Nantucket died of consumption. That meant that nearly two-fifths of the men aboard the *Dauphin* had died during the course of the three years. By contrast, not a single man from the *Maria* was killed by the plague, although young James Harnet was steadily being overwhelmed by a disease of the mind that would prove equally serious.

By the end of 1787, the overall death toll from the plague stood at 650 European and American captives and 19,000 free persons of other nationalities—more than a fifth of the total population of Algiers. In 1778, an additional 187 captives and 1,500 locals died.

It was against the background of this near-apocalyptic deathscape that the *Dauphin*'s captain Richard O'Brien sent a pathetic plea to Congress on behalf of the remaining fifteen American captives. I have edited the document but left his grammatical mistakes intact:

In Algiers, the City of Bondage.

December the 20th, 1788

Sirs—
    Informing you of . . . my captivity and sufferings during a period of three years and five months . . . without any prospect of ever being redeemed. . . .
    We have wrote many petitions to Congress, and by every opportunity writes to the American Ambassador . . . entreating them to afford us some consolation under our present afflicted situation, but we have much reason to conjecture by their not writing us, that they have not it in their power to afford us any relief. . . .
    [This] humbly sheweth that [our] situation is truly miserable and unhappy much beyond our expression and your conception. . . . We have experienced nothing but an uninterrupted scene of grief and misery . . . surrounded with the pest and other contagions, distempers, which has numbered six of our countrymen in the Bills of Mortality. . . .
    [We are] wretched and miserable. . . . Our crews being employed on the most laborious work, consuming and declining under the scorching heats of this climate, far distant from our families, friends and connections, without any prospect of ever seeing them more.

★ ★ ★

Throughout all this, James Cathcart had made it a point of honor to ensure that his dying countrymen received proper hospital treatment and that those who died were given a decent burial. Most dead captives were thrown into mass graves, but the Americans were "buried in a decent coffin at my expense," he wrote. They were carried on a bier to the graveyard by their countrymen, and Cathcart led them all in a funeral service. "Never was a single American buried without my attending them to the grave, reading prayers over them, and remaining until they were decently covered," he said. O'Brien later confirmed the contribution Cathcart had made with those important rituals.

The bleak ceremonies held in an outcasts' graveyard in sandy earth just yards from the high-water line of the Mediterranean deeply affected Cathcart. This desolate area around the northern gate of Babel Oued became to him a poignant symbol of the sacrifice of the American hostages. After presiding over yet another burial, he returned to his home and penned these darkly emotional lines of verse:

O, Babel Oued, beneath thy sand
My brother captives lie
Away from kindred hearts and land
From sad oppression die.

The sighing sea upon the shore
Their requiem will be.
The sprinkling waves will tell us more
Than teardrops o'er the sea.

Inevitably after each interment, Cathcart wondered if he himself would be the next victim. But he reminded himself that such bleak speculation was pointless. "I frequently stopped at the gates of the city to count the dead as they were carried out," he wrote, "not knowing, nor indeed caring, when my time should come." In fact, he not only remained hale and hearty throughout the two-year epidemic, but he enjoyed a surge of vigor as his system recovered from his earlier suffering at the prisons. "The plague raged all this year," he wrote in 1788, "[but] I never enjoyed better health."

At this point, he had a minor epiphany. Two years before when he had been moved out of the palace gardens to the Bagnio Belique, he had pledged himself to "be the means of alleviating the sufferings of my unfortunate fellow citizens." Yet all he had managed to do was help the dying and the dead. It was not enough. Now he needed to help the living.

His fellow Americans were falling ill, not only because they were crowded into pestilential jails, but also because they were severely malnourished. He could do nothing about the first problem, but could he do something about the second? There must be a way in which even a captive like himself could provide a decent daily meal to his countrymen and send them back to the bagnios each night with a full stomach.

There was. There was only one way.

That was the moment when James Cathcart decided to get his own pub.

★   ★   ★

It was a crazy idea, but somehow it worked. It worked only because of help from Cathcart's latest guardian angels: two Swedish brothers named Mathias and Peter Erik Skjoldebrand. Mathias was the Swedish consul in Algiers, and Peter was one of several people who were angling to be appointed the US agent in the corsair city. The two men were skilled diplomats, independently wealthy, and worldly wise. They knew exactly how things worked in the "crazy capital."

It's unclear at what point Cathcart first met the Skjoldebrands, but word had probably spread among the small diplomatic community about this twenty-one-year-old wunderkind who had somehow risen from basic seaman to the position of marine clerk. It was clear to everyone—despite his sudden demotion and house arrest—that this was Hassan's protégé and very much a young man on the rise. Cathcart made his usual good impression, and the three men became close friends.

The conversation that changed Cathcart's life took place early in 1789. We can imagine the three of them sitting at a tavern enjoying an ale when it unfolded, perhaps something along these lines:

There's a prize ship arriving in Algiers soon, Cathcart mentioned idly. It's laden with wine. Anyone who moves quickly and buys it up could make a killing.

The Skjoldebrands shook their heads. They weren't interested.

Why don't you buy it? they asked Cathcart.

Cathcart roared with laughter. Because I don't have any money, he replied.

The brothers didn't hesitate. We'll advance you $5,000, they offered. Interest free. You can pay us back when you sell the wine.

Cathcart balked at the idea. He was still a captive hostage, after all. There was nothing to prevent a hostage from investing money and making a profit—in fact, the Algerines openly encouraged this sort of enterprise. They saw it as a medium- or long-term investment with little risk, since they themselves would eventually get all the money, either in the form of ransom or in the form of property seizure after he died. On the other hand, if word went around that he had cash, he would be vulnerable to shakedowns of the type that were common in Algiers.

Cathcart tried to refuse, but the brothers were insistent. "These worthy and generous men loaned me $5,000 . . . without any interest or reward whatever, out of pure friendship," Cathcart would later recall in wonder. "Although they knew the risk they ran, for had I died or committed any fault, real or imaginary, before they were paid, the Regency would have seized all my property . . . and they would have lost every dollar." He added: "My gratitude to them is eternal, and knows no bounds."

Fortunately, the plan worked perfectly. The wine arrived safely, Cathcart's bid on it was accepted, and the taverners happily bought all the product. The Skjoldebrands were repaid, and Cathcart pocketed the profits. Suddenly, he was comfortably off.

Which leaves the question: why didn't he simply buy his freedom at that stage and get out of Algiers on the first available ship? It seems that money was not the issue. "I had property enough to pay my ransom," he recalled later, and again: "I could have been free long ago." He was evidently sincere in his resolution: he wanted to stay and help his suffering countrymen.

He scouted around for the right tavern and found it in the Mad House, a bar in central Algiers. At that time, the city had between twenty-seven and thirty bars, and not all of them were in the bagnio prisons. Once there had been taverns in each of the Janissary barracks, but they were all closed down when a foreign captive was found dead, strung up to a beam.

The Mad House was not as large as the three main city center bars, the Raphagi, the Foundaria, and the Magazine. (The Magazine was "a miserable dark hole" according to Cathcart, but it had a unique selling point: it contained a wine cask that, thanks to a miracle performed by a local saint, had supposedly flowed endlessly with wine until the streets were flooded. Patrons could visit under cover of venerating this holy cask and—as an afterthought—enjoy a drink while they were at it.)

The Mad House was on a narrow street opposite a row of private houses, with only a few feet separating pub and houses. The fact that it operated outside the bagnios was a mixed blessing. It meant Cathcart would be free of the predatory Spanish *Carneros*, the guards from Oran with their insatiable demands for money. But with less security, it was more vulnerable to acts of drunken anarchy.

Cathcart moved in right away, hired a manager and staff, and put his own stamp on the place. He was gregarious and welcoming, and the pub was soon infused with his own larger-than-life Irish American personality. Before long, it attracted a loyal clientele of soldiers, civil servants, expatriates, and diplomats, mingling with the American captives who dined there at Cathcart's invitation. Soon word spread around town: if you wanted to escape the lunacy in the "crazy capital," the Mad House was the only sane place to go.

• *14* •

Welcome to the Mad House

$\mathcal{F}$or modern readers, the parallels between Cathcart's Mad House and the bar in the classic movie *Casablanca* are irresistible. Rick's bar in *Casablanca* was called the *Café Americain*, and Cathcart's bar in Algiers was literally a café Americain, run by an American and frequented by American captives. Substitute the raucous music of fiddles, mandolins, and tabors for Dooley Wilson's sleepy piano tinkle and the atmosphere was spot on: the sultry heat, the shadows of palm trees dancing against the whitewashed walls, the tense background of war, the amiable confrontations with bribable officials, the regular raids by police.

Just as in wartime Casablanca, Cathcart's bar was frequented by diplomats, agents, and spies of all nations, intermingling and gathering information and cheerfully plotting against each other. Which nation was in favor with the dey? Which country would he choose to target next? Which powerful grandee was about to be strangled in a midlevel power grab? All these matters were discussed in murmurs in dark corners as the filigree lamps cast flickering patterns on the ceiling.

On any typical day, visiting seamen hollered shanties and tossed coins to Italian buskers as they trilled their mandolins. Grandees from the Turkish ruling caste talked business with wealthy Moorish craftsmen. Sharifs, the highborn nobles of Islam, entered with aloof majesty, selected an occupied table, and demanded that the current customers give up their seats. Janissary militiamen bristled and barked and drank too much. In the most remote corners of a back room, almost obscured by the constant fug of tobacco smoke, down-at-heels Americans hurriedly wolfed their free dinners, anxious not to draw attention, before hurrying back to the Bagnio Gallera.

And always at the center of it all was Algiers's version of Rick—James Cathcart—schmoozing the Turkish bureaucrats, greasing the right palms, smoothly defusing potential fights among the soldiers, circulating, joking, ensuring that drinks were topped up, and quietly checking that his countrymen had enough food on their plates to keep them alive and healthy for another day. As he recalled later: "Those [Americans] who survive will do me the justice to acknowledge that they never wanted [for] a good meal while I had it in my power to give it to them."

It wasn't just the ordinary American seamen who benefited from Cathcart's generosity. The officers also turned to him when they found themselves in difficulties. Until now, Captain Richard O'Brien had had a comparatively easy time living "in one consul's house or another," although he was occasionally asked to do light work at the sail loft. But now, after the dramatic reduction in captive numbers, the Algerines needed all hands on deck. "[O'Brien] was sent to hard labor," Cathcart recalled, "and put on board the Panton Grand [the harbor maintenance pontoon] to cleanse the mold, where he was kept some weeks." Cathcart moved quickly to help. "I furnished him with a good dinner and a bottle of wine daily from my tavern," he wrote. When he discovered that O'Brien's work supervisor was partial to wine, "an extra one was sent to *him*, by which Captain O'Brien was treated very kindly."

All the taverns in Algiers were run by foreign captives who were expected to provide a form of social security for the elderly or incapacitated in their ranks. There were scores of such people: for instance, in the last round of redemptions by Spain and Naples, up to 150 "very old men" had hobbled painfully aboard ship, many with the aid of crutches. The Algerines wanted to retain these captives for their potential ransom value, but they didn't want the trouble of looking after them. So they passed them on to the bar owners, who were expected to employ them as cleaners, waiters, and so on. Cathcart estimated that the taverns employed between fifty to ninety captives "and maintain more than double that number of the most indigent, who [without employment] would in all probability starve for want of food."

Other sick and injured foreign hostages hung around the taverns offering various services. Some wrote petitions for the illiterate or penned lyrical love letters for tongue-tied boyfriends. For payment, they accepted drinks in the form of bar credit. When the money for the "drinks" accrued, the bar owners paid them in cash or food.

Cathcart's change of role was reflected in the lists of captives that were regularly updated and sent home. At first, he had simply been "James Cathcart, seaman." When he became famous for his map-reading classes, he was "James Cathcart, seaman: a young man who knows navigation." But after 1788, his description must have caused no end of puzzlement to the folks back home. "James Cathcart, seaman," it read, "keeps a tavern."

★ ★ ★

Meanwhile, the plague was still roaring through Algiers. At Cathcart's old prison, the Bagnio Gallera, the death rate from pestilence had steadily increased to the point at which even the prison clerks were dying faster than they could be replaced. "Three Clerks died in less than one month," Cathcart wrote.

Soon a message reached Cathcart at the Mad House. His time in the career wilderness was over. He had been appointed as the new clerk of the Bagnio Gallera. He would also have to perform the duties of two other deceased officials, the wonderfully named clerk of the sheepskins and clerk of the charcoal. This meant more local travel and more work, but it also helped to save his life as it enabled him to spend time away from the plague-ridden jail. "[It] was probably conducive to my health," he wrote, "and the means . . . of my being alive."

Unexpectedly, the job of clerk of the Gallera carried with it a lucrative perk: the holder could operate a tavern inside the prison complex. From having one tavern in Algiers, James Cathcart had progressed with minimal effort to owning two.

★ ★ ★

If anyone in Algiers had ever doubted that Ali Hassan was hungry for power and utterly ruthless, those doubts were resolved at dawn on May 26, 1788. That was the date Hassan ordered the strangling of his own wife's father.

In a swift and brutal Mediterranean vendetta easily recognizable to any modern-day Sicilian mafioso, he waited for the right pretext and struck without warning. His target was the *Hasnagi*, the prime minister, the only man who stood between him and the throne of Algiers.

At four that morning, the *Hasnagi* appeared as usual at the dey's palace to begin his work. As usual, he was greeted in the predawn dusk by the aga, or commander of the Janissary militia, who was supposed to kiss his hand as a gesture of submission.

The prime minister immediately knew something was wrong when the aga brusquely swiped away his outstretched hand. Two other Janissary officers appeared from the gloom and grabbed him from behind. With practiced ease, they disarmed him, stripped him of his coat and turban, and bundled him off.

He desperately called out for help to his son-in-law, Ali Hassan. "Ali! Ali! What have I done?" There was no answer. "Is there no-one who will plead my cause?" Again, only his own words echoed back from the pitiless stone walls of the palace. When the realization dawned that his death was imminent, he made another anguished plea. "Oh, Ali! My wife and children. Don't let them suffer."

With his shouts ringing through the palace courtyard, the second-most powerful man in Algiers was dragged off to the strangling room, a place of execution reserved for the ruling Turkish caste who deserved "the most honorable death." One American prisoner later described it in horrific detail.

"The criminal is confined, with his back against a wall, in which is two holes right opposite the back of his neck. . . . The rope comes about the criminal's neck and when the two ends are knotted together, the executioner puts a stick in and twists the rope, which brings it tight about the criminal's neck, and he is soon dispatched. So the executioner does not see the criminal while performing his office."

The prime minister knew that any appeal for mercy would be pointless. He was slammed up against the wall. The cords circled his neck. Behind the wall, the faceless executioner inserted the stick and began to twist. His victim's face swelled and his eyes bulged. He was almost dead when . . . the cord snapped.

The aga ordered the officers to find a replacement. The victim had to wait, coughing and spluttering, until his killers could find a second cord to start the whole process all over again. Death must have come mercifully.

"This once great and respected man was carried by four [Moors] to his own new house, and laid out on the porch," Cathcart recorded. "No-one was let to visit him." Even his wife, crying and begging for one last moment alone with her husband's body, was turned away.

The funeral at two in the afternoon was a desolate affair. Not one of his friends turned up: it was too dangerous. Only his wife and children were there "to bewail his untimely fate."

Since one of these adult daughters was Ali Hassan's wife, she had to grieve alone. Her husband, the man who had organized the murder, was notably absent from the graveside.

One American diplomat later summed up the episode: "Notwithstanding he was his father-in-law, [Ali Hassan] ordered [the prime minister] to be strangled for treasonable practices. [This] never caused a moment's interruption of Dey Mahmood's confidence in [Hassan]."

That was putting it mildly. The very same day, Hassan was summoned to the palace and elevated to the position left vacant by his victim. "Sidi Hassan, Minister of the Marine, and son-in-law of the late Prime Minister, was appointed in his father-in-law's room to officiate as Prime Minister," Cathcart recorded with stiff formality. "He accordingly exercised himself in all the functions of his office, to the satisfaction of all, but those of the late Prime Minister's party."

Meanwhile, Hassan's wife was forced to continue sharing a bed with her father's killer. Unlike most rich men in Algiers, Hassan was monogamous and kept no concubines. The domestic atmosphere must have been fraught, to put it mildly.

Looking ahead, Dey Mahmood formalized the future transfer of power by designating Hassan as his successor. It was now only a matter of time before Cathcart's latest sponsor and advocate—an evil guardian angel, if ever there was one—would become the most powerful man in Algiers.

★ ★ ★

Back home in America, politicians continued to lament the plight of their kidnapped countrymen while doing absolutely nothing to secure their freedom. As we've seen, Jefferson sincerely believed that publicly ignoring the captives was the best way to reduce their ransom and eventually to bring them home. His strategy of pretending not to care was put into practice so successfully that it fooled everyone, especially the Americans in captivity in Algiers.

Two things jolted the politicians out of their inertia. The first was a widespread rumor in the late 1780s that Benjamin Franklin had been captured at sea by "the infernal crews of Algerine corsairs." Newspapers reported that he was a captive in Algiers enduring captivity "with all the patience of a philosopher." It was all nonsense, but it focused the public mind on North Africa and the rogue corsair statelet. "A voice of indignation swelled through the land," wrote one historian.

Around the same time, there were tall tales about American captives escaping from Algiers. One described how a group of twenty Americans had been captured on a single ship from Philadelphia and held in captivity in Algiers in the 1780s. (Almost correct.) Some had been put to work on farms, chained alongside mules. Others had been put on board a galley and "chained to the oars." In 1788, according to this story, these Americans rose up, killed their overseers, jumped into an unattended galley at the docks, and escaped to Gibraltar.

Sadly for the wives and families at home, it was only a rumor. The fates of the twenty-one real captives were well documented, and no such escape involving Americans was recorded by O'Brien or Cathcart in that terrible plague year.

However, rousing stories like this captured the public imagination. The outdated myth of the indomitable prisoner "chained to the oars" was much more potent than the reality of most captives' real experiences of daily drudgery and rock hauling.

Captain O'Brien's petition began to circulate more widely, but some thought it wasn't tearjerking enough. A later version was rewritten by American editors in a bombastic, sermonizing style that bore no resemblance to O'Brien's genuine, untutored, down-to-earth prose. It ended with the plea: "Thus pray your fellow citizens, chained to the galleys . . . Richard O'Brien." The captain, who knew nothing of this, would have been mortified. The truth was that thanks to the *Paga Luna* system and to Cathcart's generosity, O'Brien was more likely to be bending his elbow, raising a glass of wine at a tavern bench than hauling a heavy oar on a galley bench.

Outraged clerics began leading their congregations in special ransom collections, and groups of friends and relatives began digging deep in their pockets.

As the nation's soul swelled with righteous indignation, it took the clear and courageous voice of Benjamin Franklin to call out the hypocrisy.

How, he demanded, could a country that had enslaved hundreds of thousands of African men, women, and children take the high moral ground when its own citizens were captured and put to work in North Africa? What made the first acceptable and the second obscene? Franklin, president of an organization that wanted all forms of slavery abolished, urged Congress in 1789 to "discourage every species of traffic in our fellow men."

★   ★   ★

The second catalyst appeared in the form of a hefty *Report on Mediterranean Trade* that landed on the desks of congressmen and senators in 1790 and 1791. Prepared by Thomas Jefferson, now back in America as secretary of state, it reported what every struggling trader and shipper already knew—that the Algiers crisis was costing the United States a fortune it couldn't afford.

Before the American Revolution, the Mediterranean ports were buying a sixth of America's wheat and flour and a quarter of its fish and rice. Now the figure was precisely zero (although that figure ignored those traders who were forging passports and pretending to be English). The country had lost the income from eighty to a hundred shiploads a year, and the crisis had affected twelve hundred jobs among seamen alone.

At this stage, America was practically broke. It needed that trade back again—desperately. Government had tried, but "the sole obstacle has been the unprovoked war of Algiers; and the sole remedy must be to bring that war to an end."

If Congress were not prepared to stump up enough funds to pay the ransoms and secure a peace deal, the country must prepare for war. "Should the United States propose to vindicate their commerce by arms," Jefferson wrote, "they would, perhaps, think it prudent to possess a force equal to [that of Algiers]."

In other words, a country without a navy would have to create one. And soon.

★ ★ ★

On a chilly February day in 1791, a lone figure walked the gangway of a ship on London's docks. He probably welcomed the cold wind that swept down the Thames. The ground beneath his feet may have been damp and cold, but he was grateful at least that it didn't scorch his feet through thin-soled slippers, as it had so often in Algiers. Charles Colvill, the youthful ship's carpenter from the *Dauphin*, had just made history as the first captured US citizen to regain his freedom from the corsair city.

You may recall that young Colvill—still described as a "boy" four years after his capture—had particularly influential connections in his birth country of Scotland. Two years before, around 1789, these friends and relatives had raised the equivalent of around $1,400 to pay his ransom and had arranged with British consul Charles Logie to do the paperwork.

The process had taken many months, but at last Colvill had been released from the hell of the Bagnio Gallera, excused from his hard labor at the docks, and issued a free pass that allowed him to wander freely around Algiers until the next ship could take him to Europe. After a spell in quarantine, he began his long voyage home to Philadelphia via London.

During a debriefing session with the US consul, Joshua Johnson, he was able to give updated information on his countrymen in Algiers. He confirmed that six of his fellow *Dauphin* crewmen had died of plague and named the eight whom he'd left behind. As for the other ship, he reported that "all the crew of the schooner *Maria* . . . were living" but listed only five names, for some reason omitting or forgetting the name of a sixth, Thomas Billings.

Colvill said that their "hardship and inconvenience" had increased since their allowance had been stopped. When Johnson quizzed him about conditions for the Americans, Colvill began to open up. "The Algerines allow [us] only bread, olives and water," he told the consul. "They employ [us] in erecting fortifications, dragging stone, timber and rigging their cruisers, and frequently compelled [us] to work in chains."

He told how all six or seven hundred hostage captives of all nations were confined in the bagnios throughout the night. "The Dey only allows each man, per year, a shirt, a pair of trousers, a blanket, and one pair of slippers," he said. "[The slippers are] of no duration. . . . [We] suffer in [our] feet much more in summer from the heat of the pavement than from cold in the winter." Asked how the Americans were coping, he replied: "All of them are ready to sink under despair."

Had the Algerines become more friendly toward Americans since the first captures in 1785?

No, replied Colvill firmly. He told Johnson that, at first, the Algerines had had no idea where the United States was located and had been surprised it lay so far across an ocean. They were delighted to find a fresh source of human fodder, and now "their hopes were [of] making frequent captures" and kidnapping even more American hostages.

Amid all this pessimism, Colvill offered a solution for the standoff. The admiral of the Algerine fleet desperately wanted to upgrade his old-school navy with a smart American frigate with twenty-four or thirty guns. "Such a ship, with some naval stores and a little money, might secure [the captives' freedom]," he suggested.

· 15 ·

It's a New Dawn, It's a New Dey, It's a New Life

*F*ive months later, on the morning of July 11, Algiers woke up to discover it had a new ruler. Dey Mahmood had taken ill a few days earlier and passed away quietly just after 5:00 p.m. on July 10. Since there was every possibility of a military coup, his aides kept the news secret until nightfall.

At the prime minister's office, everyone was asleep when a German captive employed at the palace, Joseph Koenigs, heard a soft tapping at the window. He found one of Mahmood's senior aides standing outside, too terrified to use the main door. Through the aperture, he motioned at Koenigs to stay silent and to fetch the prime minister, Ali Hassan. Koenigs approached Hassan's room with terrified caution—Hassan lived in constant fear of assassination—and passed on the request. Eventually Hassan shuffled sleepily to the window, where he received the momentous news of the death of a ruler who had reigned for a quarter century.

The aide told the relieved Hassan that Mahmood had not changed his mind: on his deathbed, he had confirmed Hassan as his successor. He warned him that only one man was likely to oppose him: the aga, or supreme general of the Janissary militia.

Hassan knew he had to act quickly, for the interregnum was always an unpredictable and bloody time in Algiers. A new dey could surround himself with armed soldiers but that meant nothing: "It is sometimes a fruitless precaution," explained one contemporary writer, "as any private soldier who has the courage to murder him, stands an equal chance of becoming his successor." In the past, there had been a case of a soldier who killed a ruler and declared himself as the new dey but survived just ten minutes on the throne before he was himself dispatched by a rival.

Hassan had the advantage of surprise. He was already firmly ensconced in the dey's throne when the aga appeared on the scene, "intending to contest the right of sovereignty with him." When Hassan refused to budge, the aga "attempted to assassinate him in his seat," only to find himself bundled away by the new dey's henchmen and summarily dispatched with the strangling cord.

The episode was summed up matter-of-factly by Robert Montgomery, US agent in Alicante: "Ali Hassan . . . ordered the Aga to be strangled for an attempt to oppose him [and took] peaceable possession of the Regency." The aga, thrashing hopelessly as the cord tightened around his throat, may have disagreed with the adjective "peaceable" but everyone else breathed a sigh of relief.

Montgomery knew that this change of regime was good news from a US perspective, since Hassan had always been pro-America. Montgomery had known him personally when he was held as a prisoner of war in Cartagena two decades before and had anticipated that he would soon be "at the summit of power." Now that he had been proved correct, he appealed to Jefferson to push this open door and negotiate a peace deal. His suggestion was mostly ignored.

★ ★ ★

The regime change was also good news for James Cathcart. His old friend Angelo d'Andreis had retained his position as chief clerk under the new dey. It made his own life as clerk of the Bagnio Gallera so much easier.

Cathcart worked at the prison for three years, spending most of his nights in the elevated, airy apartment that had been bequeathed to him by his predecessor. However, life as a captive was never predictable, and the continued shortage of workers meant that he was not excluded from hard labor on Fridays. From time to time, every foreign captive—including even the bureaucrats and the *Paga Lunas*—was conscripted to load and unload ships, work at the construction sites, and cart off rubble from the site of the dey's new palace extension. In theory, those with a bit of money could bribe their way to an easier task, but that caused resentment among the penniless captives who had to work twice as hard, and so the practice was frowned upon.

At the other extreme, Cathcart spent six months at the home of the British consul's surgeon, Dr. Werner, doing accountancy work. He slept there as guest and ate at the main dining table, but as soon as the job was done and his usefulness had expired, the relationship suddenly changed. The surgeon began treating him as his personal dogsbody and refused to let him leave the house without permission. Cathcart took great offense, heated words were exchanged, and the affronted accountant stormed off back to the Gallera.

Despite his relative comfort, Cathcart still suffered bouts of an unspecified mental health problem—most likely depression—which he described as "sentimental afflictions." Overall, though, he prospered financially—"I had money enough to serve all my wants"—and he decided to invest his income in another bar.

By the early 1790s, "I owned the Mad House tavern and half a tavern in the Bagnio Gallera, and another in the Bagnio Liddi Hamuda," he listed. (The latter was the third and smallest prison.) He had begun contracting out the bars to other captives, who paid him a set fee for each barrel of wine or brandy. "This gave me a profit enough for all my purposes, and an over-plus to serve the immediate wants of my unfortunate fellow-sufferers taken in 1785 . . . some of [whom] had been at hard labor all the time. . . . Had it not pleased God to have placed me in a situation to have assisted them, they would certainly have been worse off."

For the American captives, it made no sense to hoard money, because the state would seize it all on their death. "As we did not know when it would be our turn to die, we set no great value upon money and made a merit of assisting our unfortunate brother sufferers," Cathcart explained. "Had we not been afraid of dying, I think it is likely enough that we would have been less liberal or at least more careful."

★   ★   ★

In Algiers, barkeeping had its own unique problems. Quite apart from the need to pay a fortune in formal fees and informal bribes, the tavern owners constantly lived in terror that their premises would be the scene of some unpredictable incident. Just one quarrel, just one outbreak of fisticuffs would be enough to cause an owner to lose his pub, sacrifice his assets, and end up back in the work gangs. If an incident were especially serious, the dey would close down all the bars in town and order every tavern keeper—guilty and innocent alike—to be bastinadoed.

"[The customers] frequently quarrel among themselves and proceed to blows," Cathcart explained. "Even murder often takes place . . . which generally occasions the tavern keeper to lose all his property. The tavern is in the most instances seized by the Regency, and the tavern keeper is sent to hard labor."

Tavern owners were expected to keep orderly houses, yet they had to obey the overarching rule that a captive hostage was never, ever allowed to lay hands on a "Turk," even in self-defense, no matter how serious the provocation.

Some bar owners worked out ingenious solutions. One tavern keeper was said to keep a ladder behind the bar: if a customer became troublesome, he would pop the ladder over the man's head, pinning his shoulders and arms between the rungs, and expertly propel him into the street before reclaiming his ladder. That way, he could honestly swear that he had not laid hands on anybody.

A separate problem was dealing with customers who tried to leave without paying. According to one source, a tavern keeper "is empowered to strip any of his guests if they refuse to pay . . . and herein he is protected by the Dey himself." It was much harder to put that rule into practice, especially when dealing with prickly Janissary militiamen or Turkish grandees. "[With] Turks and Moors . . . the tavern keepers were always obliged to be extremely watchful," says the same source, "otherwise they would frequently steal away without paying."

We don't know what methods James Cathcart used to maintain sanity at the Mad House, but he managed to avoid trouble for several years . . . until a serious incident at the bar almost cost him his life.

★   ★   ★

As he'd risen through the ranks, Cathcart had made some enemies in high places, and one of the most powerful was the man who had succeeded Dey Hassan as minister of the marine. His name was Sidi Ali and "he was by no means my friend."

Sidi Ali's opportunity to get his revenge came one day as Cathcart stood outside his bar chatting to a Turkish man. A Janissary militiaman was sitting by an open window in the house directly opposite. The street was so narrow that when this man made a remark about a woman, the eavesdropper took great offense. A fierce argument erupted. Grabbing a handgun, the Janissary ran into the laneway and shot the man through the thigh. Then he drew his yataghan saber and stabbed him in the torso. In his death throes, his victim dived for safety toward the pub door and fell into the domain of the Mad House.

It didn't end there. A pistol went off again and hit another Turk in the foot.

The minister for the marine took his fury out on the captives, particularly Cathcart. "The tavern was shut up, and all the Christians who were present, among whom I was one, were sent to the Marine to work," he wrote. "I remained at hard labor two days."

Cathcart escaped further punishment thanks to another long-standing tradition of Algiers: barefaced bribery. He gave a backhander to an influential grandee, who organized a return to the status quo. The Mad House reopened, and Cathcart got off, but it took a full week before all his bar staff were returned from the docks and quarries.

Meanwhile, the Janissary who had caused all this mayhem evaded justice thanks to a long-standing tradition that militiamen who committed crimes could claim sanctuary in a special tent outside the city.

Soon after, there was an equally serious incident when a fight broke out between a Greek renegado and a dishonorably discharged soldier, this time inside the tavern itself. Fueled by alcohol, the ex-soldier insulted the Greek, who "beat him unmercifully." After recovering, the former army man demanded compensation from the Mad House. He lied, claiming that Cathcart was the one who had beaten him. This time Cathcart really was in trouble. A captive who attacked a "believer" usually died a horrible death.

Matters involving blood fines were decided by the chief surgeon, who summoned Cathcart to appear before him. He thundered that he knew Cathcart was guilty and emphasized the severity of the crime.

As the American wilted under the onslaught, the chief surgeon hinted that the matter could be resolved quietly for a small consideration of two hundred sequins—around $400, payable to himself. Otherwise, Cathcart would go straight to prison.

Then, in a dramatic courtroom intervention, the real attacker—the Greek renegado—appeared on the scene and told the truth. He swore that Cathcart was not even present when the fracas had taken place.

The chief surgeon was not happy about seeing his $400 disappear.

I suppose this man has paid you well to give false evidence, he told the Greek. It's a sad thing to see a believer take the side of a Christian against his brethren.

The Greek was not cowed. He pointed to Cathcart.

This has nothing to do with religion, he told the chief surgeon. You're trying to extort money from this man. For every sequin he is forced to pay, I will give that soldier another beating.

His confrontational attitude didn't help. Faced with the prospect of indefinite imprisonment, Cathcart decided to take the path of least resistance and settled on payment—"as the price of blood which I had not drawn."

Everything went back to normal, except that the irascible Greek was as good as his word. "Every time he met [the ex-soldier] he broke his pipe over his head," Cathcart wrote, "until ultimately he was obliged to leave the city."

· *16* ·

"That Is Our Liberty in Sweet America"

$\mathscr{B}$ack in America, Isaac Stephens's wife Hannah was suffering severely during the cold winter of 1791. At her wit's end, she sent a heartrending plea for help directly to the most powerful man in America: President George Washington.

During the six years since Isaac's capture, her life had grown steadily worse. She had been able to write to her husband in Algiers, encouraging him in his captivity but also confessing that "she was obliged to put her children out [to work] for their living, and herself obliged to work hard for her bread." Isaac, distraught by the revelation that his three young children had been hired out, had written to George Washington a year earlier with the bitter comment: "That is our liberty in sweet America." He pleaded with Washington to "turn your hard hearts in America for our redemption."

Hannah had already lost her husband and her home. In 1791, however, she suffered yet another blow. Her eldest daughter, aged only fourteen, had always been sickly but had now become too ill to work and had to be supported financially. The other two still "remained a great expense to their mother": presumably she had to pay their employers a certain amount for their keep.

The original of Hannah's petition to George Washington still remains in the National Archives. Headed "The Memorial of Hannah Stephens Requesting the Release of her Husband from Prison in Algiers," it is a faded document, brown with age, with neat, well-spaced lines of handwriting that fail to convey the emotional torment of the petitioner. Hannah begins by "humbly" laying out the facts of her husband's capture six years earlier. "[He] has ever since remained a prisoner among them, deprived of his liberty and of every means of providing for himself, his wife, or children."

She tells how she not only lost the family home, but also all the money they had paid into it. She describes the distress of being evicted and her anguish at having to work as a low-paid servant just to survive.

All this was bad enough, but she added: "[Our] sufferings . . . become insupportable when added to the distress [I] feel for [my] husband, who is continually representing by his letters his melancholy situation."

She describes her condition as "destitute and forsaken" and begs the president to "devise some way by which he may be freed from his present state of captivity, that [I] and [my] helpless children may once more enjoy the great pleasure of seeing their long-lost friend, at liberty and in his native land."

Hannah ends with a plea for some sort of subsistence allowance "in order that [I] may have some alleviation of [my] accumulated load of human woe—as duty bound shall ever pray."

Hannah's plea did not go unnoticed. Together with the petition of the *Dauphin* carpenter Charles Colvill, who had just arrived home from Britain, it pricked the consciences of the politicians, and a month later, in January 1792, it was read in the Senate and passed on to an action committee.

A month later, in February, the Senate gave formal approval for a full peace deal for up to $100,000 a year (to include not only Algiers but also its neighboring Barbary states Tunis and Tripoli), to go along with the sum of $40,000 it had earlier approved for the prisoners' ransoms. If those measures failed, it resolved that a trust fund would be set up for the captives' families. In response, Washington pledged: "I will proceed to take measures for the ransom of our citizens in captivity."

However, as we soon see, that good intention was rapidly overtaken by events—and there is no evidence that this courageous and persistent woman from Concord ever received a penny in help from George Washington or the US government.

No document speaks quite so eloquently about her personal misery than the census of households in her hometown of Concord, Massachusetts. The census is filled with records of happy, united families: a head of household (almost always the husband) followed by a wife and three, four, five, or even nine children. In Hannah's case, Isaac's name is missing from the first column and her own name, misspelled as "Stevens" is listed as the sole head of household. One person is listed in another column for females, so the reader feels a slight relief that at least one of her daughters remained at home to help her out, but then it emerges that this figure *includes* the household head. Her happy, prosperous family of five has been reduced to just one. Hannah is on her own.

★ ★ ★

Figure 1. James Leander Cathcart in later life. As a captive in Algiers—we must imagine a younger and presumably much leaner figure—he began as a lionkeeper in the dey's private zoo and worked his way up to the pinnacle of power at the palace. *Source*: James Leander Cathcart and J. B. Newkirk, *The Captives: Eleven Years a Prisoner in Algiers* (La Porte, IN: Herald Print, 1899). Thanks to the General Research Division of the New York Public Library.

JAMES LEANDER CATHCART.

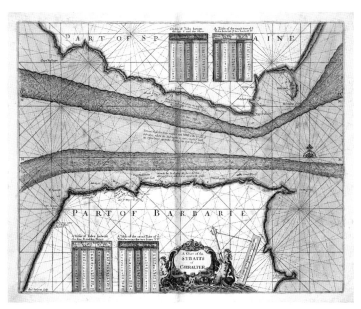

Figure 2. A natural trap for seamen: This chart of the Strait of Gibraltar from the 1700s shows the narrow bottleneck through which US merchant ships were forced to sail, running the gauntlet of predatory corsair ships. *Source*: Samuel Thornton, cartographer, *A Chart of the Straits of Gibraltar (1702–1707)*. Thanks to the Lionel Pincus and Princess Firyal Map Division of the New York Public Library.

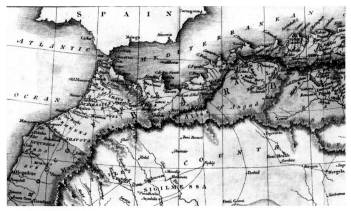

Figure 3. A chart of the western Mediterranean in the era of the corsairs depicts Morocco and Algiers, both labeled as "Barbary." *Source*: George Anson Jackson, *Algiers, Being a Complete Picture of the Barbary States . . .* (London: R. Edwards, 1817). Thanks to the British Library for placing this digitized image in the public domain under its Mechanical Curator collection.

Figure 4. A map of "Barbary" in 1798 shows Morocco alongside the three rogue Ottoman statelets—Algiers, Tunis, and Tripoli—whose corsairs terrorized the world for three centuries. *Source*: William Faden, cartographer, *Barbary, including Morocco, Algiers, Tunis & Tripoly (1798)*. Thanks to the Lionel Pincus and Princess Firyal Map Division of the New York Public Library.

Figure 5. "With its minarets and beautiful country seats, [Algiers] forms one of the most beautiful prospects in the world," Cathcart wrote, and this painting from the early 1800s seems to confirm his opinion. *Source*: Henry Parke, artist; L. Clark, engraver, in Filippo Pananti, *Narrative of a Residence in Algiers* (London: H. Colburn, 1818). Thanks to the General Research Division of the New York Public Library.

Figure 6. Newly arrived captives disembark at the harbor at Algiers in the 1600s, as depicted by the Dutch artist Jan Luiken. Approaching corsair ships would fire their guns to indicate their success in a mission, and "when no shots are fired . . . the captains are frequently bastinadoed." *Source*: Jan Luiken, engraver, *Slave Markt* (1684), in *Historie van Barbaryen en des Zelfs Zee-Roovers*. Thanks to the Rare Book Division of the New York Public Library.

Figure 7. Two decades after Cathcart's experiences, a group of captives in Algiers is depicted under the escort of a whip-wielding overseer. They include two women. In reality, Cathcart's group of captives in 1785 included a Spanish woman who was "purchased by the Regency"—effectively, she became the property of the dey himself. *Source*: George Anson Jackson, *Algiers, Being a Complete Picture of the Barbary States* . . . (London: R. Edwards, 1817). Thanks to the British Library for placing this digitized image in the public domain under its Mechanical Curator collection.

Figure 8. "O, Babel Oued, beneath thy sand my brother captives lie": This bird's-eye view plan of Algiers in 1818 shows, to the extreme right, the Babel Oued gate (9) leading out to the bleak burial ground where Cathcart interred the fallen Americans. We can also see the dey's palace (A), the port, and the mole (S). *Source*: Henry Parke, artist; Sidney Hall, engraver, in Filippo Pananti, *Narrative of a Residence in Algiers* (London: H. Colburn, 1818). Thanks to the General Research Division of the New York Public Library.

Figure 9. A belligerent city, permanently crouched ready to attack: This wonderful etching of Algiers, showing a foreshortened Mediterranean in the foreground, was created by Luca Berteli in the sixteenth century. *Source*: Luca Berteli, *Algier* (1565). Thanks to the public library of the University of Basel, Switzerland, via the e-rara digitization platform.

Figure 10. Dey Mahmood, the ruler who decided in 1785 to unleash his predatory corsairs against the United States. Although he presided over a golden age of prosperity for Algiers, he was notoriously mean and once had a servant beheaded for tidying away a few low-value coins. *Source*: Camille Leynadier, *Histoire de l'Algérie française . . .* Paris: H. Morel, 1846).

Figure 11. President George Washington: He was much admired by Dey Mahmood, who asked for a full-length portrait to hang in his palace. It didn't stop Mahmood from kidnapping US citizens, though. *Source*: Gilbert Stuart, From *Portraits of Presidents* (1828). Thanks to Library of Congress Prints and Photographs Division.

Figure 12. The notorious Badistan market where captives were put on view for possible sale to private buyers. Although Cathcart's group of prisoners was exhibited there for three days "from daylight to half past three without refreshment," only five men were purchased, and none of the Americans. *Source*: Print by Jan Luyken, *Christelijke gevangenen worden op een plein te Algiers . . .* in Pierre Dan, *Historie van Barbaryen* (Amsterdam: Jan Claesz ten Hoorn, 1684). Thanks to the Rijksmuseum of the Netherlands (www.rijksmuseum.nl) for placing this digitized image in the public domain

Figure 13. Normal life, yet not normal, in Algiers: An etching from the 1600s shows two captives walking through Algiers in animated conversation, by now oblivious to the long punishment chains they had to drag behind them. American hostages were fitted with chains weighing thirty to forty pounds, as heavy as a modern microwave oven. *Source*: Jan Luiken, engraver, *Hoe de Slaaven Met de Keetenen aen haer beenen gaen* (1684), in *Historie van Barbaryen en des Zelfs Zee-Roovers*. Thanks to the Rare Book Division of the New York Public Library.

Figure 14. The dreaded "ganches" or sharpened hooks, as depicted in a European propaganda picture. Although rarely used, one diplomat recorded three instances of this extreme punishment during his time in Algiers in the 1700s. *Source*: Pierre Dan, *Histoire de Barbarie* (1637), in Stanley Lane-Poole, *The Barbary Corsairs* (London: Fisher Unwin, 1890).

Figure 15. The petition of Hannah Stephens in 1791: In a heartbreaking plea to Congress, she begged the politicians to bring her husband Isaac home and so ease her "human woe." *Source*: *Memorial from Hannah Stephens Requesting the Release of her Husband from Prison in Algiers*, December 9, 1791. From the Records of the US Senate, National Archives ID 306398, Petitions and Memorials Relating to Various Subjects; Anson McCook Collection of Presidential Signatures, 1789–1975, Record Group 46; National Archives Building, Washington, DC. Thanks to the National Archives.

Figure 16. The town of Concord, Massachusetts, during the British occupation. This is the townscape that Hannah Stephens would have known in 1785, when her husband's capture by the Algerines left her homeless, destitute, and deprived of her beloved children. *Source*: Ralph Earl, artist; Amos Doolittle, engraver, *A View of the Town of Concord* (1775), from the Doolittle Engravings of the Battles of Lexington and Concord in 1775. Thanks to the Miriam and Ira D. Wallach Division of Art, Prints and Photographs, Print Collection, in the New York Public Library.

Figure 17. Thomas Jefferson: His instinct in 1785 was to "effect a peace through the medium of war. Justice is in favor of this opinion. Honor favors it." However, the United States would not have a national navy until the late 1790s. *Source*: Gilbert Stuart, *From Portraits of Presidents* (1828). Thanks to Library of Congress Prints and Photographs Division.

Figure 18. A French priest ransoming captives from Barbary in the 1600s. Thomas Jefferson's secret plan to back-channel US ransom money through the Trinitarian Order of Paris was tragically cut short by the French Revolution. *Source*: Pierre Dan, *Histoire de Barbarie* (1637), in Stanley Lane-Poole, *The Barbary Corsairs* (London: Fisher Unwin, 1890).

Dey of Algiers.

Figure 19. An unnamed dey of Algiers. Dey Hassan lived in constant fear of assassination, since he himself came to power by strangling his rival. Anyone in the palace could murder a ruler and declare himself as dey—one such killer lasted just ten minutes as ruler before he was himself dispatched by another candidate. *Source*: George Anson Jackson, *Algiers, Being a Complete Picture of the Barbary States . . .* (London: R. Edwards, 1817). Thanks to the British Library for placing these digitized images in the public domain under its Mechanical Curator collection.

Figure 20. "We were shown to a huge, shaggy beast, sitting on his rump upon a low bench, with his hind legs gathered up like a tailor or a bear": An English delegation meets the dey of Algiers in the early 1800s. *Source*: Abraham Salamé, *A Narrative of the Expedition to Algiers . . .* (London: John Murray, 1819). Thanks to the Schomburg Center for Research in Black Culture, Manuscripts, Archives and Rare Books Division of the New York Public Library and to the Boston Public Library.

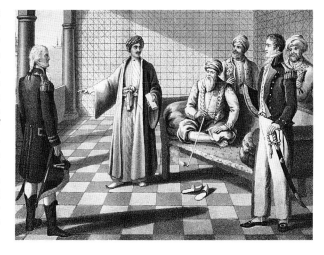

Figure 21. David Humphreys, the US ambassador to Portugal: He was alarmed when his envoy to Algiers agreed to give the predatory corsairs a warship with thirty-six guns—weapons they could easily turn against America in the future. *Source*: By James Herring and Stuart Gilbert. Thanks to the Miriam and Ira D. Wallach Division of Arts, Prints and Photographs in the New York Public Library.

Figure 22. John Adams, US minister in London: His cautious approach to freeing the US hostages made him a hated figure among some of the captives. "I must think you the greatest enemy I have in the world," one hostage wrote to him in fury, "and not a friend to liberty." *Source*: Gilbert Stuart, *Portraits of Presidents* (1828). Thanks to Library of Congress Prints and Photographs Division.

Figure 23. Joel Barlow, poet and envoy to Algiers: He blew a fortune on gifts of fashionable Parisian dresses for the ladies of the dey's court, only to discover that they were too revealing for women in an Islamic society. They were "entirely thrown away." *Source*: Portrait created 1783–1890. Thanks to the Miriam and Ira D. Wallach Division of Arts, Prints and Photographs in the New York Public Library.

When news reached Algiers that things were beginning to move forward politically, the prisoners took heart. "It affords the Americans in captivity some consolation," Captain Richard O'Brien wrote home in April 1791.

He warned that there were now only seven hundred foreign hostages in Algiers, compared to three thousand at first. The dey, he wrote, was not inclined to let any of them be ransomed "on any terms . . . as the captives are much wanted to do the public work."

He repeated his suggestion that the cost of a peace deal would be much lower if it were paid through stores and naval supplies.

O'Brien's main fear was that Algiers would make a truce with Portugal. Without that nation's patrol ships guarding the Straits of Gibraltar, more American ships would be left vulnerable, with "fatal consequences."

He ended his letter with a familiar appeal. "We hope you will finally extricate your fourteen unfortunate subjects from their present state of bondage and adversity."

Make that thirteen. In summer of that same year, 1791, a second crewman from the *Dauphin*, John Robertson, was redeemed by his friends in America. After tearful goodbyes, he boarded a ship and returned home.

And shortly afterward, the unfortunate James Harnet, seaman from the *Maria*, turned completely insane. "One of us, James Harnet, has been deprived of his senses, and confined in a dungeon," reported a letter home from the American captives. Cathcart paid for his upkeep, but in such horrendous conditions, Harnet was not expected to survive for long.

By March 29, 1792, a petition from the prisoners repeated all the earlier pleas but ended with a new twist. They were "destitute of almost all the necessities of life, and in [a] deplorable situation," it said. Yet they had always resisted any attempts to abandon their country or religion, "trusting in the justice and humanity of Congress." But if the politicians did not act soon, they warned, there would be no captives left and no problem to solve.

The plague epidemic had gradually subsided but had never been exterminated. "We entreat that some attention will be paid to our situation," pleaded the prisoners, "before the whole of us perish."

★ ★ ★

James Cathcart almost did perish around that time, thanks to a third unexpected incident in the Mad House tavern, which brought him closer to death than any other single event during his captivity in Algiers. It was an episode that could easily have sent him, within hours, to a grisly death by burning.

Here's how the incident unfolded. Cathcart had been working at the Bagnio Gallera until three in the afternoon and hadn't eaten since breakfast.

He walked to the Mad House to get a meal before his American colleagues arrived for their dinner. He was deeply worried about the death toll among his friends and made the classic mistake of drinking on an empty stomach. "Whether the thought of my situation, or not having eaten anything since the morning, or both, aided by a glass or two of wine, impaired my reason or not, I am not aware," he wrote later, "but I certainly acted very imprudently, which nearly ruined me forever."

Cathcart's dinner had just arrived on his table when a sharif, a religious noble, entered the bar and demanded his seat. Cathcart refused. I will finish my dinner, he said, before I will let you or anyone else sit in my place.

An argument erupted and the sharif called him "a dog without faith." Cathcart took exception. "I doubt if you know the tenets of your own religion as well as I do," he said.

It wasn't an empty boast. Ever since his early days in the palace garden, he had been studying the Koran in an effort to better understand this new religion and culture. He also knew the history of Islam, chapter and verse.

An elderly sheikh dared him to prove it, and the entire tavern fell silent. Cathcart had entered very hazardous territory. But the wine had gone straight to his head, and it gave him a dangerous confidence. He launched straight in, listing all the key events in the history of the religion, from its beginnings, through its great schism, right up to the present day.

Warming to his theme, he said he believed that Christianity and Islam had much in common and should concentrate on their similarities rather than their differences. Far from being "without faith," he declared, he himself belonged to a religion that shared a mutual belief in the first phrase of the *Shahada*, the Muslim declaration of faith: "There is no deity but God." They simply differed on the second part, which he quoted to his audience.

There was a roar of approval from his listeners: "He has pronounced the symbol of our faith," they shouted.

For Cathcart, the headiness of the wine evaporated in an instant as he suddenly realized that he was in "the greatest danger I had ever been in since my captivity commenced." Strictly speaking, his "conversion" was not valid since his words were a quotation, not a declaration of faith, but that didn't help. As his brain sobered, he searched hopelessly for a way to get himself out of this dangerous corner.

He was smart enough to know that any excuse would simply make things worse. *I didn't mean it?* Then he was blaspheming. *I had been drinking?* Worse still, with one sin compounding the other. *I did say it, but now I've changed my mind?* Worst of all: the Algerines reserved their very worst punishments for those who forsook their faith. Traditionally, they were roasted alive within a ring of ferocious bonfires.

As he sat in stunned silence, someone rushed out to fetch the qadi, a sharia judge, to confirm his conversion. Everyone in the bar waited eagerly for his return. Fortunately for Cathcart, the judge wasn't home. Undeterred, the messengers set off to search the city for an alternative.

By this time, it was dusk, and the Janissaries in the bar had to leave before curfew. Their departure drained the energy from the room. Only a few customers stayed to witness the climax of the episode.

Cathcart, by now perfectly sober, fell back on his default tactic. He threw open his cashbox, dug deep, and bribed every man jack in the room. The sharif, who was a practical-minded man, agreed to forget the entire incident in exchange for a fistful of cash and a free tab at the bar. The elderly sheikh who'd called him out accepted ten sequins, or around $20, and then decided—quite correctly—that Cathcart had simply been quoting a text "without any intention whatever." The other drinkers were equally amenable, and by the time the open-bar session ended and the doors were finally locked on the Mad House, Cathcart was able to heave a giant sigh of relief.

Still, Algiers was a small city, and word was bound to get around. Cathcart had a troubled night's sleep and awoke next morning to hear that the news was buzzing all over town.

Dey Hassan himself investigated the incident, but fortunately for the American, the ruler vividly remembered the time that Cathcart had refused a lucrative promotion that had been dependent upon his conversion. "That young man has a hard head," Hassan said. "He has no more intention to turn Muslim than I have to turn Christian. Had he been so disposed, he might have done it years ago, much more to his advantage."

The old sheikh met Cathcart later and told him exactly how close he'd come to suffering an agonizing death. "Had I refused after having recited the symbol of their faith," Cathcart wrote, "I would have been put to death as an apostate from it. I had a lucky escape."

He was not exaggerating. Just a few years earlier, a Genoese seaman in Algiers had converted to Islam, but changed his mind after only two months. He was sentenced to several hundred blows of the bastinado before his head was cut off.

A little later, US diplomat Joel Barlow recorded a similar incident. A man had supposedly been overheard in the street mentioning that he wanted to convert to Islam. "They immediately led him before the Dey . . . [but] his courage had failed and he refused to change his religion. The penalty for a retraction of this kind was death, and everybody was expecting [his] burning that same afternoon." Fortunately for him, "the affair was settled by means of a little money."

Burning alive was just one of the gruesome punishments that the Algerines reserved for serious offenders. If a captive murdered another captive, he was beheaded at the palace gates. But if a captive murdered a freeperson, he could be thrown on to the dreaded ganches.

The ganches were sharpened upward-pointing metal hooks set into the city walls. "A platform is built on the top, about fifty feet high, from whence criminals are precipitated down an oblique wall, in which are fixed ganches or hooks at short distances, by which the malefactor is either hung or torn to pieces," one historian wrote in the 1700s.

American John Foss recorded that the hooks "catch by any part of the body that strikes them, and sometimes they hang in this manner in the most exquisite agonies for several days before they expire."

At this stage in the late 1700s, the ganches were rarely used. But they were by no means a relic of the distant past. Joseph Morgan, an Englishman who lived in Algiers earlier in the same century, recorded three instances of execution by ganches during his stay there.

Cathcart's narrow escape had taught him a valuable lesson. "The escape prevented me from ever disputing . . . on points of religion again," he wrote.

Wise words—for anyone, in any country, and in any century. But especially sound advice for an Irishman.

· *17* ·

Cape Desolation

$\mathcal{I}$n March 1792, James Cathcart shot to the very peak of power in Algiers. He was abruptly and unexpectedly elevated to the highest position that any European or American could occupy: the coveted role of the dey's chief Christian clerk. This was a high-profile administrative position that involved dealing with consuls and foreign diplomats.

Once again, Cathcart lucked into it by being in the right place at the right time with the right money, and knowing the right people, but once again he had made his own luck by building a solid network of support. The vacancy arose out of the blue with the surprise redemption of his old friend from Boston, Angelo d'Andreis, who had been chief clerk since the mid-1780s. It was almost certainly d'Andreis who recommended Cathcart as his successor. The dey, of course, had already been impressed with Cathcart's honesty and his refusal to buckle under pressure in the dispute over the financial accounts at the prison. The previous year, the ruler had employed the young American to do the accounts for the sale of his own private house, proving that the controversies at the Mad House tavern had not affected his standing at the palace.

"[The dey] said that, as I had fulfilled the duties of . . . Clerk of the Marine, etc., that I ought to be preferred to the highest post a Christian can attain," Cathcart wrote. "He therefore appointed me the same day."

The position came with a superb perk: it entitled the holder to be included in any mass redemption by any nation whatever. This applied even if the redemption were to take place the day after he took the job. The downside was that the new chief Christian clerk had to stump up a hefty insurance payment against that happening. The payment was 1,383 sequins (around $2,800), upfront and nonrefundable.

115

The dey lamented that he did not have it in his power to waive the fee, and Cathcart didn't have enough money. However, his friends the Skjoldebrands (Mathias, the Swedish consul, and his America-friendly brother Peter Erik) lent him five hundred sequins and the dey agreed to lend him the remainder.

Frustratingly for us, Cathcart does not disclose his feelings about returning to the palace where—just six years before—he had first shuffled through the gate filthy, shackled, and bereft of all hope. He made the same walk through the execution courtyard, past the fountains, and into the arcades, but this time with a spring in his step and a new sense of empowerment. He was now a major player in the Algiers bureaucracy—more powerful than his old captain, Richard O'Brien, and in a much better position to help his countrymen. But when he glanced at the captives performing his old tasks in the garden—cleaning the lion cages and chasing the cats off the shrubbery—did he shudder at the bad memories or glow with pride at his elevation? Whatever his true feelings, it was an astonishing reversal of fortune.

Although he retained control over his three taverns, he began to move through the gilded rooms of the palace with ease. Every morning, he rose before dawn to meet the dey in his private reception room. To get there, he negotiated the five flights of stone stairs that were deliberately designed to confuse intruders. A later diplomat from America gives a vivid picture of the experience.

"We uncovered our heads and ascended a winding maze of five flights of stairs to a narrow dark entry, leading to a contracted apartment of about twelve by eight feet, the private audience room. Here we took off our shoes and [entered] the cave—for so it seemed—with small apertures for light, with iron grates."

The diplomat then recalls meeting the dey. His rather overwrought description anticipates the genre of African gothic horror long before H. Rider Haggard dreamed up Twala and the witch Gagool in *King Solomon's Mines*.

"We were shown to a huge, shaggy beast, sitting on his rump upon a low bench covered with a cushion of embroidered velvet, with his hind legs gathered up like a tailor or a bear. On our approach to him, he reached out his forepaw as if to receive something to eat. . . . [We] kissed it. . . .

"The animal seemed at that moment to be in a harmless mood; he grinned several times, but made very little noise. . . . [After] standing for a few moments in silent agony, we had leave to take our shoes and leave the den."

According to another source, "the Dey and his visitors are seated on slabs of marble or slate projecting from the wall, about three feet high, upon which are placed cushions . . . where his visitors sit cross-legged. The Dey sits with a large fan of ostrich feathers in his hand."

Cathcart had to give daily briefings to Hassan and convey his somewhat erratic decisions to anxious foreign consuls. It wasn't an easy job, because he took severe stick from both of them. The dey threw screaming fits that Cathcart attempted to de-escalate while the consuls tore their hair out analyzing the ruler's decisions and trying to find a logic that usually didn't exist. The dey accused his clerk of taking the foreigners' side against him, and the consuls accused him of being a turncoat who took the side of the Algerines. For Cathcart, it was an ominous harbinger of what was to come later.

★ ★ ★

Cathcart's role as chief clerk put him back in contact with the two *Maria* crewmen who had remained on the palace staff: George Smith, the dey's personal page, and Thomas Billings. A seaman from the *Dauphin*, Philip Sloan, also worked there as the chief sweeper, or *captain aproa*. This position, like the job of coffee maker, was much more desirable than it sounded.

However, it also carried considerable risk. One of Sloan's predecessors as *captain aproa* had served under Dey Mahmood, who had been a notorious skinflint. Despite sitting on a treasury that was worth millions, Mahmood used to walk the streets at night looking for aspers, the lowest value coin in Algiers. Spitting on his fingers to achieve better adhesion, the old dey stooped to pick up the light tin coins and take them back to his apartment in the palace.

The previous head sweeper chanced upon a little pile of the aspers, worth practically nothing, and innocently tidied them away. On his return, Mahmood immediately spotted the missing coins and "in consequence," reported one writer, "the *Captain Aproa* lost his head."

George Smith, the dey's page, seemed to have hit it lucky. He wore a smart uniform, shared in the generous tips, and lived in a pleasant room in the dey's luxurious new apartments. Yet the atmosphere there was always tense. One witness wrote in 1797 that "it is impossible to conceive the consternation that always prevails" among the workers in the palace. "Everyone is in continual apprehension of losing his life."

As Cathcart chatted with Smith, he learned that life as the dey's page also had its lighter moments—although they certainly did not seem funny at the time. For instance, there was the time when the young American servant was accused of trying to murder the dey in what turned out to be a wardrobe malfunction.

George Smith was required to dress the ruler each morning, pulling a long, unbuttoned shirt over his head. These shirts, custom-made in the Levant, were fresh from the tailor. One morning, George suddenly found to his horror that the tailor had forgotten to undo the stitching at the top. There was no hole for the dey's head to emerge through.

Hassan had made many enemies and lived in constant fear of assassination. He gave a muffled yell, convinced that he was being bundled into a sack for execution. Struggling blindly inside the shirt, he succeeded only in becoming more entangled. He "screamed with the greatest terror imaginable." He seized the razor-sharp yataghan saber that he always kept beside his bed and swiped blindly at George, who jumped out of the way just in time and fled the room. The dey struggled free and "ran naked out of the room to murder the boy, who fled for refuge into a distant apartment." When he finally realized what had happened, "instead of murdering the boy, he beat him unmercifully with a rope."

(There are two versions of this story. One maintains that the tailor's mistake was purely accidental. The other claims that a rival servant deliberately sewed up the shirt in a bid to get George into trouble.)

In the palace, even normal human weaknesses could become dangerous. For instance, one page at the palace suffered from sleepwalking, a potentially fatal condition in a place where every sound in the night was interpreted as an assassination bid.

One night the dey heard footsteps as the page wandered around the corridor fast asleep. He yelled for his guards. The guards were aware of the secret: they woke the servant, sent him back to bed, and told the dey that the noises had been made by the palace cats.

The sleepwalker asked to sleep beside a fellow servant from then on, with one of their legs tied together in the style of a three-legged race. The system worked well until the night the dey unexpectedly called for a servant in the small hours. Forgetting they were tied together, both men leaped out of bed, tripped each other in the corridor, and fell against the dey's door, which burst open with an almighty crash and sent them tumbling to the floor. Convinced he was under attack, the dey grabbed his yataghan saber and stabbed at the figures on the floor. Somehow they managed to evade his sword thrusts in almost total darkness and scrambled to their feet, running three-legged to the stairway, where they tripped again and fell headlong downstairs.

Meanwhile, the ruler's trusted guards calmed the dey and explained exactly what had happened. Hassan ordered both servants executed, but next morning, in the cold light of day, he saw the humor in the situation. He had them bastinadoed instead.

"The lives of those unfortunate youths [were] rendered extremely miserable," wrote Cathcart. "Every moment they were menaced with bastinadoes, hard labor, chains and death. . . . Their situation was by no means enviable."

* * *

Meanwhile, across the Atlantic, with public indignation at boiling point, America desperately needed a hero. Secretary of State Thomas Jefferson found one in Admiral John Paul Jones, the dashing former privateer who'd razed the British coast with fire and lead during the Revolutionary War.

Jones, a feisty forty-five-year-old Scotsman, first shot to fame in 1778, when his ship *Ranger* took on the mighty British naval sloop *Drake* and laid her low with ruthlessly forensic gunnery. His indomitable spirit was summed up in a famous quote. Facing defeat in a crucial sea battle, he was called upon to surrender and memorably shouted back: "I have not yet begun to fight!"

This was the spirit that Jefferson needed. Jones's Scottish character displayed fireworks of bristling indignation and righteous anger, but these were combined with undertones of keen intelligence and personal charm. If anyone could slice through the intractable gordian knot of Barbary politics, it was John Paul Jones.

On June 1, 1792, Jefferson wrote to Jones in Paris offering him the job of envoy. "Entire secrecy is recommended," Jefferson wrote. "Cover from the public your departure and destination." It wasn't the North Africans he was worried about. It was the British, who could easily sabotage the mission before it even began.

Once in Algiers, he said that Jones should communicate only in cipher and should trust only one man: Captain O'Brien. "The zeal which he has displayed . . . has been very distinguished."

Jefferson also warned the admiral to beware of well-meaning volunteers who had tried to negotiate ransoms for the Americans. They had done more harm than good by destroying Jefferson's carefully constructed illusion that America didn't care about its captured citizens. They had "lengthened the chains they were meant to break."

First item, the peace deal. Based on O'Brien's recommendations, Jones should offer the dey two light cruisers and a consignment of maritime stores upfront, followed by an annual tribute payment: "We would be pleased with $10,000, contented with $15,000, think $20,000 a very hard bargain, yet go as far as $25,000." He could go no higher under law.

Next item on the agenda, the ransom of the crewmen. "You will consider . . . $27,000 as your ultimate limit." Once they had been ransomed, Jones should "have the captives well clothed and sent home at the expense of the United States."

There was a certain spark of confidence and optimism in Jefferson's tone. His new appointee was a man in his prime facing into a promising political career, and Jefferson was sure he would rise to this challenge.

In an alternative universe, the revolutionary hero John Paul Jones goes straight to Algiers, charms and intimidates the dey in equal measure, secures a peace deal, and brings the thirteen captives home to national acclaim.

But real life doesn't deliver dramatic climaxes to order. Real life often gives us high expectations followed by dispiriting anticlimax. A few weeks after receiving his commission, Jones began experiencing crippling stomach pains. The ink was hardly dry on Jefferson's letter when, in July, Jones was found dead in his Paris home. The warrior who'd humbled the British navy had been floored by kidney inflammation. He never did get to Algiers.

★ ★ ★

Back in the corsair city, the Black Death finally tapped the shoulder of the unstoppable James Cathcart—the only man in Algiers who had actually emerged from the first epidemic feeling *healthier* than before.

Early in 1793, Cathcart's iron-clad immune system let him down and he fell seriously ill. He was temporarily cast out of the palace and sent back to the Bagnio Gallera.

The horrified Cathcart knew his condition could only worsen in the pestilential hellhole of the Gallera. He sent a message to his former sea captain, Isaac Stephens of the *Maria*, explaining the situation and asking if he could stay with the officers in their spacious suburban home, well clear of the plague-ravaged city. Cathcart was astonished and hurt when Stephens said no.

The two men had different interpretations of the reason for the refusal. To Stephens, it was common sense: it would only make things worse if Cathcart were to bring the plague with him into the captains' house. From Cathcart's perspective, Stephens was less worried about catching the plague than about catching lower-class contamination, since the suburban lodging was reserved for officers and gentlemen.

Stunned by the rejection, the socially ambitious Cathcart wrote a letter to Captain Richard O'Brien, pathetically addressed from "Death's Door, Algiers." It was searingly passive-aggressive in tone:

March 2 1793.

My Dear Sir,

I am sorry to be under the necessity of troubling you at this melancholy crisis of mortality . . . but I may be on the verge of eternity. . . .

I forgive Stephens with all my heart, but if I die of this distemper, he will certainly have his conduct to answer for, relative to me, before a just God who makes no difference between the captain and the sailors, as he has been the means of hindering me from being accommodated out of the reach of the plague. . . .

By the bearer, receive a watch chain and seal; if I do weather Cape Desolation, you will give it me again; if I do not, I beg of you to keep it as a small token of remembrance of a disinterested friend in the shades.

Your affectionate and unfeigned friend,

James Cathcart.

Leaving aside Cathcart's maudlin and slightly pretentious tone (he was very ill at the time), it's fascinating to see his psychological bonding skills at work. The phrase "if I weather Cape Desolation" is an adroit mirroring of O'Brien's seafaring metaphors.

Cathcart went on to make a full recovery, but later that year he informed O'Brien that one of the *Dauphin* captives, the young French passenger Jacob Tessanaer, had collapsed and died of plague in July. (A few years before, Tessanaer had been appointed as a page at the palace.)

"I am much concerned and afraid that this tremendous disorder will carry off the major part of this victim remnant," O'Brien wrote home. "They are [driven to] the greatest despair. They are on the verge of eternity . . . destined to be victims of American Independence."

Later in that dismal year of 1793, there was more bad news when Cathcart's crewmate, James Harnet, finally died in the dungeon of the "mad house" (the asylum, not the pub), where he had been confined for more than a year, mostly at Cathcart's expense.

That same year, his *Maria* crewmate George Smith had a remarkably lucky escape from the executioner's blade. Smith, the palace page and personal favorite of the dey, had a job that carried privileges such as "fine clothes, money and good living" but also the constant threat of torture and death at the hands of his capricious boss.

It seems that George had struck up a friendship with a grandee from Algiers and had been spotted visiting him at his home. This sent Dey Hassan into a jealous fury, and he ordered the young page's execution. "George Smith incurred the displeasure of the Dey," O'Brien understatedly recorded, and would soon "die an American victim."

However, "in this time of threatening danger," the Swedish consul Mathias Skjoldebrand rode to the rescue. He offered to personally redeem the young American from death row at a jaw-droppingly high cost of $2,696, trusting the honor of the United States to repay him. Young George walked free and eventually made his way home to America, liberated forever from the daily worry of being skewered on the dey's saber as a result of a social faux pas or tailoring mishap.

The rescue has Cathcart's fingerprints all over it—after all, he was the only connection among the dey, Smith, and the Swedish consul—yet in his list of the fates of the *Maria* crewmen, he simply records George Smith as "redeemed by friends." Which may have been the most diplomatic way to put it.

★ ★ ★

Meanwhile the rest of the captives, seemingly trapped forever in what O'Brien called "this city of human misery," became so desperate that they found themselves considering another way out of their predicament. It was an almost unthinkable option: they could defect to the enemy . . . and become corsairs themselves.

O'Brien, who was himself at a low ebb psychologically, began dropping dark warnings of defection in his messages home. "[They] have suffered an ignominious captivity of nearly eight years . . . left in the most distressed and humiliating situation," he warned. "I have fears that many of them will renounce their country and become subjects of this Regency."

He suggested that some of these defectors would then seek retribution against their uncaring countryfolk: "They will thirst for revenge against the U.S.," wrote O'Brien, "who have occasioned all their miseries."

It was not an empty threat. Throughout history, some of the most enthusiastic and successful corsairs operating out of Algiers had been European seafarers who converted to Islam: for instance, Yusuf Rais, formerly John Ward of England, who terrorized his homeland in the early 1600s, and Morat Rais, a renegade Dutchman who became notorious for his rapacious raids on Iceland and Baltimore in Ireland.

"Turning Turk" (as the Europeans called it) was theoretically a straightforward process, though in practice, nothing was ever simple in Algiers. It was more common among privately owned captives, usually domestic workers whose masters sometimes offered them freedom in return for conversion after eight or ten years of service. There would often be an added incentive—a share in the family business or marriage to a daughter. In this way, the owners earned respect from their neighbors and could die peacefully in the belief they had saved a soul. The conversion of a child, particularly, elevated an owner's standing in his community. Changing religion did not automatically lead to a captive's freedom, but it was considered bad form for an owner to keep a fellow believer in bondage.

None of this mattered to the Americans taken in 1785, since they were owned by the state and very unlikely to be offered freedom in exchange for conversion. "In such cases," wrote one historian in the 1790s, "the government is deprived both of their labor and the benefit of their ransom."

As it turned out, O'Brien's gloomy fears were unfounded. During the period of this story, 1785 to 1796, there was not a single instance of an American conversion. Overall, according to the same historian, the number of apostates in the city was "very small."

Years later, however, Captain Isaac Stephens of the *Maria* made a curious and cryptic remark in a letter to John Adams. He referred to "my sailor that offered himself for a Mahommitian [sic] to cruise [against] the Americans on account that the Americans would not redeem him." He never elaborated. There were only four sailors on Stephens's ship, and if we ignore the palace page George Smith and poor James Harnet, that leaves only Cathcart and Thomas Billings. But we have no evidence that either of them offered to "turn Turk." It could be that Stephens was making a confused reference to an earlier incident in which the dey had unsuccessfully offered Cathcart the command of a fighting ship in return for his conversion—an offer that turned out to be more of a test of character than a genuine proposition.

★   ★   ★

Let's pause and take stock. By the fall of 1793, only ten of the original twenty-one Americans were still alive in Algiers. The others had died. Three had made it safely home. Of the six-strong *Maria* crew, we still have Captain Isaac Stephens, mate Alexander Forsyth, Thomas Billings, and Cathcart himself. From the *Dauphin*, there were only six survivors—Captain Richard O'Brien, mate Andrew Montgomery, chief palace sweeper Philip Sloan, and the other three seamen, Peter Loring, James Hull, and William Patterson.

These ten were becoming more and more scattered. With four special-category "moon payers" in the suburbs and three other captives (including Cathcart) based at the palace, that left only three Americans doing hard labor at the docks. There must have been times when they felt a bit lonely and longed to have their countrymen by their side. If so, they did not have long to wait.

Back home in America, observers were beginning to wonder why everything had been so quiet since the two ships were captured eight years before. "Why, excepting two vessels, have not the ships of this country met with any interruption?" one writer asked curiously. "Instead of being surprised at our having suffered so much, it is rather an object of wonder that we have suffered so *little*."

It was a prescient remark, because all that was about to change.

They say that war consists of long periods of boredom punctuated by short bursts of sheer terror. And so it was in Algiers, where those eight years of grinding monotony were followed, in October 1793, by a sudden flare-up of frantic activity and intense, ferocious aggression by the Barbary corsairs. The wolf packs were on the hunt again—and their prey was the American merchant navy.

• *18* •

Clipping the Eagle's Wings

$\mathcal{T}$he crisis had begun to simmer several months earlier. Dey Hassan was rapidly losing his infatuation with this newly minted nation on the other side of the Atlantic. Like a spurned lover, he turned bitter and vindictive. Meanwhile, his corsair captains were straining at the leash, and the shortage of captive labor meant he needed more grunt workers at the docks.

In May 1793, the cold war exploded into action with an opportunistic corsair attack on an American schooner, *Lark*, just off Cabo de Gata in southern Spain. The ship had left Cartagena in Murcia and had been heading toward the strait when a small oar-driven galley from Algiers closed in. Realizing they were outnumbered, the *Lark*'s crew hurriedly launched a rowboat, abandoned ship, and hauled for their lives toward the rocky shore of Andalusia. Their attackers easily could have caught them, but they didn't want to risk a diplomatic row with Spain, so they contented themselves with capturing the unmanned ship and its cargo.

On August 18 there was an almost identical replay of that incident when an American ship was attacked off Malaga. This time the Algerines were "in an American vessel which they had taken some time before" and had fitted out with guns. (Presumably this was the schooner *Lark*.) Once again, the crew jumped ship and escaped.

While all this was happening, the English and Spanish were pressuring Portugal to make a truce with Algiers—or so the Americans believed. If that happened, Portuguese navy patrols would no longer protect the Strait of Gibraltar against the corsairs, leaving the American ships as easy targets, since they had to pass through this narrow bottleneck to enter the Mediterranean. "England and Spain seem to be plotting in what way they can most effectually clip our Eagle's wings," reported Edward Church, the US consul in Lisbon. "They are both extremely envious of her soaring."

In this tense atmosphere, the reports of the two attacks on US ships left American diplomats desperately worried. "Had the men been taken, it is more than probable that the great object in view [i.e., the peace deal and ransom] would have been defeated," Church warned. "Should one other American crew fall into the Dey's hands [our ransom fund] would be totally inadequate and [our] mission fruitless."

The consul's prediction underestimated the future reality by a mile. *One* American crew? Try eleven.

★   ★   ★

In early October, the Americans received the worst possible news. "Authentic advice is just received that a truce for twelve months is [agreed] between Portugal and Algiers," reported the US consul in the Portuguese territory of Madeira.

The dey didn't lose a moment in taking advantage of the new political seascape. "Eight Algerine cruisers—four frigates, one brig and three xebecs— passed through the Straits last night into the Atlantic," the consul in Madeira reported. "I write to you in great haste . . . that you may take such measures as you shall judge proper."

A Portuguese witness confirmed that he'd seen the eight cruisers and warned that they were carrying serious firepower: the four frigates each had between twenty-eight and forty-four guns, the xebecs twenty to twenty-six guns each, and the brig twenty-two guns.

Blindsided by the news—even though O'Brien had been warning about the risk for years—an American diplomat demanded a meeting with the Portuguese foreign minister and was told that the peace deal had come as much of a surprise to Lisbon as it had to the American consulate. The coup had actually been pulled off in Algiers by the tirelessly plotting British consul, Charles Logie, based on a general Portuguese desire for peace. He had persuaded the dey to speed things up by unilaterally declaring a twelve-month truce on September 12. As a result, what the Portuguese regarded as a slow, embryonic process had suddenly reached dramatic fruition. Portugal's foreign minister told the US envoy that he'd wanted to give the Americans months of notice of any danger to their shipping but had been decisively and dramatically outmaneuvered by the British.

As expected, Portugal was required to call off its anti-corsair patrols in the strait. It couldn't even offer informal protection to American ships without incurring diplomatic backlash from Britain and Spain (although later it secretly softened this approach).

Logie further exploited the situation by supplying the dey with full details of American merchant ships and their likely whereabouts. Simultaneously—and not coincidentally—the British navy began sailing into Spanish ports and press-ganging American sailors from US ships under the ludicrous pretext that the seamen were actually British subjects concealing their identity. A shipper in Cadiz, Spain, reported: "There is hardly left two men on board of any American vessel."

Even worse for the United States, a peace deal between Algiers and Holland had now left the Algerines at war with only America, Genoa, and the tiny Hanseatic States in northern Europe. Any US ships going into or out of the Mediterranean would be like lambs to the slaughter.

The action rapidly heated up. In October, the *Nancy*, a New York ship bound for Barcelona, dashed headlong into Cadiz. It had been chased for several hours by an Algerine warship. Its master, Captain Butler, had made the brave decision to try to outrun the corsair—an almost impossible task for a fully laden cargo ship—and "got clear by means of her superior sailing." Kudos to Captain Butler: that was quite an achievement.

Cheated of their prey, the corsairs gave up on the *Nancy* and turned on another American ship. Butler couldn't identify the other vessel but believed it had been taken. Later, a second capture was witnessed by Swedish seamen. They saw an Algerine warship seize an American vessel, dump part of its cargo of grain into the sea for extra speed, and fit it out with guns as an instant addition to its fleet of cruisers.

Peter Walsh, a shipper in Cadiz, distilled the foreboding of the American community in the Mediterranean into a single poignant phrase. "Humanity shudders," he wrote, "for the fate of those who may have the misfortune to fall into the hands of the pirates."

III

· 19 ·

Scipio

In the fall of 1793, an African American seaman named Scipio Jackson stood on the deck of the brig *Minerva* and watched the familiar wharves of New York recede into the sea mist. He was on his way to Leghorn in Italy and hoped to return to America within a couple of months. However, fate had decreed that he was never to see Manhattan, Long Island, or the Hudson River again.

Scipio was a Black freeman in a city that still practiced race-dependent chattel slavery. We know little about his background, but it is almost certain that Scipio himself was formerly an enslaved person. One modern historian has put forward evidence to that effect, and it seems more likely than not. "Scipio" is a typical slave name. White owners often named their enslaved males after classical Roman figures such as Brutus, Augustus, Caesar, and the military general Scipio Africanus. (Thomas Jefferson, for instance, owned a slave named Jupiter.) But assuming he had been enslaved, how could Scipio have gained his freedom?

There is a convincing explanation. During the Revolutionary War, the British who occupied New York offered freedom to enslaved people from other areas, provided, of course, they were able to escape and make it across the line. Thousands of fugitives took up the offer (including, as it happened, two owned by George Washington); Jackson was most likely among them.

After independence, the position of these Black freemen in New York became so precarious that thousands left for Nova Scotia, but even then, the public mood in the city was gradually shifting toward abolition. By the time of our story, a third of the Black population in New York State was free. Scipio Jackson was among them, and by 1793 he had signed up as a mariner on the *Minerva* and was headed across the Atlantic.

The *Minerva* was a small workhorse of a vessel with a minimal crew of just five mariners (including Scipio himself) serving under a captain named Joseph Ingraham and a mate named Edward Smith, both from New York. The journey across the Atlantic and through the strait passed without incident, and by early November, the brig had unloaded in Leghorn and taken on a new cargo of mixed goods, or "sundries," for the voyage back to New York. Despite the offhand description, it was actually quite a rich cargo: wine, oil, fruit, and Italian marble.

Leghorn was a nerve center of international trade, so Captain Ingraham was bound to have picked up the news buzzing around port: that the Barbary wolf packs had been unleashed a few weeks before and were scouring the Mediterranean and the Atlantic for American ships. It's possible that Ingraham thought he was safe at this time of year: after all, the corsairs didn't like braving the unpredictable winters and traditionally laid up their ships in November. What he didn't realize was that the dey had decided to milk this year's American vulnerability for all it was worth and had approved an extra-late foray into the Mediterranean.

Scipio Jackson and his crewmates no doubt felt a creeping sense of apprehension as they left the safety of Leghorn and set their prow west toward home.

They settled into their usual seagoing routine as they navigated to the north of Corsica and skirted the coast of southern France until they reached Catalunya in Spain. From there they planned to follow the Spanish coast southward and again westward until they reached the strait.

They never got that far. Just seven miles off Cape San Sebastian, a rugged headland near Girona, they spotted a ship on the horizon. It was a corsair warship. Within an hour, they were in chains and on their way to Algiers. It was November 23.

★ ★ ★

Earlier that year, another African American freeman, John Thomas, had said farewell to his home state of Massachusetts and traveled to Philadelphia to enlist as a seaman aboard the merchant ship *President*.

Whether or not he himself had been formerly enslaved—and it's certainly possible—John Thomas's status as a freeman was more secure in the Commonwealth of Massachusetts than Scipio Jackson's had been in New York. Twelve years earlier the Massachusetts chief justice had declared slavery "effectively abolished" and, despite no official change in the law, the ruling had in most cases transformed slaves into paid employees. By 1790, no slaves were recorded in Massachusetts, although many were still suffering in bondage as indentured servants.

Massachusetts had a vigorous abolitionist movement. For instance, in Hannah Stephens's hometown of Concord, there was a gravestone that reflected the views of many people in the commonwealth. Commemorating an African-born enslaved man named John Jack, it said: "Though born in a land of slavery, he was born free. Though he lived in a land of liberty, he lived a slave." The slab begins: "God wills us free: man wills us slaves."

John Thomas and his nine fellow crewmen headed off from Pennsylvania in October 1793 under the command of Captain William Penrose from Philadelphia. They were bound for Cadiz with a cargo of grain and flour. The sturdy *President* made good time and they neared the Strait of Gibraltar with only a few hours' sailing time ahead of them; they were no doubt looking forward to some shore leave. They would have to help unload their cargo, but after that . . . perhaps an evening in a taverna, a couple of glasses of *vino de Andalusia*, and a bit of conversation with some Spanish chicas before reloading and heading back home.

However, at nine o'clock on the morning of October 23, that prospect vanished like a sea mirage when a mystery ship appeared to their windward. At first its profile was indistinct, but as it drew closer it revealed itself to be a fighting xebec with sixteen guns.

John Thomas and his shipmates were at first reassured by the sight of the Spanish flag. Captain Penrose hoisted his own American colors and prepared for a friendly exchange of compliments. But as the xebec drew closer, the Spanish flag disappeared, replaced by the blue-and-white flag of piratical Algiers. Janissary troops suddenly appeared on the deck and discharged a warning volley of small arms fire.

Everything happened in eerie slow motion: there was only a light breeze, and the attack ship took forever to get close. Thirty Algerines jumped into a boat and "rowed with great violence" toward the merchant ship.

The Americans were thrown into "the most violent consternation imaginable." They dashed around, trying to stash away their money and valuables and safeguard their clothes. When the corsairs came alongside, "they boarded with pistols and drawn swords," recalled one eyewitness, "and with the greatest fury and shouting."

When Penrose stepped forward to introduce himself as captain, "the first salutation he received was a violent stroke with a cutlass." The attackers, a disorderly rabble, lost all discipline as they fought violently among themselves over the spoils. "They fell foul of the crew like so many ravenous wolves [and] tore off their clothes," the witness said.

One crewman said he was held down by four attackers and stripped naked. Two corsairs fought with each other over the man's coat. The other two disputed so violently over the seaman's trousers that they accidentally ripped the garment in two.

"Every part of the vessel was rifled," the witness said, "chests were broken open, and they seized every article in avaricious fury."

Then they rounded on the captives. "They thrust all the American crew into their boat, in this naked and insulted condition, at the point of their cutlasses," said the witness. Anyone resisting was "knocked down and kicked into the boat, where they were trampled underfoot."

Like Cathcart eight years before them, they were brought before the corsair captain. In this case it was a very elderly man named Rais Mahomet. "Through age and impotency, [he] was scarcely able to support a tottering frame."

The captain's eyes were deeply sunken, and due to some ocular problem, tears seeped constantly down his cheeks. He was also drooling: "an emaciated, loathsome figure" who sat on a sheepskin sipping coffee as he surveyed the Americans. "From his ghastly visage flowed a beard of the brightest silver," the American witness said, before adding cruelly, "except where it was sullied by the drippings of his coffee."

The xebec contained nearly 150 Algerines in such filthy, overcrowded conditions that lice and fleas crawled and hopped everywhere. Food waste had been trampled all over the unswept deck, and the stench was nauseating.

When the old rais gave the nod to signify a good prize, the crew exploded in rapturous celebration. The corsairs slaughtered a sheep (obviously the overcrowded xebec contained livestock as well) and ritually smeared its blood over the sides of the ship. After it was cooked and eaten, they assembled all the Americans, stripped them, and tossed them "a few dirty rags" to wear. Finally, they dumped all the stolen goods in a heap in the center of the deck and sold each item to the highest bidder.

The xebec was so overcrowded that the Americans were ordered to sleep on the open deck. It was late autumn, and as night fell, the bitter Atlantic winds cut through their thin rags. Captain Penrose was forced to lie on the exposed roof of a cabin, "where he was almost perished by a bitter north-east wind." He came close to hypothermia before an elderly corsair saved his life by lending him a blanket.

For the next eight days the Americans worked on deck, taking spells on watches and trying to learn the Algerines' unfamiliar roster. They survived on black bread and water, and when they were given rotten olives, "they regarded [them] as a great dainty."

Since they weren't confined belowdecks between shifts, the captives secretly formulated an escape plan: "[To] rise upon the Algerine crew, to disarm those upon watch, and to confine the rest below by securing the hatches." However, since there were only 7 of them against 150 Algerines, they reluctantly abandoned the plot.

By the time they arrived in Algiers on October 30, they were glad to see dry land. But worse was to come. "They thought themselves cruelly treated on board the cruiser," one of them said, "but their treatment there was pleasure when contrasted with the miseries they afterwards experienced."

★ ★ ★

The *President* was just one of eleven American ships that were captured in the surprise swoops of October and November 1793. The captives of 1785 could only watch with mounting dread as they came in one by one, each new arrival adding to their numbers and increasing their woes. The last vessel to arrive was the brig *Minerva*, containing Captain Ingraham, Scipio Jackson, and five others.

Richard O'Brien was dockside, totting up the dismal figures. "In addition to the ten American vessels, they have captured the brig *Minerva* of New York," he reported after the corsairs finally called off their attacks. "There are at present 112 American captives in this city."

John Foss, the prolific diarist, also witnessed the arrival of the eleventh ship. "On November 29, a prize arrived, and she proved to be the *Minerva* of New York, loaded with wine, oil, fruit and marble, command by Joseph Ingraham," he recorded dolefully. "Seven more [Americans] were now added to our number . . . on Barbary's hostile coast."

★ ★ ★

As they mingled with their captured countrymen, Scipio Jackson and John Thomas would have learned the extraordinary stories behind the captures of the other nine ships. Each captain had a different experience, and each tale was dramatic in its own way. Before we move on, let's briefly recount a few of them.

THE OTHER *MINERVA* (PHILADELPHIA)

The Pennsylvania ship *Minerva* (not to be confused with Scipio Jackson's New York brig *Minerva*) had been one of the few vessels to experience a full-scale,

Hollywood-movie-style pirate attack. With the corsairs' guns blasting and sword-wielding invaders leaping on to the sails and then rappelling to the deck, it almost could have been a scene from an Errol Flynn movie.

The *Minerva*'s captain, John McShane from Pennsylvania, had been carrying wheat from Philadelphia to Barcelona. Fifteen miles from the Strait of Gibraltar, he had been pursued by an Algerine xebec of twenty guns. "After coming within musket shot, [the corsairs] kept a constant firing with small-arms," says one account. As the terrified Americans dived for cover, the corsair ship drew alongside, and the pirates leaped directly from their sail yards onto the *Minerva*'s. "The firing then ceased. They came down, sword in hand . . . stripped them of their clothes and put them on board the xebec." As McShane put it drily in a letter home: "They spared our lives, but nothing else."

This attack was unusually violent: the Algerines normally did their utmost to keep their captives alive and uninjured. Perhaps it reflected the psychopathic personality of that particular corsair captain, who—as the Americans learned later—had been sacked from his job as a top bureaucrat because he had throttled his wife to death. "[The dey] acknowledged the right of the Turks to put their wives to death, they being considered as merely the property of their husbands," explains one history. However, the wife had been pregnant at the time, and the dey ruled that "although the Turk might exercise this privilege with impunity upon his wife, he had no power whatever over the life of the infant." For this heinous double murder, the official was merely sent off to sea to vent his violent impulses upon the Americans instead.

The capture of the ship *Minerva* probably aided his rehabilitation, because he certainly hit the jackpot in terms of captive numbers: with one stroke, he had bagged seventeen new prisoners for ransom.

THE SHIP *HOPE* (NEW YORK)

However, another vessel had beaten this record and yielded even more victims: nineteen in all. The ship *Hope* from New York, commanded by Captain John Burnham, had been sailing to Malaga from Rotterdam when it was captured thirty miles off Gibraltar. In this case, though, what they gained in captives, they lost in cargo. The *Hope* had been on its way to take on freight; the rampaging corsairs must have cursed their luck when they peered into the hold and found only the rocks and junk that was used as ballast.

The attack ship had captured so many vessels on this cruise that it was already crammed full of captives. There were so many that the rais feared an uprising. "[He] distributed them on board the other corsairs which had not taken any prizes," a witness testified.

THE BRIG *POLLY* (NEWBURYPORT)

The corsairs used the ever-reliable false-flag technique when they targeted the brig *Polly* in the open Atlantic, west of Cape St. Vincent in Portugal. (This ship is famous among modern historians, since it contained the seaman and prolific diarist John Foss from Newburyport, Massachusetts.) The *Polly*, commanded by Captain Michael Smith, had been due to sail from Baltimore to Tobago, but in a fateful last-minute change of plans, ended up carrying flour to Cadiz instead.

"We got our breakfast and ate it in the greatest jollity," Foss recalled, "expecting to reach [Cadiz] within forty-eight hours." Through a spyglass they noticed a "strange sail" and identified its flag as British. As the ship closed in, a sailor in European clothing chatted to them amiably in English. It was only then, in the classic attack tactic, that the armed Janissary troops rose together in a deafening cacophony of noise: "We saw by their dress and long beards that they were Moors or Algerines. . . . We heard a most terrible shouting [and] clapping of hands." When a hundred heavily armed men rowed across to *Polly*, the Americans had no choice but to surrender.

Once on board, the corsairs plundered everything belowdecks. The captain then demanded the men's clothes, snarling that he would teach them to work naked. "They came back on deck like ravenous wolves," Foss recounted, "and stripped the clothes off our back."

THE SCHOONER *JAY* (GLOUCESTER)

Captain Samuel Calder from Gloucester, Massachusetts, told how he had been sailing his schooner *Jay* back from Malaga to Boston with a cargo of raisins, figs, and wine. With his log recording 150 miles of progress into the open Atlantic, he probably thought that he was well out of danger. But when a war frigate closed in bearing the Algerine colors of blue and white and twenty-six guns emerged from its sleek flanks, he knew it was all over.

"We suffered much on board the cruiser," Calder reported, "for they even took the clothes from our backs and brought us on board almost naked. . . . They put us into the cable tier without anything, not even a blanket, to cover us until our arrival [in Algiers] with not even a shirt to shift us."

THE BRIG *JANE* (HAVERHILL)
AND THE SHIP *THOMAS* (NEWBURYPORT)

Captain Moses Morse from Haverhill, north of Boston, told how his brig *Jane* had been four days out of Cadiz on the way to Ostend when a twenty-four-gun corsair warship swooped. The Algerines seized Morse and his seven crew along with his cargo of hides and indigo. "We were stripped of everything," he wrote disconsolately. "A few hours after, my friend Captain Newman was likewise captured by the same ship." Timothy Newman's ship *Thomas*, from Newburyport, had been carrying sugar and wool from the same port to Amsterdam when he and his ten-strong crew were manhandled aboard to join the eight men from the *Jane*.

THE *DESPATCH* (PETERSBURG, VIRGINIA),
THE *GEORGE* (NEWPORT, RHODE ISLAND),
AND THE *OLIVE BRANCH* (PORTSMOUTH, NEW HAMPSHIRE)

The dubious distinction of being the first victim of the corsairs in 1793 had fallen to the schooner *Despatch* of Petersburg, Virginia. Commanded by Captain William Wallace, it had been taking sugar, indigo, and sarsaparilla from Cadiz to Hamburg when all six men on board were captured. Two more US brigs had quickly followed: the *George* from Newport, Rhode Island, under Captain James Taylor, and the *Olive Branch* from Portsmouth, New Hampshire, under William Furnace. Traveling in and out of Lisbon, they had fifteen crew between them. (Both ships had been carrying grain and corn, so presumably one of them must have been the ship whose captors were spotted jettisoning grain into the sea before converting their prize into a fighting ship.)

When the dey finally called off his wolf packs and laid up his ships for the winter, Richard O'Brien wrote home with a terse summary of the catastrophe. "In consequence of the Portuguese and Dutch obtaining a truce," he wrote, "the Algerines have captured ten [later eleven] American vessels. . . . The masters and crews is brought to Algiers."

Before, America had had a problem on its hands. Now it had a crisis.

"Now I Have Got You, You Shall Eat Stones"

$\mathcal{D}$ey Hassan sat back on his throne and surveyed his hundred new captives with a cold eye. "Now I have got you, you dogs," he announced frostily, "you shall eat stones."

Attitudes in Algiers had changed beyond recognition since the days when his predecessor, Dey Mahmood, had viewed the Americans of 1785 as a curious novelty. This time, the captives found themselves wilting under a withering regal glare of hostility and disapproval.

"I have sent several times to your Government, entreating them to negotiate with me for a peace," Hassan informed them. "And I never received any satisfactory answer from them. They have neglected my requests and treated me with disdain." As a result, he said, their citizens would be made to suffer.

Earlier, Scipio Jackson, John Thomas, and the rest of the new arrivals had been paraded to the palace through the town to roars of celebration that were quite literally deafening. "As we passed through the streets," recalled John Foss, "our ears were stunned with the shouts, clapping of hands, and other acclamations of joy from the inhabitants, thanking God for their great success."

Before they were taken to the dey himself, they had been vetted for nationality and citizenship. It was all highly technical. Citizens of countries protected by peace treaties were usually liberated on the spot. However, this rule applied only to passengers: regardless of nationality, anyone who'd been working professionally on an "enemy" ship was regarded as a legitimate captive. Obviously, many working seamen claimed to be passengers, so the standard of proof was high. (For instance, young Jacob Tessanaer, the French boy who had genuinely been a passenger aboard the *Dauphin*, spent years unsuccessfully trying to prove his citizenship until his premature death ended the debate once and for all.)

Now, at the palace, Hassan rose to his feet and inspected all the newcomers one by one. He took his time, "passing and repassing in front of them." Traditionally, a dey was entitled to choose one in eight captives. In this case, he chose only four of the most presentable youths as his personal pages. The rest of the Americans got short shrift: they were packed off immediately to the prison hellhole of the Bagnio Belique to join the work gangs.

The entire episode must have seemed especially bizarre to African Americans like Scipio Jackson, because no one in Algiers cared about their skin color. They weren't singled out. Algerines captured hostages based on their nationality, not their ethnicity. Once in the bagnios, the harshness of their treatment depended on the amount of petty cash they had for bribery—not the amount of pigment in their skin. Of course, being treated *equally badly* wasn't much of an advantage in practical terms. But for any African American who had spent his life being treated as a second-class citizen during that cruel era, it must have seemed remarkable to see whites treated exactly the same as Blacks.

And for a former enslaved person who'd come from the United States—what a tragedy to have started life as a bondsman in America, to have escaped from your chains, to have become a freeman only to end up back in shackles on the other side of an ocean, on a different continent, in a different kind of captivity. What a long, strange journey it must have seemed to Scipio Jackson.

★ ★ ★

By the time the prisoners arrived at the Bagnio Belique, it was four in the afternoon. As the evening shadows lengthened, the prison seemed enormous, silent, and eerily deserted. The guards made no attempt to control the prisoners' movements. "We walked from one part of the bagnio to another, not knowing where we might be allowed to remain," John Foss wrote.

Everything changed at five o'clock, when the main gate was suddenly filled with hurrying figures. In an instant, the quiet courtyard transformed into a crowded bedlam of deafening activity: "We saw about six hundred men enter the bagnio, all appearing to be in a more miserable condition than ourselves, with wretched habits, dejected countenances, and chains on their legs, every part of them bespeaking unutterable distress."

At first Foss assumed they were criminal prisoners on an especially rigorous punishment detail. Then he discovered the truth: they were hostages like himself, ordinary mariners who'd been captured at sea. This was the way they lived. He had just glimpsed his own future.

Guards eventually ushered the new arrivals into a narrow corridor. On one side, a taskmaster stood threateningly with a large cudgel, while on the other, an administrator recorded their names and handed them their annual set of bedding and clothes—a thin, worn blanket, a hooded jacket, a long shirt, voluminous trousers, and thin slippers. There were no buttons: everything went down over the head or up over the legs.

The new arrivals were dispersed to different rooms where they laid their worn blankets directly on the stone floors and tried to sleep.

"In this dismal region of misery and oppression," recalled Isaac Brooks, a seaman from the *President*, "amid the clanking of chains and the cries of suffering humanity, they were left to brood over their misfortunes at leisure . . . [with] the most poignant emotions of anguish and despair."

At three in the morning the doomlike bass voice of the guardian bashaw resounded through the prison. The Americans filed into a basement where ironsmiths fitted each of them with an iron ankle ring. This leg iron not only branded them officially as state hostages, but also—oddly enough—carried a certain degree of protection. They were state property, and any citizen who assaulted or damaged them would have to answer to the dey.

For newcomers, the ironsmiths added an extra handicap—a long heavy chain fastened to the ring at one end. "The day after our arrival here [we were] put in irons and a chain of about thirty pounds," recalled Moses Morse, captain of the *Jane*. (In terms of weight, think of doing a day's heavy manual labor while carrying a microwave oven around with you.) In order to move at all, the prisoner had to wrap the chain around his waist or shoulder: McShane's crew were "bound with iron chains, each about forty pounds weight, which reached from their legs to their hips." This was just one of many petty, vindictive extra penalties designed to encourage the prisoners to bribe the guards. "[We were] put to the hardest labor, and continue the same every day," Morse reported. "They have since taken off our irons, but the cruel treatment is too much for me to describe. . . . Nothing is allowed us but bread and water."

McShane's crew were taken to the docks and forced to work until dusk. Foss had the same experience: "We were driven out of the bagnio, and thence to the marine," he recalled, "where I experienced the hardest day's work I ever underwent."

★ ★ ★

Their first day was a master template for all the miserable, exhausting days to follow. First the voice calling them to assemble in the yard, then the march to the docks and the allocation of work. Their most pressing task was to unload the stolen cargo from their own ships. That job completed, they were allocated for a range of menial tasks, from stripping out the ships and cleaning them to dredging the harbor sludge. Much of the time they worked as human mules—complete with wooden yokes. John Foss wrote that they had to carry "hogsheads of sugar, pipes [barrels] of wine, casks of nails, cannons, and so on." He explained why this was necessary: "The streets are so narrow that no kind of carriage is used here."

John Foss himself worked at the mountain quarry, producing giant boulders for the harbor breakwater. It was hard, grinding physical labor: some workers drilled holes for explosives up to twenty feet deep into the rock face, while others carried off the debris. "Rocks less than twenty tons weight will not serve," Foss explained. The average was forty tons. Working together, the captives sweated and strained to push each boulder to the edge of the hillside and send it tumbling all the way to the bottom.

The rocks remained there until Friday, when all the available hostages—whatever their usual roles—were "driven out to haul them to the quay." Using techniques that had changed little since the Bronze Age, they had to lift each rock—some of them were twelve to twenty feet across—onto sleds and drag them across the ground for two miles using ropes. Up to two hundred men were needed to shift each sled, and their pained, forceful grunts could be heard miles away.

On the way, they used all their strength to drag the sleds up a steep hill and then hold them back on a downhill slope. At the dockside, greased timber chutes took the boulders onto floating pontoons, which had to be hauled across to the breakwater using cables. "The sun pours down the most intolerable heat," reported Isaac Brooks, "and they are drenched in sweat, and involved in clouds of dust [as] brutal overseers scourge them with the most savage severity."

The taskmasters were given an unrealistic quota of rocks to shift each Friday, and so they treated the workers with exceptional cruelty. They continually beat them "with sticks not unlike an ox goad," Foss wrote, and "if anyone chance to faint, and fall down with fatigue, they generally beat them until they are able to rise again."

One day, a notoriously savage taskmaster lost his balance trying to lunge at a worker with his goad as he walked across a high plank on a construction site. He fell onto the sharp rocks below and was seriously injured. The hostages couldn't resist cheering, and no one shed any tears when the man died shortly afterward; in fact, some workers declared it divine judgment.

"We think ourselves happy if we escape through the day without being beaten by our drivers, who carry a stick big enough to knock a man down," Captain Samuel Calder of the *Jay* wrote home, "and the innocent often suffer with the guilty."

Some of the Americans were allocated a particularly gruesome task when the dey built a road through a graveyard where the supposedly inferior

"Moors" had buried their dead. The Turkish overlords were blind to the sensitivities of these underlings, so the Americans were forced to cart off loads of human bones while the relatives and friends of the dead gathered around them, weeping inconsolably.

Hassan was building a new mosque in the city center, and some of the Americans were ordered to carry huge rocks to the site. Each boulder was suspended on ropes from a rectangular wooden frame. A group of four men, one man positioned at each corner, had to lift the frame onto their shoulders and carry the rocks all the way up the steep winding alleyways of the city—an appallingly arduous task made more difficult because the taskmasters never bothered matching the porters by height. However, if the dey happened to ride past, he occasionally tossed them a few trinkets for religious reasons.

Other gangs of workers were forced to walk seven or eight miles into the countryside to harvest reeds and rushes from the wetlands. Since the swamps thrived with leeches, the workers emerged with their skin bleeding profusely.

After such heavy work, it was unsurprising that many developed hernias and spinal injuries. Assessed medically after their release many years later, the surviving American captives would be described as broken men, some disabled for life. Several were "probably rendered incapable of gaining a living" with eye injuries and "ruptures produced by hard labor." Isaac Brooks, the seaman from the *President*, was permanently blinded.

"It is not possible to live long in this situation," wrote Captain Samuel Calder, and in many cases, he was proved right.

Two of the captains, Samuel Calder and Moses Morse, took great exception to the fact that officers and seamen were equally abused and put to work "without distinction." The officers on the 1793 ships did not immediately receive the special status of *Paga Luna*, or "moon payer," which had been granted to the officers of the *Maria* and *Dauphin* in 1785. They had to work at the docks alongside everyone else. This was not temporary, since Morse was still complaining about it at the end of 1794. But as time passed, they were excused from the hardest labors. "The American captains and mates . . . were employed in the sail-loft making sails, or in boring pumps for vessels and . . . unloading the pontoons," says Isaac Brooks.

Captain John Burnham of the New York ship *Hope* fared better than most of them. He showed just how easy it could be to get yourself out of Algiers provided you had money and the right connections. Burnham had excellent connections, and within months he had raised his own ransom of $4,000. By the following summer, the Connecticut mariner was on his way home as a free man.

The experiences of the African Americans Scipio Jackson and John Thomas lay, unfortunately, at the other end of fortune's spectrum. Not for them the pleasant house in the country nor the effortless raising of ransom money. They were treated just as badly as their white shipmates but no worse. So why single them out for special mention?

Because they had an added problem. Besides enduring all the mistreatment and psychological torture from gang masters and guards, people of color like Scipio Jackson also had to cope with racist attacks—from their fellow Americans.

· 21 ·

An Attack on Scipio

$\mathcal{S}$cipio Jackson was working down at the wharves with a group of Americans when the worst attack occurred. The New Yorker had just finished caulking the hull of a corsair ship in preparation for a war mission. This was a painstaking, dirty operation that involved filling the seams between the planks with a mix of hemp fiber and tar.

As soon as the work was done and the cruiser was ready to sail, it was customary for the captain to treat all the workers to a good meal, thereby ensuring good fortune on the cruise. Three sheep's worth of mutton was thrown into a giant copper kettle with a vast quantity of couscous and boiled over a fire. When the tajine, or stew, was ready, the men were allowed to help themselves with a long iron ladle.

Tar-spattered and exhausted, the workers thronged around the kettle to enjoy what was probably their first decent meal in months. There was much jostling for position, and some of the white Americans took exception to the sight of an African American getting ahead of them in the throng.

"While a general competition for being served first prevailed," recalled an eyewitness, "one of the Americans took Scipio by the heels and pitched him head foremost into the kettle, where he remained until one of the Moors dragged him out."

The eyewitness—obviously sympathetic to the attackers—said there was "a great laughter" because Jackson emerged with his dark skin covered in the sticky pale mash, "well whitewashed with couscous." Fortunately, he was uninjured.

The fact that this repulsive racist attack was told as an amusing anecdote speaks volumes about the attitudes of the white Americans toward their fellow captives of color, and it suggests that low-key incidents took place in private

145

all the time. It was significant, too, that none of the Americans had the basic human decency to help Jackson out of the container—it was a local, "one of the Moors," who pulled him free, but only after the victim had "remained" there for a time.

The experience of African American captives in Algiers in the late 1700s is an almost forgotten story that is as obscure as it is fascinating. It cries out for greater study, although information is limited—it was the whites, after all, who usually wrote the histories.

How many other episodes of this sort erupted in the darkness of the prison corridors and in the daily bread queues? Were Scipio Jackson and John Thomas segregated by the others, or did they mingle in the comradeship of imprisonment? Was the bigot who threw Jackson into the cooking pot representative of the rest or an outlier among a tolerant majority? It is difficult to tell. Without much information to go on, we can imagine a culture in the bagnios much like the culture at sea: a general ethos of cooperation interspersed with flare-ups of intimidation, bullying, and outright violence, such as the attack at the docks.

What we do know for certain is that sub-Saharan Africans were so commonplace in Algiers that men such as Scipio Jackson and John Thomas would not have attracted a second glance. One in every twenty-five people in Algiers was from the sub-Sahara, at least by descent. For centuries, Arab traders had been bringing caravans of captives north to nearby Tripoli for dispersal to Algiers and the rest of Barbary. Over the years many had gained their freedom and had formed a distinct community.

The ruling Turks kept the sub-Saharan Africans far down the caste system, way below the *kuluglis* and the Moors, but they had survived like most minority groups by carving out their own area of expertise: they were who you called if you wanted your house painted. They also worked as house managers and caregivers, and they did these jobs so well that private householders often set them free in gratitude after ten years or so.

It was much the same in other parts of Barbary. In Morocco in the early 1800s, for instance, a small number of African American freemen were shipwrecked along with their white shipmates in different incidents on the Atlantic coast. Both groups were taken into captivity by wandering Bedouins and most were eventually ransomed. However, the Bedouins tended to keep the African Americans for themselves, because they valued them more highly than the others.

From time to time an interesting social twist arose when white Americans, used to giving orders to African Americans at home, ended up as low-grade domestic servants and were stunned to discover that they would be taking orders from sub-Saharan house managers. After a lifetime of racist conditioning at home, they found it almost impossible to cope with the shocking reversal of taking orders from a Black superior. "I, who had commanded many men in several parts of the world, must now be commanded by a negro," lamented one English captive.

If Scipio Jackson and John Thomas had been bought by benevolent private owners in Algiers, their experiences might have been completely different. But they were not. They were the property of a harsh and autocratic state. They had been sucked into a brutal and pitiless machine, and the people who operated it thought nothing of working captives to death.

★ ★ ★

Back home, America was stunned by the scale of the corsairs' latest offensive, and the sheer number of captives that were now awaiting ransom. Nothing had changed except the quantity, yet only now was the national conscience truly aroused by accounts of their countryfolk in captivity and "in a distressed and naked situation." George Washington himself was urged to act quickly to "restore [us] to liberty" and end the nightmare.

Newspapers mounted appeals, churches held special services, and charitable efforts went into overdrive. At fundraising dinners, toasts were offered to American captives in Algiers: "May they live to rejoice in the blessings of liberty."

As the year 1793 drew to a close, the government authorized Mathias Skjoldebrand, the Swedish consul, to pay the Americans a monthly allowance. Each captain would get $8, each mate $6, and each mariner $3.75.

This extra money made all the difference. For the first time they could buy a decent daily meal without relying solely on Cathcart's tab at the bar. However, the *Cameros*, the avaricious Spanish guards, inevitably sniffed out an opportunity for further extortion. They took control of the meal buying and demanded an exorbitant fee. "They cheated us out of one half of our money," lamented Foss. Just as water always finds its own level, the corrupt system of the Algiers bagnios inevitably canceled any increase in living standards.

The large difference in payments caused unrest among the ordinary seamen: it was "a very unjust distinction," said Isaac Brooks, "especially as the privates were subjected to much greater hardships." It must also have been galling for the 1785 captives, who had been left penniless for years after their basic subsistence money had been snatched away by the well-meaning Jefferson.

The US government also provided each American hostage with a smart blue outfit. At last, the captives would not be reliant on the thin, shoddy prison gear that left them exposed to both heat and cold. The matching hats that came with them were a godsend, since they shaded their heads from the midday sun. (The Algerines had never quite caught on to the fact that workers could perform better if they weren't fainting from sunstroke.)

The effect on morale was instantaneous. The Americans felt connected as a unit, their uniforms and slightly raised standard of living setting them apart from the other international captives. Their credit was good in the shops and taverns. To the locals, they became known in the lingua franca of Algiers as caballeros—gentlemen.

Even after their day's work, when they were confined in the bagnios, they raised one another's spirits through singing, dancing, and, oddly enough, stand-up comedy. "They excited one another to laughter by ludicrous and satirical remarks," according to Isaac Brooks. "In their frolics they were often very clamorous." Sometimes a guard stormed in and ordered them to go to bed. Some things in life do not change with the centuries. These were nearly all young men, after all, and they loved to have fun, even under the grimmest circumstances. The Americans may have arrived in Algiers in thirteen different ships, but now they had become a band of brothers.

★ ★ ★

The new suits of clothes meant nothing to Philip Sloan, the chief sweeper at the palace: his gilt uniform remained the same. But in April 1794, he received something far more precious—his freedom.

It happened under the most bizarre circumstances. In fact, it could only have happened in Algiers, where the rules seemed to be drawn from the Mad Hatter's tea party. Sloan's main role as *captain aproa* was to keep the rooms well swept and clean. But the position was also one of trust: for example, he could access the outer treasury, and one of his daily tasks was to light the dey downstairs in the predawn darkness.

Toward the end of April, the bewildered Sloan was unexpectedly summoned to the dey's chambers and told that he was a free man. The Dutch had just negotiated a swift peace deal, and it was "an old custom among the Algerines, when they make peace with any Christian nation, to oblige that nation to ransom the Dey's chief sweeper of the palace." In other words, Sloan's release came as part of the package. For this sweeper, nine years of captivity had just been swept away like a bad dream. Before he knew what was happening, the grateful Sloan was aboard a ship and headed for freedom. (Astonishingly, he would later choose to return.)

Meanwhile, James Cathcart found that he was not the only one of the 1785 hostages to become a tavern owner. Over the years, William Patterson of the *Dauphin* had borrowed enough money to set up his own bar. Any enterprising captive with a background in business could negotiate a loan from the bankers "at exorbitant interest" and try his luck. "Notwithstanding the interest and duty, many have managed so well as to purchase their liberty," Isaac Brooks explained, although their ransom was set higher as a result. Nevertheless, Patterson was able to save his pub earnings, pay up, and sail home to freedom that same year. (Further proof that Cathcart himself could have left at any time but chose to remain.)

Patterson's shipmate Peter Loring was not so fortunate: he died when the plague resurfaced, along with some of the new arrivals. By the end of 1794, only a third of the original twenty-one captives were still alive in Algiers: four from the *Maria* and three from the *Dauphin*.

And as if the bubonic plague were not enough to contend with, a deadly wave of smallpox also hit the city, killing four of the seamen from 1793. Amid this wretchedness and desolation, when it seemed that there was nothing to lose, it was hardly surprising that some of the American captives began plotting their escape.

• 22 •

An Englishman and Two Irishmen
Walk into a Bar

*O*ne day in 1795, a small group of Americans decided to make a break for freedom. It was a courageous and audacious plan—and it just might have worked, had it not been for a thirsty Englishman, two drunken Irishmen, and a parlor full of Algerine prostitutes.

Over the years, the US captives had mulled over options for escape and rejected them all. Escape by land was all but impossible. Although the city was clamped down tight at night, a captive might still worm his way out through the sewer pipes or perhaps abscond from a countryside work detail, but he would find himself stranded in a vast hostile landscape with no hiding places and nowhere to run. With Barbary states on either side of Algiers, it made no sense to break for the border. The faraway city of Oran may have been Spanish, but it was a hellhole of cutthroats. Southward lay the pitiless desert with predatory bands of nomads who would treat them even worse than the Algerines.

Of course, there were the inevitable people smugglers who would happily take your money for the promise of guiding you to a waiting boat on some deserted beach, but they almost always disappeared into the darkness along with your cash.

Only one option was at all feasible, and that was a direct escape by sea. There had been some classic success stories, but these had only focused the Algerines on the same small areas of risk. All local sailing craft were disabled in port. Captains of foreign ships had to sign agreements that they would not shelter fugitives. To discourage swimmers, the dock workers were often laden with extra chains when these ships were nearby. Paid informers were everywhere. Ordinary citizens were constantly on the lookout.

Even if a group of fugitives was somehow able to hijack a boat and evade the harbor patrols, they still would have to outrun the fastest ships in the world. If the wind dropped, they would have to resort to hauling oars, and with a few exhausted escapees trying to outpace a galley of a hundred determined oarsmen, their recapture would be only a matter of time.

A heartbreaking example of this occurred only a short time earlier, in October 1793, when a group of around fifteen dock workers from various nations made a dash for freedom. They had planned their escape for weeks, somehow acquiring swords and squirreling away provisions for their voyage. One morning, when their supervisor dozed off, they jumped into an unguarded workboat and rowed frantically toward the harbor mouth.

The taskmaster awoke to find them gone. "He hallooed to them in a tremendous voice to return," says one account. In reply, the runaways defiantly brandished a sword. They all cheered and "rowed with all their might towards the Spanish coast."

Dey Hassan didn't panic when he heard the news. He calmly ordered men with spyglasses to climb to the highest vantage points and track the boat's route. He knew that this was a game of cat and mouse: the fugitives would think that they had escaped but inevitably would be defeated by their own physical limitations. Hassan launched the city's fastest galley, with two tiers of oarsmen, and took personal command.

Following the boat's route, the Algerine oarsmen rowed flat-out at battle speed. When they seemed to be losing impetus, someone would pace up and down the catwalk throwing handfuls of money to urge them on. Meanwhile, the escapees inevitably slowed as they wilted in exhaustion under the midday heat. It took three hours, but at last the pursuers closed in. The exhausted fugitives could only surrender and throw themselves on the dey's mercy.

But by this stage, the dey's mercy was in short supply. His vengeance was terrible and relentless. His troops beat the fifteen men and brought them back to the city in chains, where the two ringleaders were instantly beheaded beneath the notorious grapes of wrath outside the palace. The others were bastinadoed and sentenced for life to wear a fifty-pound chain attached to a seventy-pound metal block. They still had to do the same amount of work while carrying the block over their shoulder. By "life," the dey meant life. When John Foss eventually sailed out of Algiers three years later, his last sight was that of these gutsy ex-fugitives "still in this miserable situation."

★   ★   ★

The Americans who planned the 1795 breakout knew this story and were aware of the risks, making their own courage seem all the more impressive.

An English cutter had just arrived in port. Cutters were the precursors of modern racing yachts: light, single-masted, gaff-rigged craft built for speed. Given a fresh wind and a head start, this one could comfortably outpace any Algerine xebec.

As they worked on the docks, the Americans recognized some of the English seamen: they'd met before. The Englishmen were shocked and distressed to hear their stories of life in captivity, and the captain agreed to help to carry the Americans to freedom.

The captain was forbidden to shelter fugitives, but he agreed to take part in an elaborate ruse in which the Americans would appear to overcome his loudly resisting crew and hijack his ship. They would instantly streak out of the harbor, outrunning the patrols, and get halfway to Spain before they were followed. But all this depended on a brisk, favorable wind.

The weather could not have been better. The crew prepared the cutter, ready to cast off in an instant. Isaac Brooks mused that no captive had ever been offered "so favorable an opportunity . . . but the most singular occurrence imaginable frustrated the whole scheme."

The only missing element was the captain himself. The Englishman had gone ashore to conclude his business and had not returned as expected. Instead, he had popped into one of the bagnio taverns for a drink—just one.

He bumped into two disreputable Irishmen who for months had been doing their utmost to live up to the national stereotype. Constantly drunken, constantly fighting, these two renegadoes were "a terror to all that frequented the bagnios." However, they were also great company. One drink led to another and then to a third, and as the day passed by in a blur, the captain forgot all about the escape plan. When one of the Irishmen suggested a trip to a brothel, he cheerfully agreed.

(Algiers had brothels hidden discreetly in the upper part of the town and tolerated by well-bribed officials.)

The three drunks were welcomed—no doubt with some trepidation—by the madam and her coterie of professionals. However, the drunken men had already caused such a stir that a band of city officers burst into the brothel and "surprised our amorous captain and his friends at the height of their mirth." Hauled off to the palace, the terrified captain broke down and revealed the escape plan.

The dey ordered the man's execution but then relented and told him to leave Algiers immediately. The officials bundled the bewildered man, still half drunk, aboard his ship, and the crew were ordered at sword point to surrender their cargo and cast off immediately.

The two Irish drunks were accused of assisting the escape plan— a trumped-up charge, because, in reality, they had unknowingly done everything possible to frustrate it—and were expelled from the city. According to Brooks, the sighs of relief could be heard all over Algiers.

Strangely enough, there is no record of any punishment for the American plotters. But as the captives watched the cutter sail off, "they were thrown into a state of inconceivable despondency" and forced to return to "the gloomy cells of the bagnio."

On their way back to prison, as if to taunt them, there sprang up "the most fortunate breeze imaginable."

★   ★   ★

Having raised the subject of sex, this seems as good a time as any to ask the obvious question. Did the American captives in Algiers ever have access to female company?

The short answer is no. They were barred from the brothels, and they were strictly forbidden from associating with any females—captives or freewomen—on pain of death. If anyone were to disobey, he would find that, in Algiers, the phrase "he lost his head over a woman" could mean exactly that. "For being found with a Mahometan woman, he is beheaded," explains John Foss, "and the woman is put into a sack and carried about a mile out to sea, and thrown overboard with a sufficient quantity of rocks, or a bomb, to sink her." If the woman were married, her husband often volunteered to carry out the execution himself.

You didn't even need to be caught in the act to suffer a grim punishment. Foss claimed that a captive could be castrated simply "for suspicion of being with [a woman]," and his alleged lover would be bastinadoed.

Occasional secret trysts could take place, but informers and spies were everywhere and the risks were terrifyingly high. One captive from Naples was discovered in a tavern with a local woman. The dey immediately sentenced him to death, but after several powerful friends intervened, his sentence was commuted to five hundred blows of the bastinado "on different parts of his body."

His partner in crime fared even worse. "She was immediately carried to the seaside by two executioners, who tied a large bomb-shell around one of her legs, and threw her into the sea some distance from shore," according to some Americans who witnessed the incident from the docks nearby. "She made the most lamentable cries."

According to one version, the woman's body somehow became detached from the weight and floated free. It was washed ashore much later, in such perfectly preserved condition that the local folk decided she must have been innocent all along and began to venerate her memory. Enraged, the dey banned the practice of execution by drowning. He declared that in future cases in which a captive was caught with a local female, they would both be burned alive while chained together back-to-back.

Even if we take the last paragraph with a large pinch of salt, the reality is that the American men in captivity in Algiers had no prospect of finding female companions, whether with a view to courtship, love, and marriage or for less lofty purposes. It is often stated that the Algerines were comparatively enlightened in their treatment of their hostages since children of female captives could be made free. In practice, that applied only to the offspring of female captives impregnated by Algerine men, often against their will. In such cases the father was expected to acknowledge paternity and raise the child free as part of his family. But this didn't matter a jot to the American men held there in the late 1700s: their chances of fathering *any* children were as remote as flying to the moon.

★ ★ ★

Back in the United States, bad luck dogged the negotiations. John Paul Jones died at exactly the wrong time. Had he lived, there was every likelihood that he could have sorted out the affair within a year and prevented the mass captures of autumn 1793. The poisoned chalice was passed on to Thomas Barclay, an experienced diplomat and an old North Africa hand—but then *he* died, too.

Eventually the job was given to America's man in Portugal, Colonel David Humphreys, an intelligent, capable, and imaginative diplomat who'd fought alongside George Washington. However, he first had to finish another task and then wait a frustratingly long time for his official papers to arrive.

As the months dragged on, Thomas Jefferson began to realize that the captives in Algiers were losing all confidence in him. "I do not wonder that Captain O'Brien has lost patience," Jefferson said. "He may possibly impute neglect to me."

Jefferson began sending well-intentioned messages to Richard O'Brien, which served only to irritate the captain even more. Digging himself ever deeper into a hole, Jefferson explained that the reason he didn't seem to care was that he cared too much. (I'm doing a very liberal paraphrase here.) His *apparent* indifference should not be confused with *real* indifference. He had failed to reply to any of O'Brien's letters, not because he'd ignored them, but because he'd wanted to give the *impression* of ignoring them. In a defense worthy of a Willie Nelson song, Jefferson made it clear that—despite all the little things he could have said or done but didn't—the captives had always been on his mind.

Looking back on this period of hiatus, however, one historian concluded that Jefferson was being less than honest. According to this analyst, Jefferson had long complained that his hands were tied by his superiors, but "when he had the power in his own hands as Secretary of State, he really accomplished nothing. He was unwilling to lose his popularity with the common people [of America] by spending an adequate sum for their release or by taking any definite step against the Barbary States."

Frustrated by all these delays, Colonel Humphreys wrote an open letter to the American people in July 1794, suggesting a nationwide lottery to raise the ransom money. Everyone should "cheerfully contribute," he urged, in order to "snatch your unfortunate countrymen from fetters, dungeons and death."

Once Humphreys was free to concentrate on Algiers, however, he threw himself into the crisis with gusto. Although Jefferson had approved the new clothes and stipends for the captives, it was Humphreys who actually ensured that they were delivered. It was Humphreys, too, who ripped Jefferson's strategy of feigned indifference out of the diplomatic playbook and started afresh.

He moved to Alicante in Spain, just a short sea trip from Algiers, and sent word to the dey that he was serious about making a deal. He was ready immediately.

The response, when it came, took the diplomat's breath away. No thank you, said Hassan. Don't even bother coming; I won't see you. You Americans have been telling me for years that you're not interested in your citizens, so now I'm taking you at your word. Your captives are off the market.

And in case Humphreys thought it was just a question of money, Hassan added: "I would not treat with you, even if you were to lavish millions."

Humphreys was furious, not only with the dey, but also with his own government for delaying his formal appointment until after the 1793 captures. He believed the United States should now prepare for war. In a stirring martial poem, he urged America:

> Let us firm, though solitary, stand
> The sword and olive branch in either hand
> An equal peace propose with reason's voice
> Or rush to arms, if arms should be their choice.

He called on the nation to respond "as one man" to the war effort and to achieve "the liberation of our fellow citizens." But behind the flag-waving rhetoric, the hard reality was that America did not yet have the sword that Humphreys was keen to brandish. Although Congress had decided early in 1794 to create a new national navy, it did not yet have any ships and would not produce any until 1797.

★ ★ ★

The dey wasn't bluffing. He really wasn't in any mood to negotiate. He found it hard to believe that two newly appointed envoys had died one after the other. To lose one negotiator was unfortunate; to lose two was carelessness. "I have been soliciting the American Government to send an ambassador to make a peace for three years," he said, "and they have treated my proposi-tions with neglect." Now, with the entrance to the Mediterranean free of Portuguese patrols, everything had changed and he would continue to pick off American ships at his leisure. After all, he said with a shrug, "I cannot be at peace with all nations at once."

The captives were deeply upset when they heard about the dey's slap down. "At this dreadful news," said Foss, "we despaired of ever tasting the sweets of liberty again." They resigned themselves to ending their days as cap-tives in Algiers.

However, it was the dey who blinked first. He leaked the news, almost certainly through Cathcart, that he would be prepared to make a deal—although his price was a crazily high $2.5 million, including $354,000 in ransom.

Humphreys pleaded with President George Washington, who was a personal friend, to take a more realistic approach to the ransom payment. The Senate authorized Humphreys to raise $800,000 to pay ransoms at a limit of $3,000 per man and then to fund a peace treaty. That was a lot less than the dey wanted, but a lot more than America had ever offered before. In No-vember 1794, the Secretary of State, Edmund Randolph, sent the good news across the Atlantic to Humphreys.

But then the affair degenerated into black farce. Humphreys was so frus-trated that he decided that same month, without authorization, to sail back to America to plead his case directly. At some point in the Atlantic, the two ships crossed paths: one vessel bearing Humphreys and his personal plea for more money, and the other bearing the news that it had been granted. The diplomat landed at Newport in February 1795 to discover that his dramatic dash home had not only been pointless, but had actually made things worse.

By the time Humphreys was able to sail back to Europe, it was April. He had a new plan. Humphreys himself would concentrate on raising the $800,000 in hard cash in Europe, while a diplomat named Joseph Donaldson, from Philadelphia, would sail to Algiers to scout terms for an agreement. Don-aldson was told to go forward cautiously and leave the final agreement to an official consul, who would follow when the time was right.

After arriving at Gibraltar in May, Humphreys traveled to France to raise money while Donaldson put out feelers to Algiers. However, nearly seven months had passed and the dey was once again spitting fire and fury at the mere mention of America. He said he would talk only to a full-scale diplomatic ambassador.

The Americans, on the other hand, were unwilling to send an ambassador until they could be sure that he would not be humiliated with unrealistic demands. It was a classic standoff, with goodwill in short supply on both sides. Only one man was in a position to break the impasse. And, incredibly, one man did.

IV

• 23 •

"Get Out of My Sight,
Thou Dog without a Soul!"

James Cathcart knew he would need all his Hassan-whispering skills to handle this delicate situation without provoking a wrathful and possibly murderous reaction from the despot. The dey had made it crystal clear that he would speak only to a fully empowered ambassador. The Americans wanted to send a low-level diplomatic sherpa first, in the form of Joseph Donaldson.

"An American gentleman wishes to kiss Your Excellency's hand on terms of peace," Cathcart told Hassan carefully.

"Is this the Ambassador I have long expected?" the dey asked with dangerous calmness.

"It is not, but it is someone sent by the Ambassador as a precursor," Cathcart said. Before the dey could erupt, he added the reason: the Ambassador was in France, raising cash for the treaty.

The mere mention of cash was enough to pacify Hassan. Cathcart then schmoozed the dey by claiming that President Washington—the mighty George Washington himself—was personally invested in this mission. Washington was keen to prove "the high sense he entertains of your justice and moderation," Cathcart said, and he wanted to repay Hassan for the goodwill he had shown America.

Cathcart had gone one tiny step too far. "If you did not benefit from my goodwill, it was your own fault," Hassan snapped back. He began to show the facial tics, the poker "tells" that the astute clerk recognized as early signs of an imminent explosion. (Cathcart later explained: "His mustachios curled indicative of a squall, as O'Brien would say.") It was a tense moment. Had Cathcart backed off at that point, the squall would have worsened to a full-force gale.

This was James Cathcart's finest moment. Rather than shrink under the pressure, he delivered a courageous oration that, despite its brevity, should

161

rank alongside the finest speeches in American history. It was a heartfelt plea for peace, but it was more than that: it marked the United States as a different sort of nation, a new nation that celebrated diversity and freedom of religion and held none of the ancient Mediterranean animosities. It's worth quoting, not only as an example of superb diplomacy, but also for the values of tolerance and inclusivity that still speak to us all today:

> Permit me to ask your Excellency: what harm did we ever do to you? Have you not taken thirteen sail of our vessels, and 131 of our people? Have I not been more than ten years in captivity, which I would consider as time well spent if I could be the medium of establishing peace and harmony between our nations? . . .
>
> In our country we have no religious test, nor enmity against those of your religion. You may build mosques, hoist your flag on the tower, chant the symbol of your faith in public, without any person interrupting you.
>
> [Muslims] may enjoy places of honor or trust under the Government, or even become President of the United States. Ought not those circumstances to be taken into consideration? If you make other nations pay high for peace, it is [for] retaliation . . . but we have never been at war with you.

There was a taut silence. Then Cathcart breathed a silent sigh of relief as "the Dey's whiskers gradually assumed their natural position."

Hassan finally spoke. "Let him come," he said. "I will hear what he has to say himself."

As Cathcart thanked him and walked off to deliver the good news, one part of their exchange was still ringing in his ears.

"Will you take responsibility for this person, that he actually has full power to negotiate?" Hassan had asked Cathcart.

"Effendi, I answer my head for it," the clerk replied.

★   ★   ★

Cathcart was in an unenviable position. As the dey's chief clerk, he was supposed to be working for the ruler. But as an American, he was determined to serve his country. Dey Hassan didn't want to upset this balance, because during this cold war, Cathcart was his only backchannel to the US government. The problem facing Cathcart himself was how to walk this diplomatic tightrope and stay alive. The dey's moods swung erratically from hour to hour, even from moment to moment, and at his worst, he was quite capable of decapitating an official who irritated him. For Cathcart, it was important in an absolutely literal sense not to lose his head during these negotiations.

He had no time to lose: he had to act quickly in order to get Donaldson to Algiers before the ruler changed his mind. Besides, the dey's walls had ears, and many European consuls were standing by, ready to sabotage the mission. Cathcart prepared Donaldson's passport without anyone knowing. Under cover of the Skjoldebrand brothers, he chartered a fast ship to Alicante with no other purpose than to inform Donaldson of the news. Then Cathcart personally walked to the harbor, put the letters on board, and ensured that the ship cleared port without interference. Ever the optimist, he also arranged for the same ship to return to Algiers bearing the envoy. The whole process, from palace meeting to embarkation, took only six hours.

Meanwhile, since it was important that the American "ambassador" should have an ambassadorial home, Cathcart located a grand house and had it fully whitewashed, at his own expense, to keep up appearances.

The French consul, who had been continually plotting to undermine the US peace efforts, was furious that he had been outsmarted. He protested, with absolutely no justification, that he should have been consulted about the decision to receive an American representative. Cathcart further infuriated him by stonewalling his requests for a meeting, so the Frenchman rounded on O'Brien instead and demanded to know why he had not been informed.

I do not consider myself under any obligation to consult you, O'Brien shot back.

You have treated me with disrespect, the consul complained.

Not so much as your conduct to us merited, O'Brien replied tersely.

Cathcart was amused by the exchange. Using one of the captain's famous seafaring metaphors, he chuckled later: "As he voluntarily placed himself in the lee of O'Brien's guns, I do not wonder that he got a broadside."

★ ★ ★

Frustratingly, Donaldson took his time about making his way to Algiers, but Cathcart used the delay to his own advantage. He told the dey that Donaldson's party would include the former palace official Philip Sloan, whom the dey respected. Sloan had gone home to America only to be enlisted to the diplomatic corps and sent back to Algiers. However, at the moment, he was stuck in Alicante waiting for the Spanish bureaucrats to issue a sailing permit. This enabled Cathcart to blame the Spanish for the entire delay, which was not quite accurate. Predictably, the dey went ballistic and sent a town crier around the streets of Algiers announcing a complete trade blockade with Spain: "No person should ship even an onion," he ordered.

Cathcart was enjoying this diplomatic mayhem. "I found it to our advantage to foment this discord," he admitted.

During those few weeks of detente, relations between Cathcart and the dey became warmer, even cordial: so much so that Cathcart believed he could have negotiated a deal for peace and ransom for as little as $450,000 if he'd had a free hand. The trick, as he'd discovered as a tavern owner, was to offer presents. He hinted to the dey that an American peace deal might include $100,000 for the ruler himself and $50,000 for his family.

"It is a mere trifle," the dey snorted dismissively. But Cathcart knew all the tells and could see that he'd hit the ruler's sweet spot. "As his whiskers did not curl, nor did his beard stand erect, and I thought I could perceive a latent spark of satisfaction illuminate his countenance."

Time passed with no sign of movement from Alicante. So at 11:00 a.m. on Thursday, September 3, Cathcart was the most relieved man in all of Barbary when, under a brisk southwesterly wind, the same ship he'd chartered in August sailed into Algiers, this time with an American flag fluttering proudly at the masthead and a flag of truce on the fore topgallant.

Joseph Donaldson had arrived.

★ ★ ★

Cathcart believed he had thought of everything to make his guest comfortable—but he never imagined that he'd need a walking aid or a sedan chair. Donaldson turned out to be a man in late middle age, disabled by severe gout, and even with the aid of a crutch, he found the uphill hike from the harbor almost impossible. Cathcart was sympathetic but found himself silently wondering why, of all places, Jefferson had chosen to send this unfortunate man to one of the world's least walkable cities.

Although it was late afternoon, the day was stiflingly hot. Donaldson, dressed in warm flannel and wearing an old-fashioned cocked hat, his gouty foot encased in a giant slipper, was soon lathered with sweat.

"The mortification which he felt at being stared at, together with some children running across him, put him in a paroxysm of rage which he endeavored to suppress," Cathcart recalled, "while the perspiration ran down both sides of his face and almost blinded him."

When he finally reached the house, he threw off his hat, collapsed on a sofa, and unleashed a long string of salty curse words, so colorfully intertwined that even Cathcart, a seaman, couldn't untangle them all.

A local banker who accompanied them thought Donaldson was speaking some unknown language and asked for a translation. "The Ambassador is only saying his prayers," Captain O'Brien explained solemnly, "and giving God thanks for his safe arrival."

"His devotion is very fervent," the banker replied.

After a meal and a bottle of fine wine served from Cathcart's tavern, Donaldson's mood began to mellow. However, it became obvious that his personality would not. He was "of a forbidding countenance and remarkably surly," Cathcart recalled.

Later, Peter Erik Skjoldebrand took Donaldson aside and quietly reminded him of the huge risk Cathcart had taken. If Donaldson had failed to come to Algiers for any reason—even a genuine one—Cathcart would have been bastinadoed and perhaps even burned alive. He said America owed the young clerk a great debt.

Donaldson did not respond with gratitude, as the Swede expected. Instead, he took a perverse pleasure in revealing that he had decided on two occasions to send Cathcart's ship back empty from Alicante before finally relenting.

The Swede was horrified. "If you had," he said, "poor Cathcart would have been sacrificed."

"Well, if he had, the world would have gone on just the same way without him," Donaldson grunted.

★　★　★

Down at the marine, Scipio Jackson and the rest of the American captives had spotted Donaldson's ship from afar at nine that morning, but it wasn't until eleven that they could first discern the US flag. Word spread quickly, electrifying them with joy and excitement. "An ambassador to relieve us had arrived."

They spent that night in "sleepless anxiety," wrote John Foss. Yet the following day was Friday, the Sabbath, with no business supposed to be done. "Never was there a longer, more tedious day," he recalled, describing the tense mood of "suspense, hope, fear and agitation."

However, "tedious" was the last word Cathcart would have used to describe that fateful Friday. For him it was a day of frantic activity and brinkmanship negotiations that began at dawn and lasted until late that evening.

DAYBREAK ON FRIDAY, SEPTEMBER 4

A coldly furious Hassan broke Sabbath to summon Cathcart and demand the full $2.5 million that he had demanded earlier. It turned out that the embittered French consul had not been idle: using the same technique that the English had used during John Lamb's negotiations, he had lied to the dey, telling him that Donaldson was authorized to pay that outlandish figure but warned Hassan that the US envoy would try to plead poverty and cheat him out of the full amount.

The clerk blanched at the size of the demand and stuttered an objection. Hassan cut him short. "I command you instantly to take those demands to your ambassador," he snapped, "and to bring me his answer in return. I will have this business settled immediately."

As Cathcart made to leave, he slipped on the marble floor and fell. He made light of the mishap: "It was the weight of your Excellency's proposal that made me stumble." Hassan saw the joke and laughed.

8:00 A.M. FRIDAY

But Cathcart was in no joking mood as he trekked to the ambassadorial house with a heavy heart. Sitting amid the whitewashed walls and marble flooring of the main reception room, he reported that the dey's demands remained unchanged: $2,247,000 in cash plus two thirty-five-gun frigates, and a consignment of stores. Plus the usual list of presents and backhanders. Donaldson slumped in despair.

I knew I was wrong to come here, he said. Any offer I can make will be taken as an insult, so I won't make any at all.

Cathcart said he was under orders to bring a response. "It would be better to offer him something than not offer him anything at all."

Donaldson reluctantly reconsidered and finally came up with a counter-proposal: $543,000 in total to cover both ransoms and treaty.

A prominent Algiers banker, Micaiah Cohen Baccri, was present at the meeting. (The Baccri brothers, from Leghorn, were the most powerful financiers in the city.) Although Baccri had agreed to handle the financial side of the transaction, he refused point-blank to take that low figure to Hassan. During a rough patch in the Dutch negotiations the previous year, the dey had threatened to burn Baccri alive, and he was determined never to put himself in that position again.

He was not being paranoid. From time to time, the French and Venetian consuls received similar threats from the enraged dey. And every diplomat in Algiers knew about the fate of Jean Le Vacher, the unfortunate French consul who, a century beforehand, had been tied to the mouth of a giant cannon and shot out to sea.

As usual, it was left to Cathcart to trek back to the palace with Donaldson's offer.

10:00 A.M. FRIDAY

"What do you mean by bringing such proposals to me?" the dey shouted. "Do you want to make game of me?"

When Cathcart tried to explain that Donaldson had a limited budget, Hassan hit the roof. "You are a liar and an infidel," he roared. "The French consul has informed me that your Ambassador has carte blanche and can give whatever he pleases for peace."

Now that the real reason for the dey's rage was out in the open, Cathcart could deal with the problem. Choosing his words carefully, he hit back: "If your Excellency had told the French Minister that he was a liar, he would have richly deserved it."

He told the dey that the French consul was acting out of "private pique"—which Hassan probably knew already—and reminded him that consuls were strictly forbidden to interfere in other nations' negotiations.

Hassan grudgingly accepted the point. "You have not been so long in Algiers for nothing." He asked Cathcart to remind him of the presents the United States had offered to him and his family. When the clerk said the sums were $100,000 and $50,000, Hassan interrupted, pretending to misunderstand that he was referring to a higher valued currency: "Sequins, you mean?"

"No, sir, dollars."

"Get out of my sight immediately, thou dog without a soul!" Hassan bellowed. "Never presume to bring such trifling terms to me again under pain of my displeasure." Cathcart knew by bitter experience that this was palace code for a beating by bastinado at the very least.

NOON, FRIDAY

However, Cathcart knew in his heart that peace was a prize worth taking risks for. He headed back to Donaldson and, drawing on nothing more than gut instinct, told him that another forty or fifty thousand dollars might get the Americans over the line.

Donaldson wouldn't entertain the idea. He was all for throwing in the towel. That's it, he said. The business is at an end. I cannot give one dollar more, whatever the consequences.

2:00 P.M. FRIDAY

The dey summoned Cathcart back to the palace. After giving his clerk a roasting—verbal, not literal—he calmed down and told Cathcart to sit down and write. He dictated another proposal, this time for $982,000—a significant drop from his original $2.2 million.

3:00 P.M. FRIDAY

Back at the ambassadorial house, Donaldson was adamant. All his experienced counselors—O'Brien, Philip Sloan, and the Swedish brothers—advised him to mollify the dey by offering a little more. Donaldson shook his head. Not another dollar, he kept repeating.

The atmosphere became heated as Cathcart told him the likely sequence of events: "The Dey will get in a passion, you will be ordered out of the country, and I will probably receive a gift of five or six hundred bastinadoes on the soles of my feet."

Donaldson didn't seem to care. "If you receive a bastinadoing," he sneered, "you will have the consolation of having received it for your country."

Cathcart had had enough. "I could turn the tables on you," he snapped at the consul. "I have enough money to pay for my ransom and leave. That will leave *you* at the risk of receiving the bastinadoes that you think so lightly about. It will be an excellent cure for your gout," he couldn't resist adding.

4:00 P.M. FRIDAY

The slap down helped Cathcart's own morale, but it was cold comfort as he trudged back to the palace to give Hassan the bad news. The consequences were exactly as he had predicted. Cathcart was sentenced to five hundred bastinadoes, which were temporarily suspended. "Embark your lame Ambassador on the vessel he came in," Hassan ordered, "and tell him to leave the Regency without delay."

5:00 P.M. FRIDAY

Cathcart didn't try to argue. He returned to the ambassadorial house and conveyed the dey's expulsion order with stiff formality. "Good evening," he said coldly as he turned away, "and pleasant passage." He refused to linger any longer and was already on the street when Donaldson sent one of the advisers to bring him back. This time Donaldson seemed more flexible, especially after Philip Sloan, the former palace sweeper, told him that David Humphreys had specifically said the deal should not be abandoned for the sake of an extra fifty or sixty thousand dollars.

"You can offer up to $650,000," he told Cathcart. "Farther I cannot go."

"If you leave it up to me," Cathcart replied, "I will guarantee peace and ransom for fifty or sixty thousand less than that."

However, he insisted on directing the stagecraft for the final act. First, Donaldson must behave as though he actually were about to sail off. He was to pack his clothes, create a bustle of activity, and order the captain at the waiting ship to prepare to cast off in the morning. Captives in the bagnios were told that this was their last chance to write letters home.

The bluff was called. The stakes were high. And everyone involved spent an uneasy and restless night.

7:00 A.M. SATURDAY

Early the following morning, Cathcart went to the palace to confirm that Donaldson was indeed leaving. But he added that the envoy had drawn on his own personal finances and had made a last-minute offer of $585,000. He reminded Hassan that Donaldson would be gone in one hour and that once he returned home with the bad news, America, which had never been at war with any of the Barbary states, would be forced to arm for its defense.

Philip Sloan, who had accompanied him to the palace, tugged Cathcart's coat at that point, feeling he had gone too far. Cathcart shrugged him off. "I have come here to speak the truth," he said.

Then Cathcart softened his tone. "Your Excellency has promised to let the captives be redeemed," he said. "I now implore from your clemency. We have been here more than ten years, Effendi. Let us go for the love of God."

· 24 ·

"A Dazzling Meteor in a Dark Night"

$\mathcal{T}$here was a long pause while the fate of the treaty hung in the balance. Hassan took a pinch of snuff and inhaled it thoughtfully. "You know how to gabber," he acknowledged at last. Blowing a fingerful of snuff powder into the air, he explained: "I esteem this sum no more than a pinch of snuff." Then, at last, he relented. "Go and tell your Ambassador that I accept his terms."

Cathcart took the happy news to Donaldson, who accepted it gracelessly. Fearing that the dey might change his mind, Cathcart advised Donaldson against drawing up a treaty document from scratch, which might take weeks, but to modify the recent Swedish treaty. Throughout the morning, he worked frantically to translate the document from Turkish into English and then make the necessary changes.

Back at the palace, Hassan received Donaldson for the first time, with Cathcart translating. The envoy's mood had not been improved by the climb up the steep stairs. However, he agreed that the American captives must remain in Algiers until the money was handed over in full. And there would be no reductions for anyone who died during the interim.

In return, the dey agreed that all the American officers would move out of the bagnios and become "moon payers," or trusted prisoners, with Cathcart arranging special housing for them in the suburbs. (That turned out to be a mixed blessing since, as we see later, it deteriorated into a den of drinking and gambling that was almost as unsafe as the prison.)

Then, unexpectedly, the dey offered to excuse all of the American seamen from hard work at the docks. To Cathcart's amazement, Donaldson said thanks but no thanks. Cathcart was so taken aback by his reply that he refused to translate, but the dey got the message anyway. Until the money arrived, the unfortunate captives would remain in the work gangs.

171

What was Donaldson thinking? Perhaps he had genuine concerns about his ability to control more than a hundred disgruntled seamen as they rampaged through the streets of Algiers. But more likely, the penny-pinching envoy calculated that the longer they stayed in the bagnios, the longer the dey would have to pay for their upkeep.

As the interview ended, Hassan gravely told Donaldson that he had Cathcart to thank for obtaining peace and suggested that the envoy write to the US president with a commendation. Cathcart was too embarrassed to translate. The interview ended, and Cathcart never received his acknowledgment.

Left alone with his clerk, Hassan revealed that he had a separate problem. He still had to get the support of the divan, or parliament, for his peace deal. This contained many hawkish corsair captains who thought that war with the United States would be much more profitable than peace, especially since America "had not a single vessel of war to oppose them." The Americans were sitting ducks, they argued, and Algiers "would derive a vast revenue by the sale of the prizes and the ransom." This was a powerful lobby group that easily could derail the entire treaty and was quite capable of removing the dey himself if he didn't agree with them.

Once again, it was Cathcart who solved the problem. He suggested that the dey draw up a speech with two killer arguments.

The first was that the short-term gain of captures would be eclipsed by the long-term benefits of the treaty. By opening up a new source of naval and maritime stores from America, Algiers would be ensuring a source for these vital supplies. It would no longer be dependent on its unreliable suppliers in northern Europe.

The second point was that Algiers should not squander the opportunity to make a deal with this emerging New World nation. Europe represented the past, but America represented the future, and Algiers should choose to be part of it.

The dey gratefully accepted this advice, and his stirring delivery of Cathcart's script was just about enough to silence the hawks in the divan.

The episode reached its climax at noon on Saturday, September 5, 1795, when Cathcart personally hoisted the American jack on Donaldson's ship, and twenty-one guns roared in salute to the flag. "Thus, in about forty-two hours after the arrival of Mr. Donaldson," Cathcart later recalled with pride, "peace was established between the Regency of Algiers and the United States of America, to the astonishment of every person in Algiers."

"Nothing can equal the satisfaction of your unfortunate countrymen in captivity," Cathcart wrote proudly to Humphreys, "when the banners of the United States were displayed and saluted." Always on the lookout for an opportunity, he put his own name forward for future service.

Down at the marine, Scipio Jackson and the other American captives had never been so delighted to hear Algerine gunfire. They whooped and hollered and embraced. "Sounds more ravishing never vibrated in the air," John Foss wrote. "Our hearts were joy. We imagined ourselves already free men, our chains falling off and our taskmasters no longer at liberty to torture us. In imagination, we were already traversing the ocean, hailing our native shore, embracing our parents, our children and our wives."

It took five hours for the sobering truth to filter down from the palace to the bagnio. The prisoners had finished their day's work and were in a state of nervous anticipation, waiting to leave their despised prison, when word reached them that they would not be freed until the ransom money was raised.

In an instant, the mood darkened. How long will our country neglect us? they asked. And how many of us will die in the meantime?

John Foss vividly compared the sudden plunge from ecstasy to despair to "a dazzling meteor in a dark night, which blazes for a moment, making the succeeding darkness more dreadful."

The next day, Sunday, was devoted to the formal presentation of gifts to the dey and his officials at the palace. Even this proved to be a joyless and cynical affair, with Hassan insisting that the Americans buy his own unwanted jewelry—for cash—to present as gifts to his own courtiers. When it was the dey's turn to give a gift to Donaldson, he sent a messenger to the envoy's house with a fine stallion—and a German captive named Joseph Koenigs. (This was the same palace worker who had relayed the news of the previous dey's death to Hassan.)

Relations between Cathcart and Donaldson, never happy at the best of times, reached a new low when Donaldson refused to tip the dey's messenger, even though Cathcart had warned him that failure to do so would be a deadly insult. Cathcart ended up paying the substantial sum out of his own pocket. Donaldson refused to reimburse him.

Later, when Cathcart offered to use his own wide network of contacts to raise the ransom cash and free the captives immediately, Donaldson made it clear that he didn't trust him. "He seems very ungrateful for the risk I have already run," Cathcart mused. "He is jealous and mistrustful, and [does not] comprehend that it is possible for a man to risk his life without any other motive than the love of his country."

Cathcart's mood soured further when the tiny committee in the ambassadorial house decided they needed to send a knowledgeable person to Lisbon to explain the details of the treaty to Humphreys. Cathcart was bitterly disappointed when they chose O'Brien rather than himself. However, the delegates persuaded him—with some justification—that he was far more important to his country in his current role as chief clerk.

Typically, it was left to Cathcart to trudge the well-worn path to the palace and try to persuade the dey to send his rival, O'Brien, on the mission. At first Hassan refused flat out. Why should he send one of his precious hostages when a diplomat like Philip Sloan, a free man, could do the job just as well? With admirable selflessness, Cathcart pushed the case for O'Brien and finally secured the ruler's approval.

He conveyed the good news to O'Brien. However, although O'Brien was well briefed on the treaty, he had no knowledge of the complex negotiations that had led up to the deal. He asked Cathcart to give him a crash course, and the clerk generously obliged.

At 2:00 p.m. on Friday, September 11, Captain Richard O'Brien set sail from Algiers in the brig *Sophia*. He had been held in captivity in the city for ten years, one month, and twelve days. He had arrived as a young man of twenty-seven and had lost the prime years of his life. Cathcart saw his old friend off, giving him $160 from his own pocket to cover his travel expenses and to buy some decent clothes to wear in Lisbon. The money should, of course, have come from Donaldson, but the envoy was in no mood to part with more cash. In fact, he'd already insisted that O'Brien save money by slogging overland from Alicante to Lisbon rather than pay for a direct sea voyage.

Before leaving, O'Brien made his first-ever visit to the dey's chamber, where he embarrassed Cathcart by kissing the ruler's feet as well as his hand. ("I did not like that humiliation," Cathcart wrote.) As they left, the dey's last words were still ringing in their ears.

He warned O'Brien not to delay in returning with the ransom money. "I am an old man," the ruler said. "When I die, my successor will not be so friendly to America as I have been."

★   ★   ★

By early October O'Brien was in Lisbon, presenting the treaty to America's man in Portugal, David Humphreys. Word of his safe arrival got back to Algiers, and for a brief, ecstatic period, it seemed that the money would be sent immediately and that the captives would be free by Christmas.

Unfortunately, the timing could not have been worse for raising cash. The United States had established $800,000 credit in London to pay for the treaty, but there was no way to turn this into coin. The convulsions that followed the French Revolution had left Europe traumatized, and cautious lenders were sitting on their purses. France itself had been hit worst, yet that's exactly where Humphreys had gone in his bid to raise funds. While there, he had wasted a lot of time in an unauthorized attempt to curry favor with the

French consul to Algiers—the very man whom Cathcart had been battling to outwit.

When Humphreys returned to Lisbon with his pockets empty, his superiors in America had been unimpressed. If he had simply stayed put in his base in Lisbon instead of traipsing around Europe, they pointed out, he could have drawn the funds in Portugal at a time when there was still plenty of money available there, and the captives would already be free. But that window of opportunity had closed, and the country had become as strapped for cash as everywhere else.

Stumped for a solution, Humphreys suggested that O'Brien sail to London in the *Sophia* for the money, but by now it was winter, and the Atlantic storms left him stranded in Lisbon until December. When O'Brien finally got there, he found the financial freeze had spread to Britain. No cash could be found anywhere.

The prisoners were doomed to spend yet another Christmas and New Year in the bagnios.

★　★　★

Back in Algiers, everyone was growing increasingly grumpy. Just one letter from Humphreys explaining the situation would have kept the dey reasonably happy, but instead the ruler waited each day for news that never came. Once again, he interpreted the silence as contempt. Moreover, he was being pressured by his own captains and generals, who wanted to go back on the attack. The aga, or general in chief of the Janissary militia, was already dropping dark hints that the dey wouldn't be around to protect the Americans forever.

Thomas Billings, Cathcart's ex-shipmate from the *Maria*, was one of the few who had a lucky break. As he prepared to endure yet another night in the bagnio, the Philadelphia man was summoned to Donaldson's house along with two other Americans—Abel Willis from the ship *Minerva* and our old friend John Foss from the brig *Polly*. Bemused, the trio stood before Donaldson in their sweaty, grimy blue work uniforms. The envoy told them that the dey had granted him three captives to work as his servants. Their names had been chosen by Cathcart. The grateful trio moved into the staff quarters in the consul's elegant home and stayed there for the rest of their captivity.

In this way, Cathcart ensured that none of the original 1785 captives remained in prison. Of the six remaining in Algiers, Captain Stephens and the two mates were "moon payers" in the suburbs, Billings was at the consulate, and of course Cathcart himself was at the palace. That left only a sixth man—James Hull from the *Dauphin*, who was about to experience the most dramatic escape of any of them.

The One That Got Away

*J*ames Hull from Massachusetts was unique among the Americans from the thirteen captured ships. He was the only one who cheated the dey of a ransom, the only one who got clean away without treaty payment or permission. In short, the only one who escaped.

And the way in which the *Dauphin* crewman made his getaway could not have been more thrilling, involving a dramatic sea battle, a keg of gunpowder with a burning fuse, and a desperate race against time.

As far as I can establish, Hull was unique in another respect: he was the only one of the Americans in this story who was actually "put to the oar," as the saying went, and sent to work on a corsair warship.

After singling Hull out as a skilled seaman, the marine minister decided to put him aboard a captured European ship that had been retrofitted as a sleek fighting frigate. Although he remained a captive and a hostage of the state, Hull was given the responsible role of boatswain, the man who supervised the deckhands in order to put the captain's orders into practice.

Early in 1796, just a few months after Donaldson's treaty was signed, the entire Algerine warfleet set out on a mission against their ancient enemies the Neapolitans. (The earlier truce between Algiers and Naples had long since broken down, and the two feuding seaports were back at war.)

Dey Hassan watched his fleet sail off with pride. He was confident that the heavily armed cruisers would return with several captured vessels and scores of new captives to solve his shortage of manpower. As the corsairs cleared port, they were blessed by a marabout, or cleric, and the shrill cheers of the city's women echoed from the rooftops, encouraging them to return home safely and rich with spoil.

As usual, the cruisers split up in the open Mediterranean to hunt as lone wolves. Before long, the rais of Hull's frigate spotted a target: a Neapolitan warship. The two vessels locked in battle, and "a smart engagement ensued." It's not clear whether Hull himself was forced to take part in the fighting: probably not, because captives were usually chained during sea battles to prevent them acting as saboteurs. When the cannons finally went silent and the gunsmoke dissipated from the air, the result was clear—the Algerines had been roundly defeated and the frigate's captain had no choice but to surrender.

Yet the corsairs still had a card up their sleeves. Another Algerine ship, a xebec, had heard the gunfire and had come to investigate. Its captain lurked just under the horizon, assessing the situation and waiting for his moment to pounce.

Meanwhile, the Neapolitans boarded Hull's frigate and rounded up the crew. Along with all the others, Hull was pushed and prodded into an open boat and transferred to the victorious warship of Naples.

The Neapolitans put a skeleton crew in charge of the captured frigate, retaining only a few elderly Algerine Moors to help with the grunt work as they prepared to sail home.

Unfortunately for them, the breeze dropped and their sails flapped impotently in a flat calm. The commander of the nearby Algerine xebec now had the advantage: his light oar-driven vessel did not depend on wind. He ordered his crew to the oars and bore down on the captured frigate in the classic Barbary attack, aiming to slot his raised prow directly over its deck so that his armed troops could leap aboard. The few Neapolitans on the frigate watched them approach with mounting dread. They knew that defeat was inevitable and that if they didn't move quickly, they would soon be doomed to a bleak future in the bagnios of Algiers.

Instead, they opted to abandon ship, scuttling the frigate rather than allowing it to fall back into the hands of their enemies. They tied up the Algerine Moors and placed a powder keg with a fuse below the waterline. One Neapolitan lit the fuse while the others hurriedly launched an open boat. The last man tumbled into the boat, and they rowed for their lives.

Hull watched the entire drama from the other vessel. As the Neapolitans rowed frantically and the fuse steadily burned down, the Moorish crewmen fought feverishly to undo their ropes. They burst free, dashed below, and located the powder keg just before the deadly spark reached the end of the fuse. They were saved with only seconds to spare. Meanwhile, the xebec closed in, recaptured the ship for the dey, and speedily retreated.

On board the European warship, the Neapolitan marines chalked the episode up as a partial victory. They may have lost their big prize, but they still had most of the Algerine crew in chains. Eventually they managed to catch a breeze and head back to Italy.

However, James Hull's troubles were far from over. As a serving petty officer aboard an enemy ship, he was regarded as a legitimate captive regardless of his nationality or his prior status in Algiers. He would remain in bondage but under new masters.

When the warship reached its home port, Hull argued his case but got nowhere. He was formally declared a captive and a state hostage of Naples despite his protestations. Thus, for a time, he had the extraordinary experience of being a captive of European pirates immediately after having been a captive of North African pirates. He probably noticed little difference: if anything, his treatment may even have been worse.

However, Hull managed to get a message back to Joseph Donaldson, who wrote to his counterpart in Naples and had him liberated. Suddenly finding himself free for the first time in more than a decade, Hull opted to go straight back to sea as a mariner on an English frigate.

Back in Algiers, the dey was left "violently exasperated" by the loss of his crew. (It seems the plucky Moors got no credit for their heroism in saving his ship.) Hull's shipmates from the *Dauphin* and the *Maria* were delighted to hear that their friend had been liberated, but their celebrations were tinged with sadness because death had reduced their numbers so drastically. Once they had been twenty-one in number. Now they were down to five.

The climactic moment in that story—the slow-burning fuse leading to a powder keg—was a perfect metaphor for what was happening in Algiers. The dey was becoming increasingly incensed by the lack of progress. He began to talk openly of tearing up the treaty and going back to war. And he wasn't the only one who had reached breaking point. The American prisoners were at the end of their tether—and they had their minds set on mutiny.

★   ★   ★

Thanks to Donaldson's rejection of the dey's offer to free the men from prison, Scipio Jackson and his comrades were still being hauled from their infested bunks at 3:00 a.m., herded down to the marine yard, and forced to do a long day's work under the lash of vengeful and corrupt overseers. But the same did not apply to their officers. Once treated exactly the same as the men, the captains were now "moon payers," secure in their comfortable house in the suburbs. This seemed to fly in the face of all the democratic ideals these men had fought for during the American Revolution. They were well aware that in France ordinary citizens had even stormed the Bastille to protest such injustices. Inside the bagnio, the indignant whisperings turned into angry shouts and demands for action. And the target for their resentment was Joseph Donaldson, whom they'd nicknamed "Old Hickory Face."

Finally, their patience snapped, and they rose up in mass to storm their own version of the Bastille—the consulate where Donaldson had taken to his bed with gout. "The mates and sailors laid siege to his chamber and insisted on him procuring them leave to stay in town," Cathcart recalled, adding with some sympathy: "They said they had as much right to be exempt from hard labor as the masters."

Donaldson hobbled to the door. "I can do nothing for you at present," he called out. "Go back to your quarters and have patience a little longer."

The men cursed him but left. They could see how much pain he was in. "His frequent indisposition might have been the cause of his petulancy towards his countrymen," mused the seaman Isaac Brooks.

Christmas behind bars did nothing to improve the men's mood. On New Year's Day 1796, James Cathcart woke up to his eleventh year in captivity to be told that a full-scale mutiny had erupted: the disaffected seamen and mates had absconded from the bagnio and had taken possession of Donaldson's house.

The angry mob shouted that the house had been paid for by the people and belonged to the people. "We have as much right to stay here as you have," they yelled. "We absolutely refuse to go to any more work at the Marine."

Donaldson rose from his sick bed to address them. He could have defused the crisis with an honest appraisal of the problem, an assurance that government agents were working hard to find a solution, and an appeal to their patience. Instead, he adopted an arrogant tone. According to Isaac Brooks, "he bade them in an imperious tone of voice to begone immediately from his lodgings, or he would find means to compel them."

It was exactly the wrong approach. Enraged by his "hauteur," the mariners exploded in fury and the peaceful occupation escalated into a full-scale riot. Donaldson was unfazed. Since he had not agreed to the prisoners' release, their conduct remained the responsibility of the prison guardians. He sent a messenger asking them to quell the uprising.

The warders came out in force and waded among the mutineers with swords and cudgels. "They beat them with sticks and the flat of their swords all the way down to the Marine," recalled Cathcart, who was not present at the time.

Back at the bagnio, they were "loaded with heavy chains for three weeks." They never mutinied again.

★   ★   ★

When January passed with no news, the dey dictated an angry letter to Humphreys, all the while directing a steady tirade of abuse at his clerk. He cursed everyone involved, from Cathcart all the way up to President Washington. "I swear by my beard that I will not be trifled with any longer," he snapped. He would throw Donaldson out, return to war with America, and cut off Cathcart's head. In that order.

The letter itself was terse and unfriendly, but it also revealed the dey's deep insecurity. Four months had passed and nothing had happened. Hassan was starting to suspect that Donaldson had never been given any power to negotiate and that Cathcart had lied to him: "My Christian Clerk absolutely informed me that he [Donaldson] was authorized by . . . George Washington, President." Hassan finished with a threat. If Humphreys did not reply—and soon—there would be a revolution in Algiers "with fatal consequences." In other words, the dey's own head was on the block as well as Cathcart's.

At two o'clock on January 29, Cathcart received a summons to the palace. You have one month, the dey told him. After that, the treaty will be voided, and we will be at war.

As Cathcart was leaving, he shouted: "And as for you, infidel, I know what to do with you." He drew his hand horizontally across his neck.

Traumatized, Cathcart told Donaldson about the threat. To his astonishment, Donaldson thought it was hilarious. "The Dey would have hard work cutting off your head, or mine either," he said, "we have such short necks."

Even the normally supportive Peter Erik Skjoldebrand joined in the black humor at Cathcart's expense. "I could try to get the sentence commuted to a roasting," the Swede offered.

Understandably, Cathcart did not see the joke and remained silent throughout dinner.

Luckily for Cathcart, America's ambassador in Lisbon did take the threat seriously. When David Humphreys read Hassan's letter and realized that Cathcart's life was in imminent danger, he immediately wrote back to Hassan assuring him that his clerk had informed him correctly: Donaldson *had* been given full authority to negotiate. He assured the dey that the treaty had been officially recognized in America, and the only delay was financial. It was "beyond foresight or control" that hard cash was unavailable anywhere. The dey sheathed his scimitar, and Cathcart's head remained firmly attached to his neck—no thanks to Joseph Donaldson.

★   ★   ★

Around this time Cathcart was given the opportunity to buy his own ship. He seized the chance eagerly, knowing that once the American hostages became free, they would require a speedy evacuation before the unpredictable dey could change his mind. The vessel was a two-hundred-ton polacre (a sort of hybrid between a European brig and a Barbary xebec), which he could also use to trade goods with the eastern Mediterranean. He immediately wrote to Humphreys, putting the ship at his country's disposal. The ship—which he named the *Independent*—was indeed to play a key role in the liberation of his countrymen but not in the way that either Cathcart or Humphreys imagined.

In the meantime, Humphreys seemed to be the only US diplomat who realized the vital importance of Cathcart's role in this tense and fateful political chess game. He wrote the young American a fifteen-page letter encouraging him in his work and giving him a primer in the politics of the Mediterranean. Clearly, he could see a future for Cathcart in the diplomatic corps.

For his part, Cathcart began informing Humphreys directly of developments. "The Dey's patience is nearly exhausted," he wrote to Lisbon on February 6, stressing that Hassan's deadline of one month still stood.

That same month, Humphreys wrote to the American captives assuring them that they hadn't been forgotten. "Be of good courage, exert all your fortitude, have a little more patience, hope always for the best," he said.

They were inspiring words. But as the clock ticked down toward the deadline, they were not the words that anyone in Algiers wanted to hear.

Everyone was waiting for word from Richard O'Brien.

$$\star \quad \star \quad \star$$

Dressed in the fancy new suit of clothes that he had bought with Cathcart's money, Captain O'Brien tirelessly tramped the streets of London, plodding from bank to credit house to coffeehouse in a bid to raise half a million dollars in hard cash to ransom his countrymen. Everywhere the response was the same: "I am sorry to inform you that in London, gold or silver cannot be procured."

Ever the optimist, he hauled anchor once more and set sail in the long-suffering US brig *Sophia* for Hamburg, where he had exactly the same experience.

Then he had a brainstorm. Spain had gold and silver, thanks to its territories in the New World, but refused to release it except under special circumstances. O'Brien felt this was an avenue worth investigating. He sailed straight back to London, where Sir Francis Baring of Barings Bank personally issued him a credit note drawn on Cadiz. Then O'Brien wrote to Humphreys, urging him to put in a plea for help to the Spanish authorities.

It was a brilliant idea, and Humphreys wasted no time. He immediately put in the request in Madrid, saying that success was not only in America's interest but that of "humanity."

Meantime, as the deadline loomed closer, Humphreys sent out an alert to all American shipping. The area had become a danger zone. If any US citizens tried to enter the Mediterranean, "they may expose themselves to great danger."

Humphreys would have been horrified if he had known that the exact opposite message was spreading through the ports of America's East Coast. Word finally filtered through regarding Donaldson's surprise success in the treaty negotiations, and everyone assumed that the United States was now at peace with Algiers. Few people realized that the deal was actually under imminent threat and could collapse at any moment. Ships eagerly took on cargos bound for the Mediterranean. The warning voice of David Humphreys was lost amid the mighty roar of reviving commerce.

From as far away as Britain, O'Brien was genuinely alarmed. Any American setting sail for the Mediterranean was being "imprudent," he warned: "I am very apprehensive of some fatal consequences . . . [and that] the Dey will declare the treaty void and send out his corsairs to capture the American vessels."

★ ★ ★

Back in Algiers, the situation that could hardly get worse . . . got worse. One Sunday night in February, Cathcart was working in his office when Captain Moses Morse from Boston burst through the door with some very bad news. Three of the ships' captains—William Wallace from the *Despatch*, Timothy Newman of the *Thomas*, and William Furnace of the *Olive Branch*—had been drinking and gambling at the officers' house when a fight broke out. Wallace and Furnace, locked together in a grapple, had fallen from a high gallery into the courtyard. Wallace was killed instantly. Furnace's arm was broken. Morse was in a panic, since the booze-fueled party had broken all the rules about gaming, alcohol, and fighting.

Next day Cathcart got to the palace early, before anyone else, and lied by omission about the incident: he maintained the captain's death had been the result of an unfortunate fall and left it at that.

Hassan, already in a foul mood, crowed with pleasure at the news. He knew he would be paid full ransom for each officer, dead or alive. "I'm glad of it," he said malevolently. "It is the judgment of God because you people did not fulfill your promises." As his ire rose, he shouted that Cathcart would soon join Wallace in hell. "*Andar al diable, canaille,*" he roared at his clerk. "Go to the devil, you dog."

For once, Cathcart was glad to be shouted at. If the dey had been less furious, he might have ordered a full inquiry and uncovered the facts. "Had the truth been known," the clerk wrote with relief, "those concerned would have received five hundred bastinadoes each, and the others sent to hard labor."

★   ★   ★

Everyone held his breath as the dey's deadline of one month expired at the end of February, but no corsair ships set out because the cruising season was not due to begin for another few weeks. Meanwhile, for Cathcart, life at the palace had become a nightmarish existence. Donaldson remained inactive, stoically locked in his inner world of personal pain. On the few occasions when he emerged to face the reality of the crisis, he reacted with only dejection, defeatism, and despair. Cathcart was the obvious scapegoat for the dey's anger. The steady stream of abuse, threats, and personal insults rose in pitch to the point that the American was too embarrassed even to write them down.

And then, on March 4, 1796, everything changed. A ship named *Sally* sailed into the bay, flying the American flag, and carrying a new envoy who was to replace the ailing Joseph Donaldson. Joel Barlow was a poet, a wit, and a firebrand revolutionary. Brimming with energy and imaginative flair, he stood in stark contrast to the defeatist and risk-averse Donaldson. The game had suddenly been transformed. There was a new kid in town.

· 26 ·

A Poet in Purgatory

$\mathcal{J}$oel Barlow could hardly have chosen a worse time to sail into Algiers. Right from the start, the wind was against him, in the most literal sense. A howling March gale, blowing in exactly the wrong direction, had carried off one of the masts from his ship during the sea trip and left him stranded at anchor in heavy seas four miles from Algiers. Robbed of forward momentum, the vessel wallowed nauseatingly in all directions, giving Barlow "the most violent seasickness I have ever suffered."

The experience colored his attitude toward Algiers from day one. "After we had been cast about for three days from heaven to hell," he wrote later, "[the gale] drove us to a port which certainly belongs to neither, since they are not men who inhabit it."

Watching from shore, James Cathcart judged the weather too bad to attempt a rescue. Next day the seas were still rough but the wind had eased, so he organized eight oarsmen in a large rowboat to bring the envoy ashore. All the way into port, the waves crashed over the boat, completely engulfing Barlow in the chilly Mediterranean waters. This bleak baptism into his new role left the US envoy "completely drenched."

Once he'd dried out at the ambassadorial house, he discovered another reason why his timing had been disastrous. The city was about to enter the month of Ramadan and the period of fasting that inevitably made people tetchier than normal during the working day.

But there was no going back now. On March 5—which, Cathcart noted, was exactly six months since the signing of the peace treaty in September—Joel Barlow took over from Donaldson and formally began his posting in purgatory.

★ ★ ★

At forty-two, Joel Barlow was a relatively young man but had already become a celebrity—both through his writing and through turning his entire life into performance art in much the same way that Lord Byron would do a couple of decades later. Born on a Connecticut farm, he was a Yale man who had gone on to serve as a war chaplain and later practiced as a lawyer. He was famous both for his witty articles and for immensely weighty epic poetry such as his *Vision of Columbus*. He moved to France and became a real estate salesman, flogging land in America to would-be French emigrants. This turned out to be a scam, but Barlow claimed not to know this at the time, and most historians give him the benefit of the doubt. After leaving a trail of financial catastrophe, he decided his future lay in politics. Fired up by the French Revolution, he took French citizenship, joined the National Assembly, and helped Tom Paine publish *The Rights of Man*. He supported the use of the guillotine, so at least one thing he had in common with the dey was an enthusiasm for cutting people's heads off.

Barlow had been appointed US agent in Algiers as far back as September 1795, six months before his arrival, but he didn't really want the job. He loved Paris and hated the thought of being separated from his wife Ruth. After reluctantly accepting the post, he spent a full three months indulging in retail therapy, wandering from one Parisian jeweller to another, spending 162,000 French livres (around $30,000) of US taxpayers' money on lavish presents for the dey. Once again, it is astonishing to see how the American government, which had refused on principle to pay the ransom for the original captives, was quite prepared to blow the same amount on incidentals and expenses. If Donaldson had failed to understand the system of backhanders in Algiers, Barlow embraced it almost too enthusiastically.

Despite the importance of his mission, he didn't leave Paris until late December, and even then, turned his trip into a grand tour. He wandered slowly along the Rhone to Marseilles, where he chanced to meet a group of Algerine men who chatted to him amiably and casually cajoled him into telling them details on his trip. Of course, they turned out to be spies who reported everything back to the dey.

His leisurely tour ended with a ten-day trip through Spain on mule-back. Barlow seems to have had no idea of the urgency of the crisis until his arrival in Alicante, where he was shocked to learn that the money payable under the treaty was overdue by several months and that the dey was spitting fire.

When he read the increasingly panicky letters from Algiers, he realized for the first time that he was dealing with an emergency.

"Many American vessels are on their way to these seas," he wrote with concern. "[They] will fall into the hands of the Algerines the moment the negotiations are broken off."

The penny had finally dropped. There was not a moment to lose. Barlow left Spain immediately and set his course for the corsair city.

★   ★   ★

Once in Algiers, Barlow hoped for an early interview with Hassan. He thought that, with his reassuring manner, his legal skills, and his lavish presents, he would be able to talk the dey back from the ledge. Unfortunately, the day-time fasting of Ramadan had made the ruler "extremely irritated." Perpetually peckish and deprived of nicotine from his usual snuff-sniffing habit, Hassan refused flat-out to see him. If Barlow didn't have the cash, he said, then he was wasting everyone's time—and then war was inevitable.

"Then his wrath passed away a little," Barlow reported, "and the affair sleeps. I do not dare to waken it. If I can make it sleep for some weeks yet, I hope that all will go well."

While waiting for the fasting to end, Barlow looked around at the faces he saw in Algiers and decided that his pleasant, friendly features put him at a disadvantage in this macho city. He concentrated on growing an enormous black moustache to give himself "the air of a tiger."

Meanwhile, some of Barlow's lavish presents proved to be hopelessly ill chosen. A collection of fashionable Parisian dresses costing 41,000 French livres (around $7,600) were instantly rejected as of "no use at all" for the la-dies of Algiers—they were of course too revealing for women from an Islamic society. The gowns were "entirely thrown away."

The powerful Algiers banker Micaiah Cohen Baccri tried to get things moving. On a visit to the palace one evening, he showed Dey Hassan one of Barlow's finest gifts, a finely wrought silver trunk that had cost the American taxpayers a small fortune. He suggested that even if the dey refused to accept Barlow's gifts personally, the chest would make a wonderful present for Has-san's beloved daughter Fatima. According to one source, Fatima, aged around seven, was "the greatest favorite imaginable with the Dey."

The tactic rebounded. Send it to her if you want, the dey yawned. I'm off to bed.

And so the gift went to the delighted daughter but made zero impact on the negotiations. "Mr. Barlow got no thanks for the trunk," said Cathcart, "and little business was transacted during the whole of this month."

★   ★   ★

Cathcart and Barlow hit it off, at least in the early days. Humphreys had told Barlow about the young American's courageous efforts for peace, and Barlow obviously felt Cathcart deserved more respect than Donaldson had given him. Whenever Donaldson exploded in one of his tantrums, Barlow politely intervened and took Cathcart's side.

Barlow realized that Cathcart was smart and that he knew far more about Algiers than Donaldson or anyone else. He asked for his help. Flattered, Cathcart handed him all his journals and reports since 1785. During the lull of Ramadan month, Barlow distilled this invaluable information into an extensive report that he sent home to the Department of State. The department was astounded by how much Barlow had learned in Algiers in just two weeks. It was only later that Cathcart discovered he had received no credit at all for this, the most comprehensive and up-to-date report to come out of the little-known Barbary state. Barlow had simply plagiarized it without attribution.

As the days passed, Cathcart began to suspect that Barlow was forging a strong alliance with the banker Micaiah Cohen Baccri and freezing Cathcart out. He noticed that Baccri joined Cathcart at the palace when the dey was in a good mood after which the banker could report to Barlow that the ruler's attitude was mellowing thanks to his own benign influence. But when the dey was in foul form, Baccri stayed clear and let Cathcart shoulder the blame for the setbacks. All this left Barlow with the impression that Cathcart botched everything he touched.

Cathcart also became convinced that the banker was inventing entire conversations with Hassan. "[He] would go to the palace, sit in the coffee room, and bring a lie out to our agents, without ever having seen the Dey," Cathcart maintained.

Cathcart may have been oversuspicious, but, whatever the truth, it became clear that Baccri's influence with Barlow was increasing, and after each private conversation with the banker, the US envoy's attitude toward Cathcart became noticeably cooler.

★ ★ ★

Amid all this, the last thing Cathcart needed—in his dual role as clerk and tavern keeper—was an alcohol-fueled murder in the Bagnio Gallera. After drinking in one of the taverns, a *Camero*—one of the Spaniards from Oran— got into a fight and stabbed another prisoner five times. Two guards rushed to intervene, and they were both stabbed as well. During a tense three-hour standoff, the knifeman took control of the prison, and the entire city was alerted to the possibility of a mass revolt. Brandishing his knife, the rebel *Camero* shouted: "If you feel valiant enough, come and take it." Nobody did feel valiant enough, and when he was finally taken down, it was by a blow from a club wielded by one of his friends. By the time the fracas ended, one guard lay dead and two men were seriously injured.

Next morning the enraged dey had the killer beheaded under the grape-vines at the palace. It took three strokes of the executioner's saber before his head finally rolled to the cheers and applause from a large crowd of spectators.

The dey took out his fury on the tavern keepers. "If they had not sold intoxicating liquors," he said, "they would not have quarreled." He slapped the bar owners with an enormous fine of $4,000 and gave them just four days to find the money.

Nobody had that amount of cash, and as usual it was left to Cathcart to take the bad news to the dey. "He got in such a passion that I really thought he was insane," he recalled. Hassan immediately shuttered all twenty-five city taverns and threw all the taverners in jail except Cathcart himself.

Cathcart had to solve the impasse. He realized that the dey's extreme fury was hunger related. The ruler roused himself to such a level of indigna-tion that he couldn't easily descend again. It was Cathcart's job to provide a ladder down which the ruler could retreat with dignity. He waited until that evening, when the dey had had a good meal and was contentedly puffing a pipe of tobacco, and then brought him a personal payment of 280 sequins. The mere sight of a pile of cash mollified the ruler. Cathcart suggested that the others could pay their fines by monthly installments, but only if they could return to work in their taverns.

The dey agreed grudgingly, and everything returned to normal. "But," he warned his clerk, "I hold you responsible for the whole sum."

★ ★ ★

On March 28, James Cathcart experienced his most terrifying palace encoun-ter. For the first time, the dey subjected his clerk to actual physical violence.

That morning, the former palace sweeper turned diplomat Philip Sloan had arrived from Alicante with a new letter from Humphreys. It gave an in-kling of progress: O'Brien had arrived in Spain with the letter of credit from Barings Bank. If the dey could pressure Madrid to release the hard cash, "it would facilitate the payment in a very short time."

Word of the ship's arrival reached the dey, who had taken to sleeping for most of the day during the month of Ramadan. At six in the evening, tetchy and still a bit groggy from his doze, the ruler summoned Sloan and Cathcart to the palace. "Have you brought the money, or any account of it?" he demanded.

With trepidation, Cathcart began translating Humphreys's letter. He was still reading when the dey sprang to his feet, incandescent with rage. He ran up to Cathcart and slapped his face hard. "Dogs without faith!" he bellowed. "If you ever come to me again on such an errand, it will be the death of you both!"

Sensing that peace hung in the balance, Cathcart swallowed his anger and stood his ground. "Strike, Effendi," he said, "but listen. Things are not always what they appear to be."

Hassan's only answer was to draw out a razor-sharp yataghan saber. He moved toward the two men, who dived for the safety of the stairwell. Fortunately, the dey did not follow them: if he had, the guards outside would have killed both men in an instant.

Cathcart, stunned and traumatized by his narrow escape, walked unsteadily to the ambassadorial house and reported his terrifying experience. To his astonishment, Donaldson burst out laughing. "You should have turned the cheek," he spluttered at last, "and fulfilled the Scriptures."

Diplomatically, Barlow intervened before Cathcart could lose his cool. "It is no dishonour to be insulted either by a fool or a despot," he reassured the clerk. "Those who offer the injury are the persons disgraced."

In a later account of the incident, Barlow wrote: "As the messenger was stooping to kiss his hand, [the dey] struck him in the face. . . . He took [the letter] in his hand and threw it out the door with great fury, uttering many execrations and threats." With this wording, Barlow downgraded Cathcart to the role of a passive messenger boy, despite the young American's enormous—and courageous—contribution to the peace negotiations.

The threat of execution hung over Cathcart's head for weeks. A little later, after a furious argument at the palace, Hassan turned to his clerk. "As for you, imposter," he yelled, "you who have been the means of sending a passport for [Donaldson] to come here to deceive me, I will settle my accounts with you very soon." He rose, unsheathed his yataghan saber, and mimed the act of beheading.

Barlow summoned an emergency meeting. Baccri and the Swedish brothers joined the diplomats and agreed that peace was hanging by a thread. The Algerine corsairs would soon set sail and capture dozens more Americans: "Some means must be taken, and immediately, to avert the impending storm."

• 27 •

The Dey's Last Command

For the waiting captives, April was the cruelest month. First, the dreaded plague returned to Algiers. "It carried off many of my fellow countrymen," lamented Foss, "[just] when they were expecting every day to be called free men."

At around the same time, the dey abruptly decided to end the negotiations. His timing was not surprising since the traditional sailing season was about to begin. On April 3, he announced that he would expel Barlow and Donaldson in eight days' time, and the countdown to war would begin.

"It seems today that my sojourn here draws to a close, and that the business has failed," Barlow reported despondently. "The money has not yet come; the Dey does not want to wait much longer."

When this bleak news reached the bagnios, the American captives felt that all hope finally had been extinguished. Barlow described "a scene of complete and poignant distress . . . arising from the state of total despair. . . . [We cannot] administer the least comfort or hope."

However, the Americans had confidence in Barlow that they had never had in Donaldson: "[He] gave us all the encouragement he could, assuring us that he would never quit Algiers and leave us," one prisoner wrote.

It was just as well that the captives did not have access to his private letters, however, because Barlow was not nearly as committed to staying in Algiers as he publicly claimed to be. In a confidential letter to his wife, he hinted that he would not be overly upset if the deal were to collapse, because, whatever happened, he would be out of there. If he finalized the treaty, he told her, he could leave the city and "fly to your arms." If not, "I shall be driven from here, so I shall be free soon in any case." He didn't mention the hundred-plus Americans who wouldn't be.

★   ★   ★

As the crisis deepened, Cathcart and Barlow were working at cross-purposes. Cathcart, more attuned to the mood in the palace, heard through the grapevine that a down payment of $40,000 in cash would buy the United States six months of breathing room. Marshaling his formidable network of financial contacts, he raised this money at 2 percent interest and eagerly reported the breakthrough to Barlow.

Barlow wasn't interested in the idea. He was fixated on the banker Miciah Cohen Baccri, "who has more influence with the Dey than all the Regency put together," he explained to Humphreys, "and *who alone* has been able to soothe his impatience for three months past." (My italics: once again, Cathcart's courageous interventions were airbrushed out of history.)

Barlow decided instead to give half of that amount directly to Baccri. He dipped deep into the American taxpayers' pockets and hired the banker's services for a breathtaking ten thousand sequins (around $20,000). In return, Baccri agreed to push for new solutions at the palace.

(It hardly needs to be pointed out, yet again, that this sum alone would have gone a long way toward ransoming the original captives back in 1785.)

Baccri's solution was controversial because it established a dangerous precedent. He approached the ruler proposing what we might now describe as an "arms for hostages" deal. In return for three months of breathing space, the United States would construct a state-of-the-art, copper-bottomed warship, a thirty-six-gun frigate named the *Crescent*. The fighting ship would be given not to the State of Algiers, but to Hassan's family personally. To avoid all doubt, it would be formally presented to his daughter, Fatima.

The dey accepted. He postponed his threat of war until July, "and not a single day beyond that will be allowed on any account," Hassan warned.

Cathcart was stunned. He could have bought six months for $40,000, deductible from the final bill, but instead Barlow had "concluded that it was better to promise a frigate which was valued at $45,000 but would cost $100,000 to deliver to Algiers," all in exchange for a mere three months. (Cathcart's estimate wasn't too far off—in the end, the ship would cost $90,000.) Cathcart told Barlow that he didn't believe three months would be long enough, but the envoy simply shrugged. "I will trust to the chapter of accidents," he said cryptically.

When word reached the American embassy in Lisbon, David Humphreys was alarmed. The United States had just agreed to give the predatory Algerines a warship with thirty-six guns—weapons they could just as easily turn against America at some future date. What seemed to Barlow a brilliant coup was in reality a short-term fix that established a dangerous template for the future. Other Barbary despots would demand equal treatment. Besides, there was the personal nature of the gift: when the elderly Hassan died, his successor could justifiably demand a frigate for himself.

Unnerved by the idea, Humphreys concluded that the decision was way above his pay grade and immediately ordered Richard O'Brien to sail to Philadelphia in the trusty *Sophia* to obtain top-level clearance from the government.

Back in Algiers, Joseph Donaldson was feeling much better. He heard that hard cash was available in Leghorn and volunteered to sail there to try his luck. Never was any man so glad to leave Algiers.

Left alone in the whitewashed house with little to do, Barlow began the blame game. He blamed his old friend Humphreys for his silence on the whole affair and for traipsing off to Paris instead of staying in Lisbon, where he could have drawn the ransom cash and saved everyone a lot of trouble. Waspishly, he wrote home that America could have saved $60,000 if it had appointed "a good banker's clerk" to Lisbon instead of Humphreys.

In a letter to Humphreys himself, Barlow stressed the urgency of the situation. The mercurial dey was already on a short fuse. "He is a man of the most capricious and ungovernable temper imaginable," Barlow wrote. "I can scarcely say that I have any hope."

Both men understood the implications of war. The last offensive against American shipping had begun very late in the year, yet it still had captured eleven ships. How many more could be seized this year if the offensive were to begin in July? "The war [would be] breaking out anew at a moment when—under the idea that peace is concluded—many American ships will be in these seas," he wrote.

Barlow had hit the nail on the head with the phrase "under the idea that peace is concluded." A feeling of false security had indeed spread throughout America, fueled by President Washington himself when he declared, "with particular satisfaction," that agreement had been reached with Algiers "for a speedy peace, and the restoration of our unfortunate fellow citizens from a grievous captivity." This had sucked all the urgency out of the plan to build a national navy. Back in 1794, Congress had authorized six frigates specifically for "the protection of the trade of the United States against the Algerines" with the proviso that construction work would halt in the event of a peace agreement. In March 1796, Washington suspended the project, "the peace [with Algiers] having taken place." (Later in the year, work was to resume on just three of the six frigates.)

So even the president of the United States was under the illusion—at least at that stage—that America was at peace with Algiers. And as more American seamen prepared to travel to the Mediterranean, unaware that they were sailing into the jaws of captivity, a radical solution arose. Someone who enjoyed the trust of both the Algerines and the Americans must dash directly to the United States, meet Washington face to face, and tell him the truth—before it was too late.

★ ★ ★

After eleven years of captivity. . . . I am going home. James Cathcart hardly dared to let the thought enter his mind as he emerged from the palace, dazzled both by the late April sunshine and overawed by the implications of the orders he had just been given.

The young American had been summoned to the dey's room on the last day of April 1796—a date he would remember for the rest of his life.

He probably had felt the usual sense of apprehension as he climbed the stairway, bracing himself for another verbal assault and wondering, as always, if this would be his last morning on earth.

Instead, he had found the dey in contemplative mood. Hassan said he had lost confidence in the official envoys that America had sent to him. Their "trifling" and their empty promises had only confused matters. The clock was ticking toward war and he did not believe that those untrustworthy envoys would honor their commitments before the deadline elapsed.

There was one politician that Hassan did trust, however: the war hero President George Washington. Here was a man whose word, famously, was his bond. If Washington were to be told directly, man to man, that America's agents had prevaricated for eight months instead of keeping their side of the peace bargain, such an honorable statesman would want to act immediately to put things right.

He would personally write a letter to Washington. But he also needed someone familiar with the negotiations and the complexities of Barbary politics to explain the whole matter to the president—and then to oversee the provision of the maritime equipment that was a vital part of the deal.

That someone would be James Leander Cathcart.

He told his surprised clerk that he should use his own ship—that is, Cathcart's polacre *Independent*—to sail to America. He was to meet President Washington personally and warn him what was at stake. There was never any mention of Cathcart receiving his freedom in return for this service: even in his homeland, he technically would remain a state hostage of the Regency of Algiers, sent to America with dispatches.

You should be ready to sail in eight days, he told his secretary.

Cathcart stammered that he could not find a crew in eight days. Hassan waved the objection aside. He should take some Moorish seamen from Algiers: as soon as he reached Alicante, on the first part of his voyage, he should send them home and raise a new crew in Spain.

A few days later, he dictated a letter to George Washington, which his incredulous clerk no doubt wrote with a shaking hand:

To George Washington, President of the United States of America:

Health, peace and prosperity.

Whereas peace and harmony has been settled between our two nations . . . and as eight months have elapsed without one article of the agreement being complied with, we have thought it expedient to dispatch James Leander Cathcart, formerly our Christian secretary, with a note of such articles as are required. . . . For further intelligence I refer you to your consul resident here, and to the said James Leander Cathcart, and I pray you . . . that the said Cathcart may be dispatched with such part of the articles specified in our negotiation. . . . We have granted the said Cathcart a Mediterranean passport [from] the first of May, 1796.

Done in the Dey's Palace by our order and sealed with the great seal, on the 26th of the Luna of Carib in the year of the Hegira, 1210, which corresponds with the 5th of May 1796.

Signed, Vizir Hassan Bashaw, Dey of the City and Regency of Algiers.

Hassan affixed his seal to the letter and handed it to Cathcart.

I will wait for nine months for the president's reply, he said.

* * *

Cathcart trekked back to the consulate and passed all this to Barlow—who reacted just as you might expect a man to react when you tell him that you are about to go over his head and take up matters directly with his boss. He seemed underwhelmed by the good news that America was off the hook for nine months rather than an unrealistic three months. Instead, he chose to fixate on the notion that Cathcart wanted a free trip to America on Uncle Sam's dime.

I could not think of subjecting the United States to any part of the expense of this journey, he told Cathcart curtly: "You must undertake to make the best of your way to Philadelphia at your own expense."

Cathcart was disappointed by the ungenerous reaction. "Mr. Barlow does not consider," he wrote in his journal, "that it is putting me to a great expense." After having bought the ship—which he now needed for the trip—he had little in the way of cash. The dey had even forbidden him to offset the cost by taking on cargo. "The lowness of my finances . . . will make me feel the expense amazingly," Cathcart wrote.

After having washed his hands of the whole matter financially, Barlow turned around and, in the next breath, gave Cathcart a list of things to do during the trip. First, he was to deliver a package at Alicante. Then, instead of obeying the dey's order and heading directly for America, he was to take a long diversion to Lisbon and deliver another package there. Each curt instruction was prefaced with the peremptory words "I desire that you . . ." The envoy's brazenness left Cathcart speechless.

To his credit, however, Barlow dashed off two letters praising Cathcart and emphasizing the importance of his mission. To Humphreys in Lisbon, he wrote: "His intelligence and industry will doubtless enable him to render essential service in that business [the peace negotiations]. He has been very useful to our cause here, and on that account, I beg leave to recommend him to your protection and confidence."

To Timothy Pickering, the secretary of state in America, he wrote: "James Leander Cathcart [can] give you such details as may be useful in arranging and transporting the articles for the peace presents and annual tribute. He has rendered considerable service in our affairs here by his intelligence and zeal and I doubt not but that he might be usefully employed by you in the above business or in any other way in which you think proper."

Barlow told the secretary of state that he believed the dey was genuine in his desire for peace. "His proposing to send a person to America on this errand is a sort of proof of his sincerity."

Later, after peace was established, he was to emphasize the vital importance of Cathcart's voyage: "It is in a great measure owing to the circumstance of this mission that we are now at peace with Algiers."

I quote those passages at length because they were written immediately after Cathcart was given his mission—and they completely contradict a later version of events in which Barlow tries to portray the whole exercise as a distraction, a sleight of hand that he himself had cooked up. (Barlow's complex conspiracy theory, which collapses at the slightest scrutiny, is discussed in the notes.)

Barlow handed Cathcart a formal letter of instructions, which ended: "On arrival at Philadelphia, I rely on your intelligence and zeal in giving to the proper officers of government, the expediency of as prompt a compliance with our engagements here . . . wishing you a safe arrival and all prosperity and happiness. I remain, sir, your friend and servant."

Privately, however, he was not "friendly" at all toward Cathcart. He wrote to Secretary of State Pickering that Cathcart was undertaking the voyage "to obtain his liberty sooner than he otherwise would"—in other words, that his motivation was purely selfish and that it was aimed at jumping over his colleagues in the queue to freedom. It was a gratuitous and unnecessary slur—

even if it were true, Barlow had no need to say anything at all about it—but what made it worse was its deliberate mendacity. The truth was exactly the opposite. Cathcart was not being freed, simply sent home on license. More to the point—as Barlow well knew—Cathcart could have ransomed himself from captivity at any point during the past few years but had chosen to stay. His twin aims had been to give practical help to his suffering countrymen in real time and to work toward their liberation in the long term. He had already achieved the first objective, and this voyage was now buying enough time for the US diplomats to achieve the second.

Cathcart himself was philosophical and wrote off the financial cost of his journey. "I can only add it to the different sums of money I have advanced to my brother sufferers during the four years they received nothing from their country," he mused. "[I have] done everything in my power to relieve their distresses and alleviate their sufferings. [When] my brother sufferers are restored to their dearest connections and their long-lost *patria*, I shall be happy."

★   ★   ★

Let's ignore Barlow's petty jibes and focus on a more interesting question: what was going on in Dey Hassan's head when he decided to send his own clerk as a captive emissary to America?

There were three reasons: one political, one personal, and—I would suggest—one reason that he never would have admitted and that might even have been subconscious.

Politically, the pressure from his corsair captains had eased. In late April, the wolf packs had returned with half a million dollars' worth of Danish ships, so their lust for plunder had been temporarily sated.

Personally, Hassan had a deep and genuine affection for America. Deep down, he didn't really want to go to war with a country that could become, in future, a valuable alternative source for naval stores and armaments as well as annual cash tributes. He sincerely believed Washington would keep his word once Cathcart had met him in person.

Psychologically, Hassan always had had a father-son relationship with Cathcart. True, it was a warped and twisted relationship, with the threat of physical abuse always in the background. But Hassan had recognized the young American's talents at an early stage. He had supervised his career growth. He had given him tests of character that Cathcart had (usually) passed. He had rewarded him with lucrative perks, and, finally, he appointed him to the highest office open to an outsider and non-Muslim. For his part, Cathcart courageously spoke truth to power, a trait that Hassan had always respected.

Through reading the dey's moustache twitches, Cathcart could predict his moods better than Hassan could himself.

Yet Hassan was growing older and knew he had little time left. He knew that any successor could purge all the officials from his court with one bored wave of a hand. It is reasonable to speculate that Hassan wanted to give his young protégé one final task that would safeguard his future, opening a door through which he could walk away from captivity with honor. When Barlow wrote about the peace deal—"[The dey] considers it as a favorite child of his own, and as such he means to cherish it as long as he lives"—it may have been true in a much deeper and perhaps more Freudian sense.

★   ★   ★

The next eight days passed in a blur of frantic activity, with Cathcart preparing his ship and hastily assembling a crew. He had to pay all his debts to his creditors and to the dey, including the full 280 sequin fine for the bagnio murders. This left him almost broke, apart from the value of the ship, which of course he needed for the voyage. (Once home, he would have to hound the US government to honor even his most basic expenses. "I have subsisted on credit since my arrival here," he complained at that point, adding drily: "A person who has been eleven years in captivity cannot be supposed to be overburdened with riches.")

And so, despite the wealth he had accumulated in the corsair city, he would leave Algiers with little money. This was not unusual—on the contrary, it was designed into the system. The phrase "you can't take it with you" usually applies to wealth after death, but it applied equally well to any state hostage who'd prospered in Algiers. There were exceptions, but generally, the system of debt traps, levies, and parting gifts ensured that they departed broke. Diplomats to the Barbary States in the 1700s were often bewildered to meet well-off captives who didn't want to be ransomed because they would forfeit their savings and return to a life of penury at home.

However, these were a fortunate minority. Let's not lose sight of the fact that the vast majority of captive hostages in Algiers at this time lived brutish lives of bondage, their crippling hard work interrupted only by bouts of pestilential sickness and disability.

As an example of a captive who got the dirty end of the stick, let's catch up with Scipio Jackson, the African American New Yorker who had been captured in 1793 and was still suffering in the bagnios.

· 28 ·

Scipio "Was in His Grave before Sunset"

$\mathcal{W}$hereas James Cathcart owned three taverns and his own ship, Scipio Jackson represented the other side of the coin for American hostages in Algiers. For Jackson and nearly all of his ordinary seamen comrades, things had never improved. Thanks to Donaldson's gruff indifference to their plight, they were still laboring at the docks and quarries and bedding down at night among the rats in the bagnios.

Scipio had managed to survive it all for two and a half years, but eventually the combination of filthy surroundings, hard work, poor diet, and harsh treatment took its toll on his health, and he contracted cholera. Needless to say, the gang masters at the docks and quarries had little sympathy for sick people—they regarded them all as malingerers. "If you live, you work" was the repeated motto.

Even fainting in the hot sun was regarded as deliberate disobedience. A victim who passed out often would recover consciousness to find himself pinioned to the ground with a bastinado swinging toward the soles of his feet. For instance, around that period of time, two Americans who had been working under the direct sun on the mountainside began to feel faint. When they staggered toward a nearby spring to get water, they collapsed unconscious on the grass. Two taskmasters found them, dragged them back, and gave them each a hundred strokes of the bastinado. "Many instances of this kind I have witnessed," wrote John Foss.

When Scipio Jackson began showing all the distressing symptoms of cholera, he was admitted to the Spanish hospital. This in itself demonstrated the severity of his condition, because captive workers were never hospitalized until they were so sick that they failed to respond to threats and beatings. Once inside the building, however, they were in a different environment. A team of up to four doctors and ten priests provided medication and meticulous care. But even in this place of protection, a captive could not count on sanctuary.

At daybreak each morning, a gang master toured the wards and decided, on a whim, who was fit for work and who was not. "If he finds anyone whom he thinks is able to perform any kind of work, he drives him out, not even asking the doctors," explains John Foss. "Often times they are driven out to work, and are obliged to return within two or three hours to the hospital, and often expire within a few hours."

That was the fate of the unfortunate Scipio Jackson. He responded to treatment in hospital, and as he started his journey toward recovery, the doctors recommended that he walk a few steps around the ward. At that precise moment a taskmaster burst into the room.

If you are well enough to walk, you are well enough to work, he declared. Get down to the docks and join the others.

I'm not able, Jackson said.

If you're not able, I will make you able, swore the taskmaster, striking him several times with his stick as he forced him out of the ward.

Several doctors appeared and pleaded for their patient: after all, a healthy worker was as much in the state's interest as Jackson's. But the gang master simply ignored them. He pushed and prodded the sick man through the streets to the marine.

"He did the best he could for about half an hour," recalled John Foss, "then fell down insensible. He was again sent to the hospital, expired at two o'clock, and was in his grave before sunset."

Scipio Jackson was buried at the sandy coast near the Babel Oued, where so many American captives had been interred before him. We can be certain that Cathcart was there—one exile praying over the grave of another in the long shadows of sunset on this lonely and desolate African beach.

However, Cathcart was not able to attend the funeral of Jackson's fellow African American captive, John Thomas of the brig *Minerva*. Thomas took sick with the plague around the time that Cathcart was leaving for the United States. Joel Barlow suggested that the American captives be moved out of the city, but the dey wouldn't hear of it: "They were not yet paid for." Barlow fumed about the Algerines' "contempt of disease" and "obstinate refusal to use precautions against the plague" but it made no difference.

Shortly afterward, Barlow wrote: "Since my last [letter], Joseph Keith, a native of Newfoundland, has died with the plague. [Benjamin] Lunt is still in hospital, [as is] John Thomas, a black man from Massachusetts."

Lunt eventually recovered and was able to return home, but John Thomas died just two days later. Had he been able to stay clear of the disease for just twenty-five more days, he would have been on a ship and headed for home as a free man.

And so the two US captives from 1793 that we definitively know to be African Americans—there were probably more—both died in their final year of captivity, along with many of their white comrades, all with freedom almost within their grasp.

It is important, though, in passing to consider the different ways in which the two men died. Thomas died from plague, despite the best efforts of his doctors to cure him. Jackson would have recovered had it not been for the deliberate intervention of his sadistic overseer. Although Scipio Jackson's death was officially described as "cholera," I think many of us would agree that it was actually murder.

· 29 ·

A Voyage to Save the Peace

Just after midday on May 8, 1796, James Leander Cathcart stood on the quarterdeck of his polacca *Independent* and watched the dazzlingly white citadel of Algiers blur into a snowy thumb smudge against the distant green paintscape of the North African coast. As a benevolent wind carried him farther west toward Spain, the city faded into the Mediterranean haze, almost as though his decade of captivity had been no more than a fevered nightmare.

Cathcart had been in captivity for a total of ten years, nine months, and thirteen days, and even now he was not really free. He had not been formally liberated by the dey—officially, he was an emissary who had "left with dispatches" as he himself put it. He was now in the nebulous position in which he was still a hostage of Algiers but heading toward a land where the dey's mandate would no longer apply. Whatever his status, his life had changed beyond all recognition over the past decade. The man who had arrived in Algiers as a captured seaman was now *Captain* James Cathcart, master of his own ship and master of his own fate.

As he plotted his course westward and called out orders to his Moorish Algerian crewmen, his mind churned with emotions that he could not begin to put into words. His euphoria over his escape from the stinking, claustrophobic streets of Algiers into the fresh, salty air of the open sea was dampened by a crushing sense of his huge responsibility to "save the peace of the nation" and of his continuing duty to his fellow captives. A sense of satisfaction in having survived nearly eleven years mingled with a feeling of revulsion when he remembered how truly dreadful those years had been: the first stirrings, perhaps, of post-traumatic stress syndrome that he was unable to put into words. "Words are insufficient to describe my sensations," he confessed. "The remembrance makes me tremble with horror."

His life in Algiers had indeed been remarkable; his survival even more so. "I had endured every indignity that [the Algerines] could invent to render the existence of a Christian captive insupportable," he wrote, "from a brick-layer's laborer, carrying heavy stones through the mountains, to being the First Christian Secretary."

He could have added to the list: lionkeeper at the palace zoo, teacher of navigation classes, carpenter, docker, harbor administrator, accountant, and, of course, bar owner. In three centuries of Barbary history, perhaps no one has ever had such a varied career in captivity as James Cathcart.

During the previous eight days, he had been busy putting the final seal to his life as a captive in Algiers. His taverns had been transferred to new owners. Debts had been paid. Rooms had been re-leased. He had received his orders and papers from Barlow only that morning and had exchanged a formal farewell. The Swedish diplomat Peter Erik Skjoldebrand, the "worthy and disinterested friend" whose loan had enabled him to become the dey's chief clerk, was at the harbor to see him off. "Never was a parting more truly affecting," Cathcart recalled.

Curiously, Cathcart says little about his last meeting with the dey himself. The ruler, never a man for sentimental gestures, would not have given his clerk an emotional send-off, especially as he expected to see him again within a year. Cathcart, for his part, had too many bitter memories of the ruler's verbal and physical abuse to be anything other than courteously formal. He certainly would have avoided the mistake made by the departing courtier who thanked the previous dey for never having punished him with the bastinado, only to be told that the oversight would be rectified immediately.

However, we can confidently picture their last encounter in the palace sometime around daybreak that morning: the dey taking his normal sardonic tone and Cathcart replying with his usual polite eloquence, all the time watch-ing the ruler's face carefully, as always, for that telltale twitch of the moustache that foretold a squall of regal temper. Finally, Cathcart kissed the dey's hand for the last time and made his way down the five flights of stairs toward his new destiny.

The two men were never to see each other again.

For Cathcart, the most heartbreaking element of his departure was the knowledge that he was leaving his comrades behind—something he had stolidly refused to do even when he'd won the right to pay his own ransom and escape. The sight of their desperately hopeful faces as they shared an emotional farewell was etched in his memory. "[It was] distressing for me to part with my brother sufferers and leave them on that inhospitable shore," he admitted. "Indeed, it was one of the most affecting scenes that can possibly be comprehended."

James Cathcart could take comfort, because his mission did indeed save the peace—it salvaged the treaty and, perhaps more importantly, bought enough time for the liberation of his countrymen in Algiers.

On September 12, 1796, he finally would step ashore at Philadelphia after more than eleven years of absence from the United States. Within twenty-four hours, he would be invited to dine with the great George Washington himself. The president subsequently would admit in a letter to the dey that he had not been aware of the seriousness of the crisis until this little-known mariner had arrived from the northern shores of Africa bringing him "more full and exact information." As a result, Washington would take immediate steps to fulfil the terms of the treaty.

But all that lay in the future for the young voyager as he left Algiers on that fine spring afternoon and set his course for the Spanish port of Alicante. As the sturdy *Independent* shouldered its way through the Mediterranean waves on the first leg of its long journey to America, Cathcart was already dreaming up a final verse to the dark poem he had composed several years before while standing by the graves of his dead compatriots at Babel Oued. Then, the mood of the poem had been one of despair and desolation. Now, at last, it was one of hope.

> And I am spared to cross the wave
> For those that yet remain,
> To help you. Oh, be strong and brave
> Till you are free again.

· 30 ·

"An Adieu to the Land of Bondage"

$\mathcal{A}$s things turned out, the captives had to remain "strong and brave" for only two more months. They were free by July.

In May 1796, when Cathcart embarked on a voyage that he knew would take several months, he must have known that he would not be in Algiers to witness the last act of the ransom saga—a process that he himself had made possible through the agreement he'd helped negotiate, the treaty he'd personally drawn up, and the vital extra time he'd bought through his mission to America. The road to the captives' freedom had already been mapped out: they would be free as soon as the diplomats could find the funds, and it would have been truly extraordinary if they were *not* able to raise the cash during the nine months of leeway that he'd secured.

Cathcart had to focus his mind on an even more important task. To recap, the agreement with Algiers had always involved two distinct elements. The first was the ransom of the captives; the second was the general peace treaty that was the only thing keeping the two nations from war. Cathcart had done all the heavy lifting on the former element, and could do no more. His task now was to concentrate on the second element, and to save the peace deal that was hanging on an increasingly flimsy thread. In the long term, this would be of far greater consequence. Failing in this mission would result in the capture of many more American seamen, perhaps in quantities that would make the number of existing captives appear ridiculously small by comparison.

While the Americans were understandably fixated on bringing their citizens home, the Algerines had a different perspective. They had always considered captives as an almost unlimited resource that they could tap into at any time, especially when the victim was a nation as vulnerable as the United States. If the treaty were to collapse after this batch of hostages had been released, the voracious corsairs would simply shrug and scoop up another hundred prisoners, as they had done in 1793. To them, hostages were expendable and easily replaceable. They were a bit like the cash-float in a retail business —the individual units might come and go, but the asset remained the same.

Cathcart had taken on a challenging task that was more critical, more urgent, but also thankless. Since he would be away from Algiers for at least nine months, he knew that he could not be around to join the cheering and backslapping on the day the captives were told that their ransom money had been secured and that they would soon be on their way home.

★   ★   ★

On a hot July morning in 1796, a group of American captives were hard at work at the quarries when they spotted a shimmering figure striding toward them through the heat haze. Wiping the sweat from their brows and squinting into the sun, they recognized the US diplomat Joel Barlow. When he told them they were free, "none of them would believe him," according to the seaman Isaac Brooks. After so many false dawns, they felt as though they could not risk another disappointment.

However . . .

"Their incredulity deserted them when orders were presented for their appearance before the Dey," Brooks recalled. "They bade an eternal adieu to the huge stones of [the quarry] and repaired to the palace with the most extravagant joy."

Two days later—on July 11—the Americans were assembled in the bagnio courtyard at dawn and marched to the palace. The experience "filled our hearts with joy, and we imagined ourselves the happiest people in the world," wrote John Foss.

For most of them, it was their first trip to the palace since their initial capture. Forty-eight Neapolitans were being liberated at the same time, so it turned out to be a grand and formal ceremony presided over by Dey Hassan, flanked by the prime minister, the Janissary aga, and all the grandees of the Regency. According to Isaac Brooks, one of the Neapolitans was so overcome by the magnificence of the event that, "in a transport of joy, [he] prostrated himself before the Dey and kissed his hands and feet: but the Americans . . . were not so servile." Eventually the US prisoners, still filthy in their sweat-stained blue uniforms, were each handed a passport of freedom and told they were at liberty to leave Algiers.

★   ★   ★

The task of garnering the ransom money had proved more difficult than anyone had anticipated. Despite the extra nine extra months of latitude, the entire process had been bedeviled by the worst luck imaginable.

You'll recall that, earlier in 1796, Richard O'Brien had been busily buzzing around Europe like a frantic worker bee, flitting from bank to bank and country to country in search of hard cash before being ordered to America. Meanwhile, Donaldson was in Leghorn drumming up $400,000 worth of loans backed by the $800,000 that was held by Barings Bank in London. But as soon as he had done so, by a cruel coincidence the British navy blockaded the Italian free port. All was not lost, however, because Donaldson managed to send word to the Baccri banking family in Algiers that he was good for the money. The knowledge that the funds were solidly placed in Leghorn, the Baccris' hometown, made everyone relax a bit.

At around the same time, Richard O'Brien returned to Lisbon from America to find that ambassador David Humphreys had managed to accumulate $225,000 in cash there. O'Brien gamely loaded the bulk of it on his ocean-battered brig *Sophia* and set off for Algiers. It was a daring trip—some would say foolhardy—because the cargo of cash could not be insured at anything other than a sky-high premium, which Humphreys refused to pay. There was a terrifyingly high risk of the *Sophia* falling victim to storms, maritime mishaps, or attack by pirates or privateers of all hues. O'Brien's only safeguard was a US passport and an Algerine pass from Dey Hassan.

Right from the start, it all went chaotically wrong. "Captain O'Brien was delayed from sailing by one day," Humphreys reported dolefully, "on account of a sad accident which happened to his Chief Mate, who lost his hand by discharging an overloaded blunderbuss."

Once at sea, O'Brien sailed safely through the Strait of Gibraltar—and promptly disappeared off the map. Forty-four days later, US representative Joel Barlow, who had been notified about his voyage, was still waiting in Algiers for the *Sophia* to appear on the horizon. "The wind has been good, the ship does not come," he bewailed. "It is probably taken or lost." He was being charitable: cynics were imagining a runaway O'Brien living the high life on some remote island.

The truth was harder to believe. O'Brien had been seized and thrown into captivity all over again by Barbary corsairs—but this time by corsairs based in Tripoli, farther along the coast. The Tripoli pirates had seized the *Sophia* along with one other American ship and were hungrily counting out the huge stash of coins, scarcely believing their luck. Even when O'Brien waved his official Barbary pass and explained that this money had been on its way to the dey of Algiers himself, it made no difference: Tripoli was a different statelet with a different ruler. Hassan was incensed and threatened war, but the diplomatic mess took weeks to sort out, and O'Brien did not make it into Algiers with his hoard of coins until October.

★ ★ ★

In the meantime, something unexpectedly wonderful had happened in Algiers itself. By sheer serendipity, a new French diplomat had arrived in the corsair city, laden with lavish gifts for Dey Hassan. It turned out that the consul needed to borrow the equivalent of around $200,000 from the state treasury, one of the few sources of coin around the Mediterranean at that time. Mollified by the presents, the dey agreed. The money was hauled out of the state treasury and counted out in hard cash. The consul, understandably reluctant to trot around the streets of the world's most dangerous city with bags of silver coins, immediately lodged it with Micaiah Baccri's bank.

Word reached US consul Barlow, who leaped at the opportunity. Baccri often had told Barlow that his bank would happily lend money to America if only he'd had the cash at hand. Now he had no excuse, especially since the banker knew that Donaldson had solid collateral in Leghorn. "I immediately asked [the Baccris] to prove the sincerity of their friendship by lending me this sum," Barlow recalled.

And so, the same money was counted out once more and handed over to Barlow, who in turn handed it over to the dey, who replaced it in the treasury as though it had never left the vaults.

Barlow himself modestly described this whole exchange as a lucky "accident," as indeed it was. However, and just as an aside, some commentators have depicted this story as a brilliant coup by Barlow, maintaining that he outsmarted the dey by paying him with his own money. But of course, economics does not work that way. Think about it: if I repay you a $10 loan in a café, using the same $10 that you paid for your coffee and that I received as change from my purchase after you, I am not outsmarting you or paying you back with your own money. In reality, Barlow was paying the dey with the hard-earned money of American taxpayers, albeit money that had taken a long and complex journey through London, Leghorn, Algiers, France, and the Baccris' bank.

The dey agreed to accept Baccri's guarantee for the balance of the ransom money in Leghorn, and the ransom for the American hostages was finally paid in full. That meant that O'Brien's money, which would not reach Algiers for another three months, could instead be used toward the bill for the peace treaty itself.

Joel Barlow became a hero. "The captives speak in terms of the warmest affection for his exertions in rescuing them from this region of horror," according to Isaac Brooks. "To this worthy character, whose heart vibrated with finer feelings of philanthropy while his life was in imminent danger, the most ardent tribute of gratitude is due."

John Foss agreed. "[His] compassionate services for his distressed countrymen can never be estimated too highly, nor praised too much."

Barlow himself described the grateful ex-captives that surrounded him. "What benedictions, what tears of gratitude!" he wrote. "They all said that, without me, and without the operations which have astounded them, they would all have perished [in captivity]. And that is true." He believed the hostages really were indebted to him for their liberty, but "as to the operations, they have attributed to me more than I have done."

That was his nod to the contribution of James Cathcart, whose life had been genuinely in danger—more directly than Barlow's had ever been—and who had forged the treaty that enabled their freedom. At an earlier point, Barlow had openly admitted that peace would probably not have been achieved without Cathcart's dramatic voyage home. Yet the freed prisoners obviously had no knowledge of this, and as a consequence, Cathcart's name was never mentioned.

Instead, Barlow expertly brushed off the praise with just the right degree of bashful modesty that actually allowed him to take nearly all the credit. At one point, he quoted a diplomat from Denmark as saying about him: "The American agent is not a man, he is an angel."

★   ★   ★

When the cheering died down, Barlow knew he had to get his men out of Algiers—and fast. The notoriously capricious dey could change his mind at any moment on any pretext. Barlow chartered one of Micaiah Baccri's ships, *La Fortune*, for immediate departure to Leghorn.

He faced several obstacles. The most urgent problem was the plague, which still raged through the city, killing as many as forty people a day. The disease had recently claimed five American lives. By cramming the men together in a small ship, was he actually sentencing them to death? Yet that choice was his least-worst option. "Although they cannot embark without risk," Barlow concluded, "it is much more dangerous for them to stay."

However, he made the heartbreaking decision to leave one sick man behind in the hospital. Sources disagree on the number of Americans who actually boarded the ship—eighty-five according to Isaac Brooks and eighty-nine according to Joel Barlow.

At 9:00 a.m. on that memorable day, July 11, the scarred and broken survivors filed aboard *La Fortune*. Barlow was moved by pity as he watched the sad procession. "Several of them are probably rendered incapable of gaining a living," he wrote. "One is in a state of total blindness, [another almost blind], two or three carry the marks of unmerciful treatment in ruptures produced by hard labor, others have had their constitutions injured by the plague."

Coming from a dispassionate observer, this was a harrowing description indeed—and one that refutes the notion that the Americans captured in the late 1700s were well-treated in Algiers.

The Americans' last sixty hours in Algiers were tense and uncomfortable. Crammed on board the ship along with the forty-eight ransomed Neapolitans, they waited impatiently from early morning on July 11 until the night of July 13. The Bostoner Captain Calder, formerly of the *Jay*, was given command of the vessel. That evening, he finally took the ship out of harbor. However, he neglected the usual protocol of informing the port officer first.

As they cleared the harbor mouth, the freed captives all cheered and "bade an eternal adieu to the land of bondage." But it wasn't quite that simple or quite that eternal. The departure was a fiasco and all the men on board narrowly escaped death. A fresh west wind blew up, the unpracticed seamen botched the rigging of the sails, an emergency anchor failed, and the ship was swept backward, stern-first, toward the rocks. Totally out of control, she was saved only by the swift intervention of the Algiers port officer, who sailed to the rescue and ordered *La Fortune* to be towed back to harbor. "In a great rage, he struck Captain Calder several blows, and asked him how he dared to get under way before he came," Isaac Brooks recalled.

For the second attempt, the Algerines themselves towed the ship safely out to sea before cutting her loose. But fate was still against the ill-named *Fortune*. Two hours out, one of the Neapolitans took ill with plague, and Captain Calder decided it would be safer to return him to Algiers than to risk a raging contagion belowdecks.

Once they had left Algiers for a third time and were out in the open sea, death stalked the ship the entire voyage. Another Neapolitan died of plague, and the following day they lost an American officer, Captain Samuel Bayley of the *Polly*. Calder immediately ordered the sort of basic sanitary precautions that the Algerines had always disdained: he set up a deck hospital and ordered his crew to perpetually scrub all the surfaces of the ship. Men were not to remain below, but to move around in the open air. The measures proved effective and the outbreak was contained.

Calder knew that a plague ship would not be welcome in Leghorn, so he altered course for the French port of Marseilles—to the great distress of his Neapolitan passengers, whose state was at war with France. (The Neapolitans were jailed but later repatriated.) After eighty days of quarantine, the Americans were cleared, and on November 12, they finally set off in a specially chartered Swedish ship bound for Philadelphia and for home.

★ ★ ★

In the meantime, a lot had been happening back in the Americans' homeland. Two months earlier, in September 1796 James Cathcart had finally landed in Pennsylvania after a long and eventful voyage. He had come very close to running out of cash to fund the expedition: in Spain, he personally spent $100 chartering a ship to take his Moorish crew back to Algiers (rather than simply abandoning them in Spain to make their own way home, as many others might have done). He had been forced to sell a third share in his beloved ship the *Independent* to raise cash for this and for the final transatlantic leg of his journey.

On his arrival in Philadelphia, he had found himself once again overwhelmed with emotion, unable to find the words to express the joy of "standing once more on American soil, after so many years of trial and degradation."

Word of his arrival went straight to the very top, and over dinner at the President's House, he had briefed George Washington about the knife-edge political situation in Algiers.

Once the president's eyes had been opened to the true danger that his citizens were under, he moved fast. He wrote this letter to Dey Hassan:

> To the most excellent and illustrious Vizer Hassan Bashaw, Dey of Algiers.
>
> Health, peace and prosperity.
> I have received your Excellency's letter of 5th of May last, by James Leander Cathcart, informing me that although eight months had then elapsed since peace and harmony had been settled between our two nations, not one article of the agreement had been complied with. This unlooked-for event has been to me a subject of extreme regret. . . .
> It has afforded me great satisfaction that you dispatched Mr. Cathcart to give me more full and exact information. . . . Rest assured that the solicitude of our Government will not cease until the whole shall be accomplished. . . .
> May God long preserve Your Excellency and crown your days with happiness and honor.
> George Washington
> President of the United States.

Washington had promised to rectify the situation, and he was as good as his word. Throughout that autumn, the shipyards were loud with the sound of hammers and saws as they rushed to complete the promised frigate. Meanwhile, officials worked flat-out to assemble the marine stores for Algiers.

In December, President Washington felt confident enough to announce a breakthrough: "After many delays and disappointments . . . the final arrangements for fulfilling the [treaty requirements] will, in all present appearance, be crowned with success."

As a result, in early 1797, Cathcart's ship the *Independent* set sail for Algiers with the first consignment of stores to honor the peace treaty. With almost incredible courage, Cathcart himself had intended to travel back to the North African hellhole with this initial shipment. Instead, he received formal orders to stay in the United States for two years in preparation for returning to Barbary in an official capacity. A diplomatic role would give him some degree of protection in Algiers, because his position was complicated. In May 1796, he had been released on parole. Legally, he had been included in the general redemption of American captives in July 1796, and it seemed obvious that this superseded the May parole. However, it remained to be seen whether the Algerines would see it in the same way. He had not taken part in the formal liberation ceremony there, and had never been issued with the official pass declaring him to be a free man. The dey could easily argue that he was still under an obligation that would not be discharged until his mission was fulfilled. If Cathcart returned to Algiers to find that the dey was not happy with his efforts, could he end up back in captivity? These were grey areas, and nobody in America wanted them to be decided in Barbary on the whim of a capricious ruler.

Sourcing the rest of the stores and gifts for the dey was a nightmare in itself. It turned out that O'Brien and Donaldson had specified certain items without any idea of their stratospheric cost. Some items cost exactly double what they had reckoned. Others were impossible to get; at one point the secretary of state, Timothy Pickering, wrote to Humphreys in exasperation: "The golden coffee pot and salver are omitted, for no such things exist in the United States, which I hope will be admitted as an apology for not furnishing them."

The cost of the project mushroomed to the point that the entire treaty ended up costing the United States close to a million dollars instead of the $500,000 to $600,000 originally estimated. (For context, the entire annual federal budget at the time was just $6.3 million.) O'Brien's brainstorm of offering stores instead of cash had been a good one, but neither he nor Donaldson had had the expertise to price them with any accuracy. If Barlow's claim was true that a good banker's clerk sent to Portugal could have saved the United States $60,000, then a good quantity surveyor sent to Algiers could have saved them a good part of a million.

★ ★ ★

On a freezing February morning in 1797, a Swedish-owned ship named *Jupiter* entered the icebound Delaware River at Marcus Hook in Pennsylvania, carrying the freed American captives. The men's excitement at seeing their homeland was only slightly cooled by the arctic chill—perhaps the greatest possible contrast to the withering heat of the summer they had left behind in Algiers. It was so bitterly cold that their ship was stranded on the icebound river for a day or so.

Throughout the United States, the people of America were waiting to welcome them. "A thrill of joy went through the land," recalled one senator.

When Captain Olaf Schale finally deposited them safely on shore, the first sound they heard was the deafening roar from hundreds of people who had assembled to cheer them home. Carriages would bring the returning heroes all the way to Philadelphia, about twenty miles away, where their route into the city was jammed with well-wishers. A pub opened its doors to throw a welcome home party.

"Upon their arrival at the Indian Queen Tavern," writes one witness, "the streets were so thronged as to render their passage difficult, and as they entered the house, an ardent acclamation expressed the satisfaction of the people at their return."

On the way through the city, one returning captive craned his neck, scanning the crowd for a familiar face that he had not seen for nearly twelve years. Captain Isaac Stephens, master of Cathcart's former ship the *Maria*, was desperately searching for his loyal wife Hannah, who during his years in captivity had moved mountains in a bid to get her husband home again. Stephens must have been tense with nervous anticipation. Would Hannah even recognize him at this stage? If she did, would she still feel the same toward him?

He was not disappointed. Hannah had been running through the throng of former captives, searching for Isaac. At last, their eyes met and Hannah burst out of the crowd to fling her arms around him.

The new president-elect, John Adams, was there to witness their emotional reunion. As we've seen, Adams came from Braintree, the same small town where Isaac and Hannah had married, and he recognized the forty-nine-year-old seaman immediately. "Captain Stephens is among them," Adams wrote to his wife Abigail. "A woman rushed into the crowd and picked out her husband, whom she has not seen for fourteen years. *I am and ever shall be yours and no other's.*"

Apart from recording that emotional scene (and getting the duration of Stephens's captivity wrong), Adams was surprisingly curt in his account of the captives' homecoming. "The prisoners from Algiers arrived yesterday in this city," he wrote tersely, "in good health and looking very well."

Two other men from the *Maria* accompanied Stephens: his mate, Alexander Forsyth, and the seaman Thomas Billings. Since Cathcart and George Smith had both left Algiers before the redemption, this meant—quite remarkably—that the half dozen strong band of brothers from the *Maria* had lost only one man in their eleven years in Algiers. This was, of course, the unfortunate James Harnet, who'd died insane in a dungeon.

The other ship captured in 1785, the *Dauphin*, had not fared as well. Only one of its crew, First Mate Andrew Montgomery, had been included in this mass ransom. More than half the *Dauphin*'s complement of fifteen men had died in Algiers—seven of plague and one of consumption. Three had been redeemed by friends, one freed in a sea battle, one ransomed in a peace deal by the Dutch, and one—Captain Richard O'Brien—sent from Algiers to find cash for the treaty.

Altogether, only sixty-five men were recorded as returning to Philadelphia in February 1797, although seventeen more made their way home separately from Marseilles. Those seventeen included John Foss of the brig *Polly*, which had lost five of its original nine crew to plague.

It's reckoned that 133 Americans had been held in Algiers at various times between 1785 and 1796, and more than ninety got out alive at different times: a survival rate of (roughly) two of every three. Cathcart's ship *Maria*, with its extraordinarily high ratio of survivors, was obviously an outlier. There were two reasons. First, given its small complement of six men, it had a greater proportion of officers who were excused from the plague prisons and the hardest labor. Second, Americans were regarded as such a novelty in Algiers in 1785 that the other crewmen were originally given jobs as palace workers, a perk that most later arrivals did not enjoy.

★ ★ ★

While he was working to fulfill the terms of the treaty, Cathcart had no official job title or income. Pickering assured him that President Washington wanted him to be given a position but added sorrowfully: "At present there [is] no vacancy." Soon Cathcart was destitute. He'd had to bear the full expenses of his mission and lamented that he had "never received one cent either for my services or maintenance since I left Algiers."

Cathcart wanted to be appointed US consul in Algiers—a role for which he was uniquely qualified. However, in the class system of the late 1700s, this was a huge ask. He was a basic seaman who had only recently become a captain. And, unknown to Cathcart, Joel Barlow had been busily poisoning the air against him. In one letter to the secretary of state, Barlow delivered this crushing put-down: "I am told that Mr. Cathcart has hopes of obtaining the consulate to this place. He has neither the talents nor the dignity of character necessary for the purpose."

Coming from a former salesman for a firm of property scammers, that was a bit rich. Nevertheless, Barlow added: "I sincerely wish that he might be employed in the business of the peace present and tribute, in which I think his intelligence and industry would enable him to render essential service."

Richard O'Brien was regarded as the natural choice for consul, and so he became. However, Cathcart was appointed as US consul for the neighboring Barbary state of Tripoli.

Meanwhile, word arrived from Algiers that Dey Hassan had developed gangrene in his leg and died. Cathcart wrote no eulogies for the man who had been both his guardian angel and his relentless persecutor. He later frequently would describe him as a "tyrant" and a "despot." If he felt any emotion due to the dey's passing, he never recorded it.

In early January 1799, the new US consul for Tripoli boarded the travel-worn brig *Sophia* (O'Brien's former ship) on his way to his post in Barbary. But first, he had outstanding business to settle. He was sailing to the Mediterranean as part of a fleet carrying the articles required to finalize the peace deal that he'd made with the late dey.

James Cathcart was going back to Algiers.

★   ★   ★

Thirteen days after his return to the corsair city, Cathcart was summoned to an audience with Dey Muhammad, the new ruler of Algiers. It must have been a nerve-racking experience, since there was no telling how the new ruler would react to him—after all, Cathcart had been Hassan's protégé, and Muhammad hated his predecessor so much that no one at court was even allowed to mention his name.

The familiar trek up the well-worn stone staircase must have been a dizzying experience for the man who had last trod them as a captive bereft of any human rights and who now was returning as a diplomat empowered by his government. However, Muhammad officially welcomed him as the consul for Tripoli and sent him onward with his good wishes.

The frigate *Crescent* was officially handed over to the state of Algiers. (After the change of regime, there was no longer any question of the ship being given to the late dey's daughter Fatima.) The treaty obligations were almost complete, but there was a last-minute hiccup when Dey Muhammad—predictably—demanded an extra frigate as a personal gift for himself. After a lot of hard bargaining, he agreed to accept some stores instead, and at long last the treaty between the Regency and the United States was finalized.

Cathcart's time in Algiers was over, and his new life as a diplomat on the world stage was just beginning.

JAMES CATHCART'S LEGACY

Today, the name of James Leander Cathcart has been almost forgotten.

Yet his contemporaries—including two US presidents—were lavish and generous in their praise of the man who saved the peace at a time when his country was under clear and present danger.

Perhaps the most eloquent tribute to Cathcart came from President Thomas Jefferson, who said he had built up "a pretty full acquaintance" with him when they were both in Philadelphia. "He is personally known to me," he wrote in February 1802. "He is the honestest and ablest consul we have with the Barbary powers: a man of very sound judgement, and fearless." Nearly twenty years later, Jefferson wrote to Cathcart personally praising "your integrity and experience."

A later president, John Quincy Adams, praised Cathcart's "long, faithful and important services" to the United States.

David Humphreys, the US ambassador to Portugal, was equally generous in his praise: "I consider [him] a very faithful and diligent public officer," he wrote.

Peter Erik Skjoldebrand, who served as American agent in Algiers, wrote that Cathcart had "rendered . . . his country signal services" and that America would "never have obtained peace on the favorable terms on which it was concluded, had it not been for [his] exertions for years."

And, as we've seen, even the hypercritical Joel Barlow praised his "considerable service" and his "intelligence and zeal."

Robert Montgomery, American consul to Spain, went even further when he praised Cathcart's human qualities—particularly his generosity toward the less fortunate Americans during a dark period in their captivity. He referred to Cathcart's "goodness of heart and humane disposition" and lauded his "good services and friendship to our fellow citizens." This was all the more surprising, he said, because Cathcart easily could have enjoyed the benefits of his own rise to power and ignored his less fortunate comrades. Montgomery found this particularly moving because, in his experience, it was uncommon to find it in a person who "by the caprice of fortune" had escaped from bleak captivity "to become the favorite and useful Secretary of a Prince."

With such glowing tributes clearly on the record from such high-level sources, it is disheartening to see how Cathcart is depicted in those few modern writings in which he is mentioned at all. (In many cases he is simply airbrushed out of history: all his achievements are credited to Donaldson or Barlow.) The casual reader comes away with the impression that James Cathcart was—at best—a helpful messenger boy or—at worst—a collaborator who joined the bureaucracy in Algiers, thereby taking sides against his own countrymen and helping to disunite them. This book has presented enough evidence to show that Cathcart was far more than a messenger—as Peter Skjoldebrand attests, he was an energetic, fearless, and proactive voice for America at a time when everyone else seemed to be trapped under a dark spell of lethargy and inaction. Robert Montgomery's tribute confirms that he used his elevated position to help his American comrades rather than to subjugate or control them. As his fellow prisoners drifted further and further apart, divided by the contemporary obsession with social class, Cathcart was a meritocrat who became a powerful unifying factor rather than a divisive one.

James Cathcart was the very first citizen of the newly independent United States to be taken hostage in Algiers. He did not ask for that destiny. Once there, he had none of the privileges of the officers: as a basic seaman, he seemed fated to be a grunt worker, shifted back and forth among whatever tasks his overseers allotted him. Cathcart's remarkable achievement was that he refused to accept that role passively. Right from the start, when he found himself resenting the Spanish female captive's attempt to "reconcile everyone to their fate," he refused to be cast in the role of a human beast of burden. His only weapons against his temporary overlords were his talents: his language skills, his personal charm, his formidable networking skills, and what we would now call emotional intelligence.

As a young lad of twenty laboring in the palace gardens, he laid down his marker from the beginning. He would not yield to the psychological torture of his bosses. Instead, he very firmly let them know that he would maintain his dignity and individuality. Their savage beatings—he was bastinadoed three times—did not break his spirit.

He understood how the system worked and used it to rise steadily up the ladder, aided by a series of "guardian angels" whom he had won over with the sheer positive force of his personality. And this must indeed have been a potent force: otherwise, he would never have won over so many powerful friends who trusted him so much that they took enormous risks to help him rise out of the stinking bagnios toward the pleasant and airy rooms of the bureaucracy. Cathcart would never have won their enduring friendship if he had had a negative or off-putting personality—at least at that stage in his life. On the contrary, he was very obviously an intelligent, humorous, and amiable young man, a person whom most people liked instinctively. Flawed, absolutely. Ambitious, of course. Cynical, yes. Self-serving, to a point. But he never forgot his comrades once he had risen to power.

No one knows how many lives he saved by providing free meals to his malnourished comrades after their grueling twelve-hour shifts at the docks and the quarry. Admittedly, his decision to become a tavern-keeper was not entirely altruistic, because the role also made him prosperous and influential; but, as Montgomery points out, he did not *have* to help his fellow citizens. The fact that Cathcart remained in Algiers even when he had enough money to pay his own ransom was proof enough of his good intentions. He also ensured that plague victims had a decent burial and intervened, over and over again, to protect his officers from the worst effects of the work details. When his fellow bar owners—all hostages like himself—were threatened with jail and five hundred bastinadoes, he risked everything to save them.

Human beings are never angels nor demons. I see Cathcart as more of a flawed antihero, a bit cynical and selfish but with a good heart that would never allow him to turn his back on his friends. As I mentioned earlier, if we think of Humphrey Bogart's depiction of the fictive bar owner Rick in *Casablanca*, we probably are not too far from the truth.

Born a quarter of a millennium ago, Cathcart cannot be expected to be a modern man. Because his views were so advanced in certain ways—anti-Islamophobia, anti-class prejudice, emotionally intelligent—it sometimes jolts the researcher to be reminded that he was a man of his time. He fell in line with some thought patterns and behavioral standards that today would raise eyebrows to say the least. This book does not attempt to nominate him for sainthood but simply to present the fascinating tale of an everyman struggling to survive under extreme pressure in a foreign land and an alien culture during one of the most explosive decades in world history.

Politically, his achievement can be summarized in a few words: through his quick thinking, courage, daring, and ingenuity, he bought precious time for the infant United States to build a navy with which it could successfully challenge the Barbary States before those predators could deal a deathblow to the new nation's morale. The new navy went on to do exactly that during the conflicts that have become known as the First and Second Barbary Wars, and many historians agree that its first test of strength gave America a new sense of confidence and unity.

Writing a quarter century after the event, Cathcart analyzed his own contribution: "I arrived at the highest station a Christian could attain, which enabled me to render essential service to my country in laying the basis of our first treaty with Algiers, at the risk of my life, and on very favorable terms, considering that at this period we had more than one hundred of our fellow citizens in chains, and not one vessel of war afloat to protect our commerce."

He went on: "My life was for many months in jeopardy in consequence of my exertions to repress the Dey's impatience. . . . To prevent a rupture,

I purchased a polacre at Algiers, manned her with Moors, and navigated her at my own expense, with dispatches to Alicante, Lisbon and Philadelphia, and a letter from the Dey to [President] George Washington, which ensured a further respite of nine months . . . and preserved the peace of the nation."

Without Cathcart's work on the 1795 treaty and his epic dash to America, the peace negotiations would have become deadlocked, the influence of the rapacious corsair captains would have overridden the less hawkish instincts of the dey, and American seamen would have been captured by the hundreds, and perhaps thousands, by the Barbary States before the United States was in any position to wage war. (And by that stage, the presence of so many American hostages in Barbary would have left the navy at a considerable disadvantage.)

Joseph Donaldson's treaty, which surprised everyone at home due to its supposed ease, had not come easily at all. Cathcart's work in enemy territory had laid down the landing lights: persuading the dey, with great difficulty, to allow Donaldson to come to Algiers at all; negotiating calmly between the two men while the shadow of the executioner's scimitar hung over his head; brilliantly outwitting the scheming French consul; arranging the dramatic stagecraft of Donaldson's fake "exit" that forced Hassan's hand; cleverly adapting an earlier treaty at high speed to enable a quick signature; formulating the killer argument that allowed the dey to sell the deal to his snarling, impatient corsair captains; and, of course, using his own ship, at his own expense, to dash to Philadelphia to save the peace. The treaty deal could have fallen apart due to any one of those obstacles, but Cathcart ensured that, at each point, it survived. His unique contribution to the early history of the United States has never been fully recognized and possibly never will be, but perhaps this book will help in some small way to remedy the oversight.

Afterlives

A relived life I wish for.

—Isaac Stephens

In alphabetical order . . .

John and Abigail Adams moved into the President's House in Philadelphia one month after they welcomed home the Algiers captives in 1797. John succeeded George Washington and, in 1800, became the first president to occupy the White House. He built the US Navy. Abigail died in 1818, leaving a historical treasure trove of wise and perceptive letters. She shares with Barbara Bush the distinction of being the wife of one US president and the mother of another (in her case, John Quincy Adams, 1825–1829). John Adams died, aged ninety, in 1826.

Joel Barlow stayed in Algiers until July 1797 and hated every minute of it. Upon leaving, a surly Barlow said that he was handing all of Barbary back to the devil. He helped draft the peace treaty for Tripoli, including its controversial clause stating that the US government was "not in any sense founded on the Christian religion." After reuniting with his wife in Paris, he returned to America where he worked on his enormous epic poem *The Columbiad*. However, he is best known today for his lighthearted early poem *The Hasty Pudding*, which appears in many school poetry textbooks. A town in Ohio bears his surname.

Interesting fact: According to one biographer, this man who helped to liberate more than seven dozen captives from Algiers returned to America—and bought a Black couple to serve as his personal slaves in his Washington household. (He later sold them for $400 but stipulated in the deal that they should be freed after another six years of work.)

Barlow's death was Tolstoyan. He became caught up in the French army's retreat from Russia and died of exposure, aged fifty-eight, in a Polish village during Christmas 1812.

Isaac Brooks, the sailor and journal keeper who was captured along with John Thomas in the ship *President*, went almost totally blind in Algiers as a result of "the miseries of this unparalleled servitude." Back home in Philadelphia, he turned this challenge into an advantage by dictating his memories of life in Algiers to a ghostwriter named James Wilson Stevens. His accounts were featured in a best-selling book with the unelectrifying title *An Historical and Geographical Account of Algiers*. Stevens paid tribute to Brooks as "a gentleman of veracity and intelligence." The book was dedicated to Joel Barlow.

James Cathcart lived to seventy-six. His near half-century of life post-Algiers must be reserved for another book, but here's a quick gallop through it.

His tenure as a consul in Tripoli ended abruptly in 1801 when the pasha had the flagstaff at the US consulate chopped down in a declaration of war. The conflict that later became known as the First Barbary War lasted until 1805 and established the reputation of the new American navy—as celebrated in the phrase "the shores of Tripoli" in the "Marines' Hymn." After a US naval blockade of Tripoli proved unsuccessful, Cathcart helped concoct a plan to provoke a regime change. A force of four hundred men under General William Eaton marched across five hundred miles of desert and were about to move toward the capital when a peace deal was brokered. Cathcart went on to serve as US consul in Leghorn, Madeira, and later Cadiz before taking domestic positions.

It would be nice to report that he lived happily ever after, but he was as damaged as one might expect of a man who had been subjected to severe physical and psychological torture during nearly eleven years of traumatic captivity. Crippled by rheumatism in limbs that had been distorted by systematic beatings and hard labor, he became increasingly crabbed and querulous. Jobless in his fifties, he was forced to write humiliating letters to his government seeking employment. He married and raised a family of twelve children—born in different places around the world—whom he described as "my wandering tribe of Africans, Italians, Spaniards, Portuguese and Americans."

He died on October 6, 1843. It was only after his death that the government finally agreed to pay $30,000 to his family in compensation for the huge personal expense he'd incurred in saving the peace with Algiers.

John Foss, the American hostage and indefatigable diarist, took a very long time getting home. When most of his freed countrymen headed directly home from Marseilles, Foss volunteered as first mate on a trading mission in the Mediterranean, along with a captain and fourteen crewmen who were all former US captives from Algiers. Staying with the same ship, *La Fortune*, they sailed to Bona, near Algiers, to pick up a cargo of wheat to bring back to Marseilles. But near the coast of France, they were captured by two British ships, taken to Elba, and given the choice of either joining the Royal Navy or being left stranded. A few crewmen agreed to join the navy but Foss and the others—abandoned in Elba without money or clothes—refused and had to beg a passage back to Leghorn on another ship.

After much shuttling around the Mediterranean, he finally secured a ticket on a passenger ship to Philadelphia. On the way he was captured again, three times, by Spanish and French privateers and once again by the Royal Navy. On each occasion he was set free.

Foss hadn't even cleared the Mediterranean when he was captured for a fifth time near Gibraltar, again by privateers from Spain. By this time Foss was growing antsy, and he lashed out with a sword, wounding one of his attackers on the arm. He was chained up and thrown into a dungeon in Ceuta in Spanish North Africa.

Once he was freed and headed for America, his troubles didn't end. A Spanish privateer attacked his homebound ship in the open Atlantic and stripped it of almost all its provisions before setting it loose. The men subsisted for forty days on a starvation ration of less than one biscuit a day until they were lucky enough to encounter an American ship and obtain food and water. Foss finally arrived in Philadelphia in April, promptly fell ill, and did not arrive home in Newburyport until late August—more than a year after leaving Algiers. He was one of only four survivors of the brig *Polly*.

John Foss had written his diary in Algiers in an attempt to take his mind off the daily drudgery of his life as a captive. He thought no one would ever read it, but when it was published in two editions in 1798, it became an instant success and was the forerunner of a series of similar "captivity narratives." It remains a valuable resource for historians of this period.

Hassan, Dey of Algiers, died in 1798 after a reign of seven years, when a leg wound was left untreated and became gangrenous. Although utterly ruthless and unprincipled, Hassan had the vision to see the potential of the United States as a trading partner in the modern sense but missed the opportunity to drag Algiers out of the medieval era. Just like every dey before him, he was stuck firmly in the piratical hit-and-run ethos of an earlier epoch and could not adapt to a changing world that would soon be carved up by giants of commerce and naval superpowers.

David Humphreys, the US minister in Lisbon, moved on to Madrid and served two years there before leaving the diplomatic corps. His later life was surprising: he obtained permission from the Spanish government to import a hundred merino sheep into America, and, after their superior quality wool proved an instant sensation in the New World, he became acknowledged as the founder of the US woolen industry. A celebrated wit, he also wrote a hit play, *The Yankee in England*, that introduced the stock character of the innocently comical "Yankee" abroad, which remained popular as a theatrical and Hollywood stereotype until the mid-1900s. He died in Connecticut in 1818.

Thomas Jefferson became, of course, the third president of the United States in March 1801 and served two terms. His presidency is remembered for his tough stance against the Barbary corsairs and for the United States' westward expansion. Later, he went on to found the University of Virginia. Apart from his master achievement, the Declaration of Independence, he is best known today for his quirky neo-Palladian mansion Monticello. His shining reputation as a champion of equality has dimmed in the modern era with the increasing acknowledgment—hardly a revelation—that he owned hundreds of slaves and enthusiastically encouraged others to invest in this free source of human labor. Most historians now accept that he fathered four children with his enslaved concubine Sally Hemmings, whom he never formally emancipated. However flawed, Jefferson remains a towering figure in world history.

Richard O'Brien remained as US consul in Algiers until 1803. During that tense time he had a dramatic falling-out with his old friend Cathcart. The power balance between the two consuls had shifted dramatically—they were now equals—and there was tension in the air when they met for dinner in Algiers.

The dispute began over a trivial matter, with Cathcart cantankerously refusing O'Brien's request that they be joined at the meal by a young female employee from Cathcart's traveling entourage. It somehow escalated into a furious row. Harsh words were exchanged, and the young woman resigned in tears. O'Brien arranged temporary accommodation for her in Algiers, and the couple ended up marrying, much to Cathcart's annoyance.

The quarrel festered, and this epic huff between the two US consuls proved a major handicap for American political decision making in North Africa.

The O'Briens had a long and happy marriage and went on to have a family of eight children—four sons and four daughters, half of them born in Barbary. After returning to America in 1805, O'Brien set up house in Philadelphia and went back to work in the merchant marine until one of his sons was lost at sea. He bought a farm, settled down, and entered state politics.

Like Cathcart, he faced an uphill struggle to reclaim his expenses from the government. He received some compensation in 1820, but he never lived to see his family receive the full amount due to him. In the meantime, US politicians had begun the usual revisionism, looking back on his career with a jaundiced eye. "[His] only qualification for being Consul was his having been ten years in Algiers," John Quincy Adams grumbled sourly. In 1824, Richard

O'Brien died—or as the incorrigible old sea dog might have put it, he finished his last watch on the ship of life as he rounded Cape Demise.

Captain Isaac Stephens, master of the *Maria*, returned home to an emotional reunion with his loyal wife Hannah. However, he complained that the government refused to give him any financial assistance and he ended up "dependent and very indigent," along with so many others among the former American hostages from Algiers who were welcomed home but soon forgotten.

As we've seen, the returnees of 1797 enjoyed a rapturous reception in a bar in Philadelphia. However, when the celebrations ended and the pub closed its doors, the party ended on a decidedly sour note. Those who lived far away, in Boston or New York, found themselves abruptly stranded in the bitterly cold streets of the icebound city. The citizens' welcome extended only so far. "They were left entirely destitute," wrote one witness, "to wander the streets of the city at that inclement season of the year, without friends or a single cent to provide for their subsistence."

It was a harbinger of their future lives, because during the following years the government was reluctant to provide any financial assistance to its traumatized, vulnerable, and often disabled citizens who had suffered so much in Algiers.

Three months after his return, we find Isaac Stephens writing a letter to President John Adams reminding him of the "misfortunes" of his life in captivity and pleading for a position as a lighthouse keeper on Cape Cod. He didn't get the job. A year later he told Adams that he had been given "no employ . . . of any kind" since his return, although he said pointedly that his counterpart Richard O'Brien had since "done very well for himself." Isaac moved from Concord to Boston in 1798. Adams recommended Isaac for a position with a sailmaker, but he did not get that job either. A year later, Stephens wrote once more to the president, saying: "Distress wrings the soul. . . . I do not ask for great appointments, [just] something small to keep me from sinking to the bottom." The letter finishes with an almost audible sigh: "A relived life I wish for: so long in Algiers." And on that sad note, both Isaac and Hannah fade from history.

★   ★   ★

As for Algiers itself, by the nineteenth century, the writing was on the wall for "the corsair city." The United States had built up its navy, and when a later dey resumed capturing Americans in the early 1800s (maintaining its long tradition of breaking peace agreements) the United States sent a fighting fleet under Commodore Stephen Decatur to quell the menace once and for all.

After some heated action—the Second Barbary War—the dey of that era backed down and promised never to capture American hostages again.

This was the beginning of the end for Algiers. In August 1816, the British admiral Lord Exmouth blasted the city into submission with an awesome bombardment of shells, rockets, 500 tons of shot, and 118 tons of powder. He forced the dey to agree to stop capturing "Christians" but rather shamefully allowed him to continue capturing and exploiting free labor from captives who did not fall into that category. However, Exmouth did not follow up his victory, so, in all other ways, nothing much changed in Algiers—until 1830.

Now you may recall Hassan's super-indulged daughter Fatima, who received Barlow's valuable silver trunk on her dad's bored whim and who was even offered her own warship by the United States? (The frigate *Crescent* ultimately was given directly to the State of Algiers, whereupon it was renamed *El Merkane* and allowed to rot away by the Algerines, who had to break it up in 1806.) Fatima had a close-up view of the final collapse of the corsair city. She married a man named Hussein, who served as the last dey of Algiers from 1815 to 1830. Hussein's term as dey ended, along with three centuries of Barbary rule, after he arrogantly swiped at a French consul with his fly whisk. That was mild by Algerine standards (remember, a previous French consul had been shot from a cannon), but France took great offense and sent thirty-four thousand troops to take over the city. Hussein, Fatima, and their family fled the country. Left in full control, the French victors embarked on a vengeful fury of murder and looting, which set the tone for their colonization of Algeria. The new boss was, if anything, worse than the old boss. However, the corsairs of Algiers no longer prowled the seas capturing mariners at will. The long era of the Barbary pirates was effectively over. They would not be missed.

Notes

$\mathcal{T}$his is a factual narrative based almost entirely upon primary sources—that is, letters and reports written in real time by the main participants; their recollections after the event; and some histories written during the Barbary era. For this reason, and also because this is not intended as an academic work, I have not compiled a bibliography listing the scores of authors who have since analyzed this fascinating period in US history.

The main players are also referred to by their initials—JC for James Cathcart, TJ for Thomas Jefferson, and so on—which I hope will be obvious from the text. To avoid confusion, initials that are employed as abbreviations for frequently used sources are marked with a double asterisk; a key for those follows.

ABBREVIATIONS USED

★★FO: *Founders Online*, the portal provided by the US National Archives for public access to the historical documents of the founders of the United States, with helpful explanatory footnotes. Speedy, efficient, clearly laid out, and a joy to use. Highly recommended.

★★JLC/JBN-TC: James Leander Cathcart and J. B. Newkirk, *The Captives: Eleven Years a Prisoner in Algiers* (La Porte, Indiana: Herald Print, 1899).

★★ND: *Naval Documents Related to the United States Wars with the Barbary Powers, Volume 1: 1785–1801* (Bolton Landing, New York: American Naval Records Society, 1939), published under direction of Claude A. Swanson and supervision of Captain Dudley W. Knox. Also highly recommended.

CHAPTER 1

JC first captive: JC to James Madison, Nov. 30, 1803, ★★FO.

Capture of Maria: Thomas Jefferson, *Report* to Congress on U.S. citizens in captivity in Algiers, Dec. 28, 1790, ★★ND, p. 18; *List of American Prisoners*, July 9, 1790, ★★ND, p. 1; M. Carey, *A Short Account of Algiers* (Philadelphia: J. Parker, 1794), p. 41.

United States had no national navy: The Continental Navy of 1775 had been disbanded and the last of its ships (*Alliance*) was sold off that same summer of 1785. The cash-strapped new nation was trying to get by without one.

Captain and crew: ★★JLC/JBN-TC, p. 274. Note: endless confusion has been caused by the names Thomas Billings and John Gregory, who appear to be one and the same man: for some reason he used an alias.

Cargo and name of Algerine Rais: from Cathcart family oral history as recalled by JC's granddaughter-in-law, interviewed by Eleanor Lee Reading Templeman, *Arlington Heritage: Vignettes of a Virginia County* (Arlington, VA: E. Templeman, 1959).

Twenty-six days, location: Richard O'Brien to TJ, Aug. 24, 1785, ★★FO.

"Without strength . . . contemptible": ★★JLC/JBN-TC, p. 4.

"To escape . . .": John Foss, *A Journal of the Captivity and Sufferings of John Foss* (Newburyport, MA: Angier March, 1798), p. 10.

Betsey capture: TJ, *Report on Mediterranean Trade*, Dec. 28, 1790, ★★ND, p. 22. The captain was James Erving.

Passports, notched sticks, forgeries: Carey, *A Short Account of Algiers*, pp. 41–42; ★★JLC/JBN-TC, p. 5.

Stephens was straight shooter: e.g., in his letter to John Adams, Oct. 24, 1787, ★★FO; magazines and history, IS to JA, Feb. 7, 1786, ★★FO.

First foreign war: The First Barbary War (1801–1805) against Tripoli would be the first to be fought on foreign soil. There would be a quasi-war against France in 1798, but it was undeclared and fought at sea by privateers.

Sleeping conditions, sleep impossible: Foss, *A Journal of the Captivity and Sufferings of John Foss*, p. 13.

Prisoner before: See next chapter.

CHAPTER 2

JC early life, Seth Harding: ★★JLC/JBN-TC, preface.

Learned languages, navigation, "learned how to survive," "liberated at end of war": Cathcart family history in Eleanor Lee Reading Templeman, *Arlington Heritage: Vignettes of a Virginia County* (Arlington, VA: E. Templeman, 1959).

Harding career; Tyrannicide, Penobscot; prison ships, conditions of prisoners: Gardner W. Allen, *Naval History of the Revolution*, vol. 2 (Boston: Houghton Mifflin, 1913), chap. XII and XVIII; Harding capture, p. 556.

"Attempts to escape": Allen, *Naval History of the Revolution*, p. 649.

JC escape: ★★JLC/JBN-TC, preface.

JC on xebec, Spanish woman: ★★JLC/JBN-TC, p. 4.

Marriage in Braintree, Hannah's early surname and her birthplace: *Records of the Town of Braintree 1640 to 1793*, p. 876.

IS born in Braintree; "by misfortunes . . .": IS to JA, Apr. 15, 1786, ★★FO.

Moved to Concord: *Memorial from Hannah Stephens Requesting the Release of Her Husband from Prison in Algiers*, Dec. 9, 1791, Records of US Senate.

Status of sea captain, "high repute," future prospects, dangers at sea, widows, Boston pubs, "lowest ranks": Clark Joseph Strickland, "Who Was Jack Tar? Aspects of the Social History of Boston, Mass. Seamen 1700–1770" (thesis, College of William and Mary, 1972).

Master's earnings, seaman's earnings at that time: US Department of Labor, *History of Wages in the United States*.

Two Italians, de la Cruz mate on Leghorn ship, etc.: ★★JLC/JBN-TC, pp. 120–22; Angelo d'Andreis, ★★JLC/JBN-TC, p. 156; JC to Thos Appleton, Nov. 27, 1800; Boston fiancée Sarah Moody, *Records of Trinity Church Boston*, vol. 56, Oct. 9, 1785. (Angelo's name is often spelled "Angiolo"—I have used the spelling from the legal documents in Boston.)

CHAPTER 3

"At the distance . . .": ★★JLC/JBN-TC, p. 88.

"The town appears . . .": Carey, *A Short Account of Algiers*, p. 7.

Snow bank comparison: Foss, *A Journal of the Captivity and Sufferings of John Foss*, p. 41.

White marble, etc.: John Clark Kennedy, *Algeria and Tunis* (London: Colburn, 1845), pp. 3–5.

"Detestable place": in Charles Burr Todd, ed., *Life and Letters of Joel Barlow* (New York: Putnam, 1886), p. 126.

"Demonstrations of joy . . .": ★★JLC/JBN-TC, pp. 82, 89.

Facedown, etc.: Foss, *A Journal of the Captivity and Sufferings of John Foss*, p. 13.

Woman separated, captives' first night, unloading, parade: ★★JLC/JBN-TC, pp. 8, 61, 78.

Barlow quotes: Todd, *Life and Letters of Joel Barlow*, pp. 116, 126.

"The roofs are flat . . .": Carey, *A Short Account of Algiers*, p. 7.

Barrels: *A Journal of the Captivity and Sufferings of John Foss*, p. 29.

"Drunkard" and "unsavoury reputation": Report of Dr Philip Werner, 1788; also recommended: ★★FO editorial notes to Isaac Stephens–John Adams, Feb. 7, 1786, and to Jefferson's *Report on Mediterranean Trade*, ★★ND, p. 22.

Logie role in captures, "allegiance": ★★JLC/JBN-TC, p. 4.

Weaponize, emissaries, Lord Sheffield, "turn loose": Lord John Sheffield, *Observations of the Commerce of the American States* (London: Debrett, 1784); Carey, *A Short Account of Algiers*, pp. 44–45.

Badistan: ★★JLC/JBN-TC, pp. 11–12.

Rev. Ólafur Egilsson (1564-1639) *The Travels of Rev. Ólafur Egilsson* in *Litil Saga* (Reykjavik, 1852), p. 23.

Questioning: Laurent D'Arvieux, *Mémoires du Chevalier d'Arvieux* (Paris, 1735).

"The crier . . .": Carey, *A Short Account of Algiers*, p. 17.

Sitting in a circle: Perceval Lord, *Algiers with Notices* . . . (London: Whittaker, 1835), vol. 2, p. 58.

Result of auction: ★★JLC/JBN-TC, p. 11.

CHAPTER 4

Palace, cats, pigeons, lions, executions: ★★JLC/JBN-TC, pp. 93, 100.

Barlow quote: Todd, *Life and Letters of Joel Barlow*, p. 127.

"The criminal . . .": James Wilson Stevens, *An Historical and Geographical Account of Algiers* (Philadelphia: Hogan, 1797), p. 250.

Velvet pillows: ★★JLC/JBN-TC, chap. 5.

Mahmood biography, era of stability: Maurice Le Clercq, *Le Tombeau des cinq deys d'Alger* (Clairmont, 1888), pp. 46– .

Amount in treasury: $15 million, RoB to the Irwins, Dec. 20, 1788, ★★FO; Michael Morphy to Secretary of State, Dec. 4, 1793, estimates $20–$30 million in total, ★★ND; Barlow estimates $54 million, see JB to Secretary of State, Mar. 18, 1796, ★★ND.

"One for gold . . ." quote and harem description: Kennedy, *Algeria and Tunis*, pp. 21, 19; harem and fate of women captives, Stevens, *An Historical and Geographical Account of Algiers*, p. 242.

Cleaner theft: Stevens, *An Historical and Geographical Account of Algiers*, p. 267.

Paga Lunas (moon payers): ★★JLC/JBN-TC, p. 139. Sometimes called "papalunas"— a corruption of the same term, *paga luna* or *pagar luna* in lingua franca.

Jobs allocated to crewmen: ★★JLC/JBN-TC, p. 12. Two were made "upper servants" in the palace—one of them was George Smith, who was appointed page to the dey (RoB to TJ, July 12, 1790). Two, JC and Harnet, were sent to the gardens; if we ignore Stephens, that leaves one man sent to menial work in the kitchen (certainly Billings rather than the higher ranked Forsyth), leaving Forsyth the mate as a temporary upper servant before his discharge as a *Paga Luna*.

Scavenger, garden, lionkeeping, work, rules, chamberlains, alchemy, Genoan, JC beating, depression, "being confident . . .": ★★JLC/JBN-TC, pp. 13–31.

JC put in charge of lions: According to Cathcart family history, via Templeman, *Arlington Heritage: Vignettes of a Virginia County*.

Problems of lionkeeping (enclosure, necessary space, stress in captivity): A. H. Shoemaker, E. J. Maruska, and R. Rockwell, "Minimum Husbandry Guidelines for Mammals: Large Felids," American Association of Zoos and Aquariums; "Captive Big Cat Welfare Issues (Factsheet)," The Humane Society of the United States.

CHAPTER 5

Capture of Dauphin: US Consular Archives at Tunis, RoB *Narrative*, ★★ND, p. 115; Thomas Jefferson *Report* to Congress on US citizens in captivity in Algiers, Dec. 28, 1790, ★★ND, p. 18; *List of American Prisoners*, July 9, 1790, ★★ND, p. 1; Carey, *A Short Account of Algiers*, p. 41; date, location, course, RoB to TJ, Aug. 24, 1785, ★★FO; three captains to John Adams, Aug. 27, 1785, ★★FO; RoB to Irwins, Dec. 20, 1788, ★★FO; Mathew Irwin to George Washington, July 9, 1789, ★★FO with editorial notes; ★★JLC/JBN-TC, pp. 5, 17, 274. (Note: The *Dauphin* is incorrectly referred to as the *Dolphin* in some contemporary documents.)

RoB as old sea dog, JQA quote, Smollett comparison: John Quincy Adams *Memoirs of John Quincy Adams vol. 4 1795-1848* (Philadelphia, 1875), p. 403; Cathcart made the same comparison, see ★★JLC/JBN-TC, p. 170; also see maritime phrases (e.g., "it blows a heavy gale of wind") regularly used to describe political problems throughout RoB correspondence in ★★ND.

JQA on RoB: Eugene Schuyler, *American Commerce* (New York: Scribner, 1886), p. 206.

RoB birthplace: There are conflicting versions of his early life. This is from his obit in *The American Volunteer*, Feb. 19, 1824. He was, in any case, a proud Irish American.

Captives on board Dauphin: ★★JLC/JBN-TC, p. 274; *List of Prisoners*, ★★ND, p. 1; RoB to Irwins, Dec. 20, 1788.

Coffin consumptive: ★★JLC/JBN-TC, p. 24.

Tessanaer French passenger: List of Prisoners; TJ to JP Jones, June 1, 1792, ★★ND.

Sloan: Foss, *A Journal of the Captivity and Sufferings of John Foss*, p. 57. More in chap. 21.

Colvill: More in chap. 14.

Crew numbers and conscripts: RoB *Narrative*, ★★JLC/JBN-TC, pp. 81–82.

"One third . . .": RoB to TJ, June 8, 1786, ★★ND, p. 3.

Janissaries, cacophony: Stanley Lane-Poole, *The Barbary Corsairs* (London: Fisher Unwin, 1890), p. 224.

Used in same manner; Maria *and* Dauphin *crews meet:* ★★JLC/JBN-TC, p. 17.

RoB in war: Irwin to GW, July 9, 1789, ★★FO.

Sent "to hard labor": ★★JLC/JBN-TC, p. 18.

"Seeing our . . .": RoB to TJ, Aug. 24, 1785, ★★FO.

Heroism myth: American Volunteer, Feb. 19, 1824.

Three captains to John Adams: On Aug. 27, 1785, ★★FO.

Stephens, Adams acquainted: IS to JA, Oct. 24, 1787, ★★FO.

RoB letter: RoB to TJ, Aug. 24, 1785, ★★FO.

Replies, from TJ: Sept. 29, 1785, ★★FO; and from JA, Oct. 6, 1785, ★★FO.

Coffee money, JC to Logie's house and prison: ★★JLC/JBN-TC, p. 45, 23–24.

RoB "aged mother": RoB to TJ, June 8, 1786, ★★ND, p. 6.

CHAPTER 6

Concord: For details about life in the Stephenses' hometown just after the Revolution, including the topography, the economy, the shocks caused by farming changes, the care of the poor, and the role of the Middlesex Hotel as the nerve center of news, business, and gossip, I am indebted to the following sources: Lemuel Shattuck, *A History of the Town of Concord* (Boston: Russell, Odiorne, 1835); Mary Babson Fuhrer, "The Revolutionary Worlds of Lexington and Concord Compared," *New England Quarterly* 85, no 1 (2012); www.concordlibrary.org; and William F. Kelly, "A History of the Town of Braintree, Mass." (master's thesis, Boston University, 1956).

Voyage duration, long delays: A transatlantic trip was faster west to east (approx. thirty days) than east to west (easily twice that), plus time in port. Delays were frequent: Ben Franklin once left England in July; it took twenty days battling headwinds before even clearing the English coast and eventually arriving in Philadelphia in October.

"Few places . . .": Shattuck, *A History of the Town of Concord*, p. 196.

Husking bee: Kelly, "A History of the Town of Braintree, Mass.," p. 24.

Captain McComb: *Salem Gazette*, Oct. 25, 1785.

"On the 25th of July . . .": Early report in Carey, *A Short Account of Algiers*, p. 41.

Irwin quotes: Irwin to GW, July 9, 1789, ★★FO.

$80,000 allocated, early negotiations: TJ to Alexander Hamilton, Feb. 4, 1793, ★★FO; *Report on Mediterranean Trade*, ★★ND, p. 23; Gardner W. Allen, *Our Navy and the Barbary Corsairs* (Boston: Houghton Mifflin, 1905), chap. 3.

"As long ago . . .": JA to Stephen Higginson, Oct. 4, 1785, ★★FO.

"Nearly three centuries . . ." to "pay up": Author's summary.

"I very early . . ." and "proceed by way . . .": TJ to JA, July 11, 1786, ★★ND, p. 10; also see JA to TJ, July 31, 1786, ★★ND, p. 11.

No navy until late 1790s: The Naval Act would come in 1794, but the first three of six frigates would not be launched until 1797.

Abigail Adams: AA to JQA, Oct. 18, 1785, ★★FO.

"With one black eye . . .": For bringing this magnificent quote to my attention, I am indebted to Priscilla H. Roberts and Richard S. Roberts, *Thomas Barclay, Consul in France, Diplomat in Barbary* (Bethlehem, PA: Lehigh University Press, 2008), p. 26. Recommended reading.

"Degenerate American": JC to James Madison, Nov. 30, 1803. (A US consul, James Simpson, also called JL "that unworthy man," JS to TJ, July 25, 1795.)

Spoke no French, "I have not seen . . .": TJ to JA, Sept. 24, 1785, ★★FO; also recommended, Allen, *Our Navy and the Barbary Corsairs*, p. 30.

"Drunk as a lord": Roberts and Roberts, *Thomas* Barclay, p. 169.

"Dispersed . . .": T. J. *Report on Prisoners*, Dec. 28, 1790, ★★ND, p. 19.

Instructions: See chap. 7.

Stephens to Adams: IS to JA, Feb. 7, 1786, ★★FO.

Reply from Adams: JA to RoB, Oct. 6, 1785, ★★FO.

CHAPTER 7

The saga of Lamb's ill-fated mission to Algiers is recounted in the following, all of which can be found in ★★ND: RoB to TJ, June 8, 1786; RoB to William Carmichael, Sept. 13, 1786; TJ, *Report* to Congress on U.S. citizens in captivity in Algiers, Dec. 28, 1790; Petition of Prisoners at Algiers, Mar. 29, 1792; TJ to John Paul Jones, June 1, 1792; James Simpson, Gibraltar consul, to TJ, July 25, 1795. In addition, these can be found in ★★FO: John Jay to American Commissioners, Mar. 11, 1785; TJ to JA, Sept. 25, 1785; John Lamb's Supplementary Instructions, Oct. 1–11, 1785; JC to James Madison, Nov. 30, 1803; JL to TJ, June 5, 1786; TJ to William Carmichael, June 20, 1786; TJ to JL, June 20, 1786; JA to TJ, June 25, 1786; Barclay to US Commissioners, Apr. 10, 1786; JL to TJ, May 20, 1787; JL to TJ, Oct. 10, 1786; JL to JA, July 18, 1786.

"Illiterate . . ." and other JC quotes: ★★JLC/JBN-TC, pp. 35–42.

"Ungentlemanlike" behavior, *"a few days," bosom friend, sabotage, what sum*: RoB to TJ, June 8, 1786.

"Mr. Logie received me . . .": JL to American Commissioners, May 20, 1786, ★★FO.

Price of ransoms: Speculative. Overview in TJ, *Report on Prisoners*, Dec. 28, 1790, ★★ND, p. 21. Other guesses appear throughout correspondence.

"We do not expect . . .": Supplementary Instructions to JL, Oct. 1–11, 1785, ★★FO.

Portrait: Charles Sumner, *Speech on Bill for Abolition of Slavery*, US Senate, Mar. 31, 1862, p. 10.

Offer, counteroffer: RoB to TJ, June 8, 1786; TJ, *Report on Prisoners*, Dec. 28, 1790; JL to Commissioners, May 20, 1786. Reports vary on specifics; Lamb may have offered $6,000 or $280 per head.

Lamb $48,300, JC "confused": ★★JLC/JBN-TC, pp. 40–41; RoB to TJ, July 12, 1790 (figures in sequins); also see RoB petition, Mar. 29, 1792; IS to JA, Apr. 15, 1786, ★★FO.

"Mr. Lamb had five . . .": RoB to TJ, July 12, 1790.

TJ denied, "never settled": TJ to John Paul Jones, June 1, 1792, ★★ND, p. 36.

Lamb meeting, $400, Hassan, JL report home: JL to Commissioners, May 20, 1786, ★★FO; ★★JLC/JBN-TC, pp. 39–40.

"Badly planned": RoB to William Carmichael, Sept. 13, 1786.

JL letter to captives: IS to JA, Oct. 24, 1787.

Lamb expenses, "not censurable," "no harm": JA to TJ, Jan. 25, 1787, ★★FO.

Lamb background, no formal appointment: John Jay to American Commissioners, Mar. 11, 1785; TJ to JA, Sept. 24, 1785, ★★FO. Also recommended: Editorial Note to Adams Papers, https://founders.archives.gov/documents/Adams/06-17-02-0237-0000.

"Unhappy mess": JL to TJ, May 20, 1787.

Stephens letter: Mostly IS to JA, Apr. 15, 1786, but incorporating a quote from IS to JA, July 18, 1786, ★★FO.

JC cast out of garden, etc.: ★★JLC/JBN-TC, p. 44.

CHAPTER 8

Arrival at bagnio: ★★JLC/JBN-TC, pp. 47–56.

D'Andreis invitation: ★★JLC/JBN-TC, p. 59 (d'Andreis is identified as dey's chief clerk, p. 156); describe room, pp. 55–56; night, morning parade, job allocation, carpenter, pp. 59–60; "merchants, doctors," p. 75.

"Dreadful clanking": Foss, *A Journal of the Captivity and Sufferings of John Foss*, p. 18.

Rules of Algiers: ★★JLC/JBN-TC, p. 122, also see pp. 142 and 187; Emanuel d'Aranda, says, "A Christian is not to strike a Turk upon pain of death" (*History of Algiers*, [1666], p. 156).

Janissaries bristling for fight: ★★JLC/JBN-TC, p. 107.

Hierarchies, twelve thousand Turks: Barlow's report, Mar. 18, 1796 (and drawing on JC's report to him!), ★★ND; also see Todd, *Life and Letters of Joel Barlow*, pp. 122–23; Foss, *A Journal of the Captivity and Sufferings of John Foss*, pp. 46–47; Stevens, *An Historical and Geographical Account of Algiers*, p. 142; William Spencer, *Algiers in the Age of the Corsairs* (Norman: University of Oklahoma Press, 1976), recommended; "Barbary" in *Encyclopaedia Britannica* (1911).

Aqueducts: Carey, *A Short Account of Algiers*, p. 9.

Three thousand, etc: RoB to TJ, July 12, 1790, ★★FO.

Planks, goads: Foss, *A Journal of the Captivity and Sufferings of John Foss*, p. 20.

Heavy labor: RoB to anon., Apr. 28, 1787, ★★ND, p. 15.

Stephens: IS to JA, Apr. 15, 1786, ★★FO.

"Death would be . . .": Later quote from Captain Samuel Calder, to David Pearce, Dec. 4, 1793, ★★ND.

CHAPTER 9

"One of my crew . . .": RoB to anon., Apr. 28, 1787, ★★ND.

"Agreeable," conditions for officers: RoB to William Carmichael, Sept. 13, 1786, ★★ND; also see Expilly refs in RoB to TJ, June 8, 1786, ★★ND.

Allowance: Petition of Prisoners, Mar. 29, 1792, ★★ND; also ★★JLC/JBN-TC, p. 116.

"In any normal conflict . . .": This section sums up the unique dilemma facing the United States. Author's paraphrase of RoB's musings in his various reports home, esp. RoB to TJ, June 8, 1786; RoB to Congress, Apr. 28, 1791, ★★ND.

Guineas quote: Compte D'Estaing to TJ, May 17, 1786, cited in Allen, *Our Navy and the Barbary Corsairs*, p. 39.

"Rivals chained" . . . : David Humphreys, 1793, in Carey, *A Short Account of Algiers*, p. 45.

Louis XIV: Quoted in Carey, *A Short Account of Algiers*, p. 45 (but perhaps apocryphal).

Foreign citizenship card: For a rare successful example, see Colvill in chap. 14.

JC in Royal Navy: I first discovered this arresting fact in Brett Goodin, "The Business, Personality and Discretionary Power of American Consuls in North Africa 1797–1805," *Huntington Library Quarterly* (December 2017): 615, citing details of ships' pay books in the UK National Archives. Recommended reading.

Mathurins: Jefferson gives an overview of this secret enterprise in his *Report* to Congress on the American captives on Dec. 28, 1790, **ND, p. 18. George Washington refers to it in his diary Mar. 23, 1790. Also see TJ to Pere Chauvier, Dec. 27, 1788; Pere Chauvier to TJ, Dec. 30, 1788; TJ to Chauvier, Dec. 30, 1788; TJ to Chauvier, Sept. 16, 1789; TJ to JA, Jan. 11, 1787; JA to TJ, Jan. 25, 1787; TJ to John Jay, Feb. 1, 1787, Sept. 19, 1787, and Aug. 11, 1788; TJ to Treasury Commissioners, Sept. 6, 1788; and William Short to TJ, June 14, 1790, all **FO, with editorial footnotes.

"Can redeem at lower price": TJ to JA, Jan. 11, 1787, **FO; *"deserve our thanks"*: JA to TJ, Jan. 25, 1787, **FO.

Amounts estimated: The estimates are often contradictory and confusing since they are based on speculation. TJ, *Report* on the American captives. See also TJ to JA, Jan. 11, 1787, and RoB to TJ, July, 12 1786; June 2, 1788; Dec. 12, 1789; July 12, 1790, **FO.

CHAPTER 10

DH poem: "Poem on the Happiness of America," cited in Carey, *A Short Account of Algiers*, p. 45.

Hannah petitions: To my knowledge, only two petitions from Hannah Stephens made it into the records: the first is *A Petition from Hannah Stephens Praying That Her Husband Be Redeemed from Captivity at Algiers*, referred to by John Jay on July 18, 1787, which proved vital in provoking the release of funds to the Mathurins project (see Resolution of Congress, same date), and *Memorial from Hannah Stephens Requesting the Release of Her Husband from Prison in Algiers*, Dec. 9, 1791, Records of US Senate; also HS letter to George Washington, Dec. 9, 1791. (All HS quotes here are from 1791.) Also see IS to GW, Sept. 23, 1789, and **FO editorial note from HS to GW, Dec. 9, 1791.

Eviction: HS to GW, Dec. 9, 1791.

Maid's earnings: US Department of Labor, *History of Wages in the United States*.

Welfare in Concord, "generosity": Shattuck, *A History of the Town of Concord*, pp. 218–19. See also note on Concord sources in chap. 6 notes.

Stephens to Adams: IS to JA, Oct. 24, 1787, **FO.

RoB stoked him up: IS to JA, Mar. 23, 1798, **FO.

TJ follow-up with Mathurins: See Mathurins sources in chap. 9 notes.

"We were for some time . . .": Petition of Prisoners, Mar. 29, 1792, **ND, p. 35.

"We were allowed . . .": **JLC/JBN-TC, pp. 116–17.

Shortage of workers: RoB to Congress, Apr. 28, 1791, says 3,000 in 1786 and now 700; TJ, *TJ Report on Prisoners* of 1790, says 2,200 in 1786, now 655.

TJ and Sally Hemings, children, life at Monticello, treatment of TJ's slaves: This fascinating subject is explored in the website www.monticello.org/slavery. Highly recommended reading.

CHAPTER 11

Life in the bagnios: D'Aranda, *History of Algiers*; chap. XVI; Foss, *A Journal of the Captivity and Sufferings of John Foss*, pp. 30–33; Laurent d'Arvieux, *Mémoires du Chevalier d'Arvieux* (Paris, 1735), vol. 5, pp. 228–29; J. Morgan, *Complete History of Algiers* (London: Bettesworth and Hitch, 1731); **JLC/JBN-TC, chap. 4 (including *Carneros*).

Bagnio Gallera (or Galleria, or Gallaro): Stevens, *An Historical and Geographical Account of Algiers*, pp. 197–98; Foss, *A Journal of the Captivity and Sufferings of John Foss*, p. 33; **JLC/JBN-TC, p. 56– ; *JC's experiences there*, **JLC/JBN-TC, pp. 115–16.

CHAPTER 12

Naples and Spain ransoms caused shortage: RoB to anon., Apr. 28, 1787, **ND.

Naples and Spain, JC list of jobs, JC move, new role: **JLC/JBN-TC, pp. 116–21.

De la Cruz: **JLC/JBN-TC, pp. 120–21; *Hamet*: **JLC/JBN-TC, p. 121; *dining*: **JLC/JBN-TC, pp. 73–74.

Hassan description and background: Stevens, *An Historical and Geographical Account of Algiers*, pp. 205–7; Foss, *A Journal of the Captivity and Sufferings of John Foss*, p. 44.

"Uncommon abilities," Hassan jailed: Robert Montgomery to TJ, July 26, 1791, **ND.

Million dollars, "ungovernable temper," "whims": Todd, *Life and Letters of Joel Barlow*, pp. 123–24, latter quote by Todd.

Plague, Peter Smith death, 215 lives: RoB to anon, Apr. 28, 1787; **JLC/JBN-TC, p. 274; RoB to Irwins, Dec. 20, 1788, **FO; Foss, *A Journal of the Captivity and Sufferings of John Foss*, p. 71 (though Foss says Smith died of smallpox).

"Tolerable," de la Cruz death, staffers died: **JLC/JBN-TC, pp. 118–20.

CHAPTER 13

Passions, countenance, satisfaction, dey offer to JC: **JLC/JBN-TC, pp. 168, 149.

Stephens letter: IS to Congress, Feb. 9, 1788, **FO.

Embezzler incident: **JLC/JBN-TC, p. 122.

US deaths, overall toll: RoB to Irwins, Dec. 20, 1788, enclosure, **FO; **JLC/JBN-TC, p. 274; Foss, *A Journal of the Captivity and Sufferings of John Foss*, p. 71.

"City of Bondage" letter: RoB to Irwins, Dec. 20, 1788, enclosure, **FO.

Burials: **JLC/JBN-TC, pp. 112, 136; *poem*: **JLC/JBN-TC, p. 270; *"means of alleviating"*: **JLC/JBN-TC, p. 44.

Prize ship, loan: **JLC/JBN-TC, p. 157; *had money for ransom*: **JLC/JBN-TC, pp. 168, 178.

Bars of Algiers: **JLC/JBN-TC, pp. 107–9, 262; *bought Mad House*: **JLC/JBN-TC, pp. 138, 140.

CHAPTER 14

Scenes in tavern: ★★JLC/JBN-TC, p. 53; *sharifs demanded seats:* ★★JLC/JBN-TC, p. 146; *soldiers prone to fight:* ★★JLC/JBN-TC, p. 107; *good meal:* ★★JLC/JBN-TC, p. 136; *RoB hard labor:* ★★JLC/JBN-TC, p. 138; *welfare role:* ★★JLC/JBN-TC, p. 109; Laurent d'Arvieux, *Mémoires du Chevalier d'Arvieux* (Paris, 1735), vol. 5, p. 229; Emanuel d'Aranda, *History of Algiers* (1666), pp. 152–58.

"Seaman" or "mariner": e.g., RoB to Irwins, Dec. 20, 1788, ★★ND (also "crutches" reference); *"knows navigation":* e.g., RoB to TJ, July 12, 1790; *"keeps a tavern": List of American Prisoners,* July 9, 1790, ★★ND.

Clerk of Gallera, sheepskin and charcoal, second tavern: ★★JLC/JBN-TC, p. 123; 136.

Strangling of Hasnagi: Mongomery to TJ, July 26, 1791; *"Notwithstanding . . .":* ★★ND; ★★JLC/JBN-TC, pp. 131–34.

Strangling process: Foss, *A Journal of the Captivity and Sufferings of John Foss,* p. 26.

Franklin rumor, voice of indignation, tall story of escape: Rumor in the *Boston Independent Chronicle,* May 18, 1786, cited in Charles Sumner, *Speech on Bill for Abolition of Slavery,* US Senate, Mar. 31, 1862; Charles Sumner, *Lecture on White Slavery in the Barbary States* (Boston, 1847), p. 32; *escape:* Sumner, *Lecture on White Slavery in the Barbary States,* pp. 33–34; *Franklin broadside against US slavery:* Sumner, *Lecture on White Slavery in the Barbary States,* p. 39 footnote.

"Thus pray . . .": RoB to gentlemen of the clergy, cited in Sumner, *Lecture on White Slavery in the Barbary States,* p. 37.

Report on Mediterranean Trade: ★★ND, pp. 24–26.

Colvill debriefing: Joshua Johnson to TJ, Feb. 25, 1791, ★★FO; also see RoB to TJ, July 12, 1790, ★★FO; Report on Petition of CC, 1791, ★★FO with editorial footnote; TJ to GW, Nov. 14, 1791, ★★FO with footnote; Draught of a Secret Resolution of Both Houses, Dec. 2 1791, ★★FO with footnote; Senate Resolution to Ransom Prisoners at Algiers, Feb. 22, 1792, ★★ND.

CHAPTER 15

Hassan becomes dey: Le Clercq, Maurice, *Le Tombeau des cinq deys d'Alger* (Clairmont, 1888), p. 46; Stevens, *An Historical and Geographical Account of Algiers,* pp. 205–6; ★★JLC/JBN-TC, p. 150.

Montgomery: to TJ, July 26, 1791, ★★ND.

Everyone put to labor; Werner; afflictions; third bar; money: ★★JLC/JBN-TC, pp. 137–140.

Quarrels: Closure and bastinadoed, see ★★JLC/JBN-TC, p. 260; fights and murder, ★★JLC/JBN-TC, pp. 53–54.

Never lay hands; ladder solution: D'Aranda, *History of Algiers,* p. 156.

Empowered to strip clients: Stevens, *An Historical and Geographical Account of Algiers,* pp. 241, 249.

Two crises at bar: ★★JLC/JBN-TC, pp. 140–42.

CHAPTER 16

HS plea: HS to George Washington, Dec. 9, 1791, ★★FO.

IS letter. IS to GW, Sept. 23, 1789, ★★FO.

HS Memorial: *Memorial from Hannah Stephens Requesting the Release of Her Husband from Prison in Algiers*, Dec. 9, 1791, Records of US Senate.

Senate response: HS to GW, Dec. 9, 1791, plus editorial footnotes, ★★FO.

$100,000 authorized: Senate Resolution, Feb. 22, 1792, ★★ND; *earlier $40,000*: Senate Resolution, Feb. 22, 1791, ★★ND; also see Sumner, *Speech on Bill for Abolition of Slavery*, US Senate, Mar. 31, 1862.

Census: *US Federal Census* (1790) for Concord, Middlesex County, MA.

RoB letter. RoB to Congress, Apr. 28, 1791 (between resolutions).

Harnet insane, "destitute": Petition of Prisoners, Mar. 29, 1792, ★★ND, p. 35; also ★★JLC/JBN-TC, p. 274.

Confrontation at the Mad House: ★★JLC/JBN-TC, pp. 148–50.

Genoese: Stevens, *An Historical and Geographical Account of Algiers*, p. 267.

Barlow on near burning: Todd, *Life and Letters of Joel Barlow*, p. 128.

Ganches: Stevens, *An Historical and Geographical Account of Algiers*, p. 200; Foss, *A Journal of the Captivity and Sufferings of John Foss*, p. 24; Morgan, *Complete History of Algiers*.

CHAPTER 17

JC's role as chief Christian clerk: footnote to treaty in ★★ND, p. 116; David Humphries to Joel Barlow, Feb. 16, 1796, ★★ND; Dey Hassan to GW, May 6, 1796; ★★JLC/JBN-TC, pp. 156–57.

Description of meeting with dey: from the Diary of General Eaton, cited by Todd, *Life and Letters of Joel Barlow*, p. 124; *slate seats, fan*: Stevens, *An Historical and Geographical Account of Algiers*, p. 206.

Mahmood, aspers: Stevens, *An Historical and Geographical Account of Algiers*, p. 279.

Wardrobe malfunction: Stevens, *An Historical and Geographical Account of Algiers*, p. 269, ★★JLC/JBN-TC, p. 19. Neither account names Smith, but both describe him as an American. Smith was the only American to work as a page to the dey at that stage.

Sleepwalker. ★★JLC/JBN-TC, p. 21. It's probable that the two servants were Smith and the Frenchman Jacob Tessanaer of the *Dauphin*; both worked as pages around this time. Tessanaer was to die of plague in 1793. (See RoB to TJ, July 12, 1790, ★★FO.)

John Paul Jones, death and "not begun to fight" quote: Library of Congress, *Today in History*, July 18, 1792.

TJ to Jones: TJ to John Paul Jones, June 1, 1792, ★★ND.

JC plague, letter to RoB: ★★JLC/JBN-TC, p. 154.

"Much concerned," "human misery," "renounce their country," deaths of Tessanaer and Harnet: RoB to David Humphreys via anon., Mar. 26, 1793, ★★FO, in footnote to

DH to GW, May 5, 1793; also ★★JLC/JBN-TC, p. 274; Foss, *A Journal of the Captivity and Sufferings of John Foss*, p. 71.

G. Smith friendship, dey fury, saved: RoB to DH via anon., Mar. 26, 1793, ★★FO, in footnote to DH to GW, May 5, 1793; RoB to DH, Nov. 5, 1793, in State Papers, vol. 1. Skjoldebrand was repaid (DH to R. Montgomery, Nov. 5, 1793, in State Papers vol. 1).

Conversion: Stevens, *An Historical and Geographical Account of Algiers*, pp. 241 and 266–67; *marriage and share in business, e.g., story of William Joyce in Algiers; incentives*: Spencer, *Algiers in the Age of the Corsairs*, p. 113 (recommended); John Braithwaite, *History of the Revolutions in Morocco* (London, 1729), pp. 185–87, 191; Joseph Pitts, *A Faithful Account* . . . (London: T. Longman, 1738); William Okeley, *Eben Ezer* (London: Nat. Ponder, 1675); Norman Robert Bennett, "Christian and Negro Slavery in 18th Century North Africa," *The Journal of African History* 1, no. 1(1960): 80 (recommended); Sumner, *Lecture on White Slavery in the Barbary States*, footnote 138.

"Deprived of labor," "very small": Stevens, *An Historical and Geographical Account of Algiers*, p. 266.

"My sailor that offered . . .": IS to JA, Mar. 23, 1798, ★★FO. Stephens's phraseology is very ambiguous. The original possibly read: "my sailor that [was?] offered him Self." He also wrote "to cruise for the Americans" but presumably meant it in the sense of "to hunt for."

"Suffered so little": Carey, *A Short Account of Algiers*, p. 40.

CHAPTER 18

Schooner Lark: Report from James Simpson, US Consul in Gibraltar, June 1, 1793, ★★ND.

August 18, second ship off Malaga, England-Spain plotting, Church quotes: E. Church to TJ, Sept. 22, 1793, ★★ND.

Advice received on truce, eight cruisers: John Pintard to David Humphreys, Oct. 6, 1793, ★★ND.

Portuguese witness confirmed: E. Church to DH, Oct. 12, 1793, ★★ND.

U.S. diplomat meeting, Logie coup, no convoys: E. Church to TJ, Oct. 12, 1793, ★★ND.

Press-gangs, "hardly two," Nancy and other ship, "humanity shudders": Peter Walsh to TJ, Oct. 17, 1793, ★★ND.

Swedish witnesses: E. Church circular, Oct. 14, 1793, ★★ND.

CHAPTER 19

This chapter lists the eleven American ships taken in 1793 using details from the *List of American Vessels Captured by the Algerines in October & November 1793* (in James Simpson to TJ, Nov. 25, 1793, ★★ND; hereafter *1793 List*); RoB's list in RoB to

GW, Nov. 5, 1793, in State Papers vol. 1; letters from Samuel Calder, Nov. 3 and Dec. 4, 1793, ★★ND; list in Foss, *A Journal of the Captivity and Sufferings of John Foss*, p. 71– ; and details of captures in Stevens, *An Historical and Geographical Account of Algiers*, chap. 4.

Jackson: He is listed as "Scippio [*sic*] Jackson, mariner" among the crew of the brig *Minerva* by Foss, *A Journal of the Captivity and Sufferings of John Foss*, p. 75, and described as "a black man" in a sympathetic account of his ill-treatment on p. 22. Stevens also refers to him as "an American black [man]" (*An Historical and Geographical Account of Algiers*, p. 275).

Jackson may have been former enslaved person: SJ's personal history is obscure, and in view of the upheavals of war we may never know for sure. Author Lawrence A. Peskin points out that SJ's experience was "eerily similar" to those contained in narratives written by former American slaves in the 1800s. In his (recommended) book *Captives and Countrymen* (Baltimore: Johns Hopkins University Press, 2009), Peskin speculates that SJ may have suffered under the US chattel slavery system: "One wonders whether [SJ] had ever been enslaved in the United States and, if so, whether he found it a more 'bitter draught' there or in Algiers" (p. 9). In my opinion, the giveaway name of Scipio and his location in New York at that time makes it highly likely that he was a former enslaved person who'd sought and gained freedom in New York. Statistically, as an African American in the antebellum era, he was nine times more likely to have been born as an enslaved person than as a free man. (See National Humanities Center, *The Making of African American Identity*, vol. 1.)

New York as a sanctuary for enslaved people: "New York became a sanctuary for 10,000 freedom-seeking African-Americans from up and down the coast," according to *Revolutionary War and the Struggle for Black Freedom* in the New York Historical Society's Slavery in New York Exhibition. Recommended.

Sidenote regarding the term "African American": After much thought and based on quotes like the above, I have opted to use the term "African American" to describe enslaved people and former enslaved people, even those born in Africa, who remained in the United States to live and work after gaining their freedom. Once reserved solely for *descendants* of enslaved people from Africa, the term is now generally accepted in a much wider context.

Brig Minerva *captain, crew, voyage, course, capture*: *1793 List*; RoB to DH, Nov. 16 and Dec. 6, 1793, in State Papers, vol. 1; Foss, *A Journal of the Captivity and Sufferings of John Foss*, pp. 53, 71– .

John Thomas was African American and from Massachusetts: Todd, *Life and Letters of Joel Barlow*, p. 133.

Slavery in Massachusetts: Massachusetts Constitution and the Abolition of Slavery, www.mass.gov. Recommended.

John Jack: Shattuck, *A History of the Town of Concord*, p. 210.

President with captain, crew, cargo, voyage, capture: *1793 List* (misnaming it *Prudent*); RoB list; Foss, *A Journal of the Captivity and Sufferings of John Foss*, pp. 71– ; Stevens, *An Historical and Geographical Account of Algiers*, pp. 69–71, 235–39.

Arrival in Algiers of brig Minerva, *number of captives*: RoB to DH, Dec. 6, 1793; Foss, *A Journal of the Captivity and Sufferings of John Foss*, pp. 53, 75; Stevens, *An Historical and Geographical Account of Algiers*, chap. 4.

The other Minerva, McShane, *corsair captain*: John McShane to DH, Nov. 13, 1793, in State Papers, vol. 1; Joel Barlow certificate, July 8, 1796, **ND; Foss, *A Journal of the Captivity and Sufferings of John Foss*, pp. 71– ; Stevens, *An Historical and Geographical Account of Algiers*, pp. 69, 276–78.

Ship Hope: *1793 List*; Foss, *A Journal of the Captivity and Sufferings of John Foss*, pp. 71– ; *"distributed"*: Foss, *A Journal of the Captivity and Sufferings of John Foss*, pp. 8–9.

Brig Polly: *1793 List*; Foss, *A Journal of the Captivity and Sufferings of John Foss*, pp. 4–13, 73. (Foss lists Bayley as master and Michael Smith as mate, but *1793 List* names Smith as master.)

Schooner Jay: *1793 List*; Calder to Terry and David Pearse, Nov. 3 and Dec. 4, 1793, **ND.

Brig Jane, *ship* Thomas: Moses Morse to Dominick Terry, Dec. 1, 1794, **ND; *1793 List*; Foss, *A Journal of the Captivity and Sufferings of John Foss*, pp. 71– .

The Despatch, *the* George *and the* Olive Branch: *1793 List*; Foss, *A Journal of the Captivity and Sufferings of John Foss*, pp. 71– ; ND, p. 56 (although *1793 List* names Wallace as "Wallsey"); *grain reference*: see chap. 18.

Captured ten: RoB to James Simpson, Nov. 25, 1793, **ND, p. 55.

CHAPTER 20

Palace scenes, treatment on arrival, dey's selection, transfer to bagnio, hard labor, graveyard, new mosque: Foss, *A Journal of the Captivity and Sufferings of John Foss*, pp. 14–22; Stevens, *An Historical and Geographical Account of Algiers*, pp. 72–76, 241–44; Calder to Dominick Terry, Nov. 3, 1793, **ND.

Tessanaer: See chap 17.

Morse and McShane quotes: Morse to Terry, Dec. 1, 1794; Stevens, *An Historical and Geographical Account of Algiers*, p. 70.

Overseer's death: Foss, *A Journal of the Captivity and Sufferings of John Foss*, pp. 20–22; Stevens, *An Historical and Geographical Account of Algiers*, p. 77.

Calder quotes: Calder to David Pearce, Dec. 4, 1793, **ND.

Wetlands: Foss, *A Journal of the Captivity and Sufferings of John Foss*, p. 16; also see **JLC/JBN-TC, p. 87.

Left disabled: Todd, *Life and Letters of Joel Barlow*, p. 136; *Brooks blinded*: Stevens, *An Historical and Geographical Account of Algiers*, preface.

Officers' complaints: Morse to Terry, Dec. 1, 1794; Calder to Pearse, Dec. 4, 1794; *Brooks quotes*: Stevens, *An Historical and Geographical Account of Algiers*, p. 249; **JLC/JBN-TC, p. 245.

Burnham: DH to GW, Aug. 30, 1794, **FO.

CHAPTER 21

Racist attack on SJ: Stevens, *An Historical and Geographical Account of Algiers*, p. 275.

Sub-Saharan Africans in Algiers, shipwrecked African Americans: Bennett, "Christian and Negro Slavery in 18th Century North Africa"; Braithwaite, *History of the Revolutions in Morocco*; Spencer, *Algiers in the Age of the Corsairs*; James Riley, *The Loss of the Brig Commerce* (New York, 1859).

"I, who . . .": *Memoirs of Abraham Brown, Sallee* (1600s), cited in Sumner, *Lecture on White Slavery in the Barbary States*.

Consciences aroused, "restore to liberty," appeals, etc: Sumner, *Lecture on White Slavery in the Barbary States*, pp. 35–41; RoB to GW, Nov. 5, 1793, State Papers, vol. 1.

Money and clothes: DH to R. Montgomery, Dec. 1, 1793, State Papers, vol. 1; Foss, *A Journal of the Captivity and Sufferings of John Foss*, p. 54, including "cheated us" and "gentlemen"; Stevens, *An Historical and Geographical Account of Algiers*, pp. 239–40, including blue outfits and hats, "unjust," and "caballeros."

Songs and comedy sessions: Stevens, *An Historical and Geographical Account of Algiers*, p. 247.

Sloan, tradition of liberating captain aproa: Stevens, *An Historical and Geographical Account of Algiers*, p. 279; Foss, *A Journal of the Captivity and Sufferings of John Foss*, p. 57; *Sloan as* captain aproa: RoB to William Carmichael, May 11 or 15, 1790 (enclosure), ★★FO; *freed*: Foss, *A Journal of the Captivity and Sufferings of John Foss*, p. 57; ★★JLC/JBN-TC, pp. 16, 166, 190, 274.

Patterson tavern owner: List of Prisoners, July 9, 1790, ★★ND.

Borrow cash, Brooks quote: Stevens, *An Historical and Geographical Account of Algiers*, p. 241.

Foss, *A Journal of the Captivity and Sufferings of John Foss*, p. 71; ★★JLC/JBN-TC, p. 274.

CHAPTER 22

Americans' escape bid: Stevens, *An Historical and Geographical Account of Algiers*, p. 261–63.

October 1793 dash for freedom: Stevens, *An Historical and Geographical Account of Algiers*, p. 255; *Attempt of Fifteen Slaves to escape*; *Foss quote*: Foss, *A Journal of the Captivity and Sufferings of John Foss*, p. 25.

Brothels in Algiers: Spencer, *Algiers in the Age of the Corsairs*, p. 95.

Barclay and Humphreys: DH to TJ, Feb. 8, 1793, and TJ to DH, Mar. 21, 1793; F. L. Humphreys, *The Life and Times of David Humphreys*, vol. 2 (New York: Putnam, 1917), pp. 153–60 and chap. 9.

RoB irritation, TJ quotes: TJ to DH, Mar. 22, 1793, in Humphreys, *The Life and Times of David Humphreys*, pp. 167, 206; *"accomplished nothing"*: Humphreys, *The Life and Times of David Humphreys*, p. 162.

DH letter to people: From Lisbon, July 11, 1794, cited in Sumner, *Lecture on White Slavery in the Barbary States*.

Navy, 1797: The first of three frigates was launched in May 1797. See notes in chap. 1 and chap. 27.

Clothes: DH to R. Montgomery, Dec. 1, 1793, State Papers, vol. 1; DH to TJ, Nov. 23, 1793; *details*: Humphreys, *The Life and Times of David Humphreys*, p. 196.

DH overture, Hassan response, "unfortunate," unite for war: DH to TJ, Nov. 23, 1793; Humphreys, *The Life and Times of David Humphreys*, pp. 188–89.

DH poem: cited in Carey, *A Short Account of Algiers*, p. 45.

Hassan quote, Foss quote: Foss, *A Journal of the Captivity and Sufferings of John Foss*, pp. 52–53.

Hassan's new terms: RoB to DH, dated "October, 1794" ★★ND.

$800,000, DH trip to United States, new plan: Humphreys, *The Life and Times of David Humphreys*, pp. 222–26; *ships passed at sea*: Humphreys, *The Life and Times of David Humphreys*, p. 226; *DH and Joseph Donaldson*: Todd, *Life and Letters of Joel Barlow*, p. 116.

Dey wanted ambassador: Foss, *A Journal of the Captivity and Sufferings of John Foss*, p. 59; ★★JLC/JBN-TC, pp. 158–59.

CHAPTER 23

The arrival of Joseph Donaldson and the treaty negotiations are described in James Monroe to James Madison, Oct. 29, 1795, ★★FO; in Todd, *Life and Letters of Joel Barlow*, pp. 117–21, including letter from JB to James Monroe; Todd, *Life and Letters of Joel Barlow*, pp. 117–21; Foss, *A Journal of the Captivity and Sufferings of John Foss*, p. 59; ★★JLC/JBN-TC, pp. 158–71; *DH instructions*: TJ to DH, Mar. 28 and Apr. 4, 1785, ★★ND; DH to JD, May 18 1785, ★★ND; *Notes to treaty*: ★★ND pp. 115–16, and in the treaty itself.

JC/Dey conversation, JC secret actions, French consul: ★★JLC/JBN-TC, pp. 158–68.

Donaldson ship arrival: Foss, *A Journal of the Captivity and Sufferings of John Foss*, p. 59.

Walk to house: ★★JLC/JBN-TC, pp. 169–71; *Skjoldebrand and JD*: ★★JLC/JBN-TC, pp. 162–63.

Captives' reaction: Foss, *A Journal of the Captivity and Sufferings of John Foss*, pp. 59–60.

Jean le Vacher: *Mémoires de la Congrégation de La Mission*, vol. 2 (1864), p. 358.

Negotiations: ★★JLC/JBN-TC, pp. 172–84.

CHAPTER 24

Final stages of the treaty negotiations: ★★JLC/JBN-TC, pp. 179–85; *Dey's meeting with JD and his refusal to agree to the immediate release of the prisoners*: ★★JLC/JBN-TC, p. 187; *JC's translation of the treaty*: *Notes* to the treaty, ★★ND, pp. 115–16; *the Treaty itself*: ★★ND, p. 107; *Salute to the US flag*: JC to DH, Sept. 7, 1795 ★★ND; ★★JLC/ JBN-TC, p. 188.

JC's formula for selling the treaty to captains: ★★JLC/JBN-TC, pp. 198–99.

JC letter to DH: JC letter to DH: Sept. 7, 1795, ★★ND.

Foss quotes: Foss, *A Journal of the Captivity and Sufferings of John Foss*, p. 60.

Events on Sunday, RoB departure: ★★JLC/JBN-TC, pp. 189–94.

DH trip to France: Humphreys, *The Life and Times of David Humphreys*, pp. 235–40; *superiors unimpressed, RoB to London and cash freeze there*, Timothy Pickering to DH: Humphreys, *The Life and Times of David Humphreys*, p. 239.

Pressure on dey: ★★JLC/JBN-TC, p. 226.

Billings, Foss freed: Foss, *A Journal of the Captivity and Sufferings of John Foss*, pp. 60–61.

CHAPTER 25

Escape of James Hull (aka Hall): *Naval Expeditions* in Stevens, *An Historical and Geographical Account of Algiers*, pp. 279–81; ★★JLC/JBN-TC, p. 274 ("taken by a Neapolitan cruiser, 1796"); Foss, *A Journal of the Captivity and Sufferings of John Foss*, p. 71 ("taken by the Neapolitans").

Mutiny of crew: ★★JLC/JBN-TC, pp. 233, 241; Stevens, *An Historical and Geographical Account of Algiers*, p. 273.

Dey's anger, letter to DH, new deadline: ★★JLC/JBN-TC, pp. 243–45.

DH letter to dey: Feb. 16, 1796, ★★ND.

JC bought and offered own ship: JC to James Madison, Sept. 18, 1821, ★★FO; DH to Barlow, Feb. 16, 1796, ★★ND; ★★JLC/JBN-TC, pp. 200, 227, 265, 267–68, 272–73.

Patience exhausted, DH "primer" to JC: JC to DH, Feb. 6, 1796, and *Note*, ★★ND.

DH to captives: Feb. 16, 1796; DH to Barlow, Feb. 16, 1796.

RoB to London, Hamburg, and Spain; "great danger": RoB to Timothy Pickering, Feb. 16, 1796, ★★ND; DH to US Chargé d'Affaires, Madrid, Feb. 29, 1796, ★★ND; DH to Thomas Pinckney, Mar. 9, 1796, ★★ND; Hamburg, DH to Barlow, Feb. 16, 1796, ★★ND; DH circular, Mar. 9, 1796, ★★ND.

Warning unheard: e.g., GW to Congress, Mar. 15, 1796, ★★ND.

RoB warning: RoB to Pickering, Feb. 5, 1796, ★★ND.

Brawl among captains, Wallace death: Foss, *A Journal of the Captivity and Sufferings of John Foss*, p. 74; ★★JLC/JBN-TC, p. 245.

CHAPTER 26

Joel Barlow arrival, quotes: Barlow to wife, Mar. 8, 1796, in Todd, *Life and Letters of Joel Barlow*, p. 125; *JC rescued him*: ★★JLC/JBN-TC, p. 248.

JB backstory: Todd, *Life and Letters of Joel Barlow*; *his appointment*, DH circular, Feb. 10, 1796, ★★ND; *reluctance, present buying, grand tour*: Todd, *Life and Letters of Joel Bar-*

low, pp. 117–18; *many presents useless*: ★★JLC/JBN-TC, p. 217; *spies*: Todd, *Life and Letters of Joel Barlow*, p. 118; ★★JLC/JBN-TC, p. 248.

"Many vessels . . .": JB to DH from Alicante, Feb. 26, 1796, ★★ND.

Irritated, wrath, moustache: Todd, *Life and Letters of Joel Barlow*, pp. 124–26, 150.

Dresses debacle: ★★JLC/JBN-TC, p. 217.

Trunk, daughter, JB and JC early contact, Baccri: Stevens, *An Historical and Geographical Account of Algiers*, p. 208; ★★JLC/JBN-TC, pp. 250–52.

JB report: JB to Pickering from Algiers, Mar. 18, 1796, ★★ND (he'd only been there for two weeks); *JB received credit but plagiarized from JC*: ★★JLC/JBN-TC, p. 251.

Prison fight: Todd, *Life and Letters of Joel Barlow*, p. 127; ★★JLC/JBN-TC, pp. 258–64.

Dey violence to JC: JB to Pickering, Apr. 17, 1796, ★★ND; ★★JLC/JBN-TC, pp. 252–53, 257.

CHAPTER 27

Foss, plague: Foss, *A Journal of the Captivity and Sufferings of John Foss*, p. 64.

April 3, eight days: Stevens, *An Historical and Geographical Account of Algiers*, p. 81.

"Sojourn . . .": Letter, Apr. 2, 1796, Todd, *Life and Letters of Joel Barlow*, p. 128; *"distress," letter*: Apr. 5, 1796, Todd, *Life and Letters of Joel Barlow*, p. 129.

"Never quit": Foss, *A Journal of the Captivity and Sufferings of John Foss*, p. 62.

Barlow on leaving city: Todd, *Life and Letters of Joel Barlow*, pp. 131–32.

JC $40,000: ★★JLC/JBN-TC, p. 201 (20,000 sequins equaled approx. $40,000).

Baccri "more influence": Todd, *Life and Letters of Joel Barlow*, p. 129.

$20,000 to Baccri, frigate to daughter: Donaldson and Barlow to DH, Apr. 5, 1796, ★★ND; Todd, *Life and Letters of Joel Barlow*, p. 130; ★★JLC/JBN-TC, p. 201. The *Crescent* was named later. See ★★ND, p. 204, July 7, 1797.

JC estimates of cost, JB reaction: ★★JLC/JBN-TC p. 201; *$90,000 actual cost*: Stevens, *An Historical and Geographical Account of Algiers*, p. 81.

DH worried, sent RoB to United States: Stevens, *An Historical and Geographical Account of Algiers*, p. 81.

JD to Leghorn: JB and JD to DH, Apr. 5, 1796, ★★ND, p. 145; JD to Pinckney, June 20, 1796, ★★ND.

"Banker's clerk": Todd, *Life and Letters of Joel Barlow*, p. 131.

JB to DH: Apr. 3, 1796, ★★ND.

GW "satisfaction," etc.: GW to Senate, Dec. 8, 1795, State Papers, vol. 1, pp. 27–28.

Six frigates: Secretary of War to Congress, Jan. 29, 1796, ★★ND; *work suspended*: GW to Congress, Mar. 15, 1796, ★★ND. On April 20, GW signed a supplementary Act authorizing three frigates (launched 1797), with the three others to be left in their half-constructed state.

JC summoned, instructions from dey, letter, JB reaction and letters to DH and Pickering, JC's "great expense," JC philosophical, final eight days: ★★JLC/JBN-TC, pp. 264–69.

JB refuses to pay for voyage, "proof of sincerity," and JC "liberty sooner": JB to Pickering, May 4, 1796, ★★ND; ★★JLC/JBN-TC, p. 268.

"It is in great measure . . .": JB to Pickering, July 12, 1796, ★★ND.

Special note: Barlow's conspiracy theory: The dey's surprise decision to send JC to America took Barlow completely unaware. But afterward, in a letter to TJ, the envoy tried to rewrite history by claiming that the whole trip had been his—Barlow's—own idea. He claimed—ludicrously—that he had somehow planted the notion in the dey's head while cleverly making Hassan believe he'd thought it up himself.

Barlow's overriding motive for this, or so he claimed, was simply to get Cathcart out of the way so that his friend Baccri could operate without the clerk interfering. The voyage itself was merely a feint, a distraction, although it would also help speed things along and stop Hassan from harassing Barlow. The fact that nobody else knew anything about Barlow's ingenious plan at the time was, he argued, proof that it had worked so well.

Crucially, however, his story had no follow-through. We are left waiting to hear the Machiavellian masterstroke that Barlow and Baccri achieved once they were freed of Cathcart's supposed interference. But there was none: by that stage, Baccri had become a spent force as a palace advocate. He "now seemed unable to make the least impression" and the dey "forbade him . . . to speak to him any more about the Americans," as Barlow himself admitted [JB to DH, Apr. 5, 1796]. When success eventually came, it unfolded through a combination of JC's mission to America, the dogged financial footwork of RoB and JD, and, as we see later, the serendipity of the French consul's loan. (The gift of the frigate was arranged *before* Cathcart left.)

Yet almost in the same breath, Barlow couldn't resist claiming credit for the eventual success of the voyage that he claimed was a distraction: "It is in great measure owing to . . . this mission that we are now at peace." So, which was it? Fool's errand or game-changing mission? Barlow can't have it both ways.

Another problem is that Barlow's later revisionist account does not chime with his views at the time, when he claimed that the trip to the United States was "proof of his [the dey's] sincerity." Again, Barlow can't have it both ways—either the dey was a stooge, a puppet totally manipulated by Barlow, or he was acting of his own free will and showing sincerity. The two ideas cannot coexist.

Besides, if Barlow's prime motive was to get Cathcart out of the country, why would he have placed so many obstacles in the clerk's way? Why take such an icy attitude, and why refuse to expend a single dollar in helping him to leave? Why all the snide remarks about Cathcart's wanting to jump the queue to freedom when, according to Barlow's revisionism, the idea was Barlow's own and Cathcart had no say in the matter?

I think that by this stage readers know Hassan well enough to recognize him as a shrewd, battle-hardened statesman whose ruthless political intrigues were legendary. This was not a man who was likely to allow anyone to plant ideas in his head. Yet Barlow claims to have managed this remarkable feat of telepathy remotely via Baccri. One suspects that if anyone were playing anyone, it was probably Baccri playing Barlow. But by its very nature, the envoy's "mind meld" theory is as unfalsifiable as it is unverifiable.

I suspect the US government wasn't fooled for a moment by Barlow's reverse-engineered fantasy. Yet some nineteenth-century historians have cited it as fact—proof, I suppose, that Barlow's mind-melding powers continued long after his death.

Dey's three reasons: Author's views; *Danish plunder.* ★★JLC/JBN-TC, p. 257; *"favorite child"*: JB to Pickering, May 4, 1796, ★★ND.

"Subsisted on credit": JC to JA, Mar. 25, 1797, ★★FO.

Prosperous captives sometimes wanted to stay: e.g., Shaler's *Sketches*, p. 77, cited in Sumner, *Lecture on White Slavery in the Barbary States*, footnote 150; Laurent D'Arvieux, *Mémoires*, vol. 4 (1735); Braithwaite, *History of the Revolutions in Morocco*, pp. 185–87.

CHAPTER 28

Scipio Jackson's illness and murder. Foss, *A Journal of the Captivity and Sufferings of John Foss*, pp. 22, 75. Foss also describes beatings administered for fainting at work (p. 56). JC was at every American's funeral.

Keith, Lunt, Thomas: Todd, *Life and Letters of Joel Barlow*, p. 133 (on June 16).

CHAPTER 29

JC's departure from Algiers, quotes and poem: JC to TJ, Aug. 27, 1821, ★★FO; ★★JLC/JBN-TC, pp. 269–70, 274; JC to James Madison, Sept. 18, 1821, ★★FO.

"His mission did indeed save the peace": JC to James Madison, Sept. 18, 1821, ★★FO. JB seems to confirm this: "It is in a great measure owing to . . . this mission that we are now at peace with Algiers" (Todd, *Life and Letters of Joel Barlow*, p. 134).

JC voyage and arrival, dined with GW: ★★JLC/JBN-TC, p. 272; JC to JA, Mar. 25, 1797, ★★FO.

GW letter to dey: Dec. 3, 1796, ★★FO.

CHAPTER 30

Captives receive word, palace: Foss, *A Journal of the Captivity and Sufferings of John Foss*, pp. 64–65; Stevens, *An Historical and Geographical Account of Algiers*, pp. 86–88.

JD acquired funds; RoB voyage with cash, no insurance: JB to JD, July 12, 1796, ★★ND; DH to Secretary of State, Aug. 5, 1796, ★★ND; Stevens, *An Historical and Geographical Account of Algiers*, p. 82.

RoB captured in Tripoli: DH to Secretary of State, Oct. 6, 1796, and footnote, ★★ND; JB letter, Oct. 9, 1796, in Todd, *Life and Letters of Joel Barlow*, pp. 138–41; Stevens, *An Historical and Geographical Account of Algiers*, p. 82.

"The wind . . .": Todd, *Life and Letters of Joel Barlow*, p. 138.

French consul's $200,000 recycled: JB to Secretary of State, July 12, 1796, ★★ND; Todd, *Life and Letters of Joel Barlow*, p. 134; but in JB to JD (July 12, 1796, ★★ND), Barlow simply tells JD he has freed the captives "by drawing bills on you" (i.e., the Leghorn funds).

Barlow hero and quotes: Foss, *A Journal of the Captivity and Sufferings of John Foss*, p. 62; Stevens, *An Historical and Geographical Account of Algiers*, p. 88; *"benedictions," "angel"*: Todd, *Life and Letters of Joel Barlow*, p. 137.

Chartered ship, plague: JB to JD, July 12, 1796, ★★ND; JB to Calder, July 12, 1796, ★★ND; JB, *Passport*, July 12, 1796, ★★ND; JB to Secretary of State, July 12, 1796, ★★ND.

Eighty five or eighty-nine passengers: Stevens, *An Historical and Geographical Account of Algiers*, says 85 (p. 87); JB in *Passport* says 137 total on board, less 48 Neapolitans is 89.

Departure and disabled men: Todd, *Life and Letters of Joel Barlow*, pp. 135–36; Stevens, *An Historical and Geographical Account of Algiers*, p. 87.

"Eternal adieu" and voyage to Marseilles: Stevens, *An Historical and Geographical Account of Algiers*, pp. 88, 92–93, 281–82; Foss, *A Journal of the Captivity and Sufferings of John Foss*, pp. 65–68, 71– .

JC expenses, sold share in ship, "standing once more," briefed GW: ★★JLC/JBN-TC, pp. 272, 275; JC to JA, Mar. 25, 1797, ★★FO.

GW letter to dey: Dec. 3, 1796, ★★FO.

"Crowned with success": GW, *Speech*, Dec. 7, 1796, State Papers, vol. 1, p. 30.

Independent back to Algiers, JC's intention versus his orders: Pickering to JB, Dec. 3, 1796; ★★JLC/JBN-TC, pp. 275–76.

Stores and gift list: Pickering to DH, June 11, 1796, June 17, 1796, and May 13, 1797.

Cost close to $1,000,000: Allen, *Our Navy*, p. 56.

Swedish ship to Philadelphia, arrival at Marcus Hook, ice, Indian Queen: Stevens, *An Historical and Geographical Account of Algiers*, pp. 92–93; *Captain Schale*: Pickering to JB, May 13, 1797, ★★ND; *"thrill of joy"*: Sumner, *Lecture on White Slavery in the Barbary States*.

IS reunion with Hannah: JA to Abigail Adams, Feb. 9, 1797, ★★FO, the last sentence quoted is ambiguous; *Surprisingly curt*: JA to Abigail Adams, Feb. 9, 1797, ★★FO.

List of returnees: *American Captives released by Algiers, arrived in Philadelphia, Pa.*, ★★ND p. 116; author's analysis of numbers based on that list, on Foss's list (*A Journal of the Captivity and Sufferings of John Foss*, p. 71–), and on JC's list, ★★JLC/JBN-TC, p. 274; *Foss's separate trip*: See notes to final chapter. Either eighty-five or eighty-nine Americans had left Algiers.

JC unemployed and low on cash: JC to JA, Mar. 25, 1797, ★★FO.

JB's putdown: JB to Pickering, May 4, 1796, ★★ND.

JC nominated consul: JA to Senate, July 7, 1797.

Dey Hassan death: Maurice Le Clercq, *Le Tombeau des cinq deys d'Alger* (Clairmont, 1888), p. 49; RoB to Secretary of State, Jan. 23, 1799, ★★ND.

JC left for Algiers, arrival, meeting with new dey, demand for frigate: ★★JLC/JBN-TC, pp. 276–80; *new dey's hatred for predecessor*: RoB to Secretary of State, ★★ ND, p. 290.

TJ quotes about JC: TJ to Senator Abraham Baldwin, Feb. 10, 1802, ★★FO; TJ to JC, Sept. 10, 1821, ★★FO; also see preface to J. L. Cathcart and J. B. Newkirk, ed., *Tripoli . . . Letter Book* (La Porte, IN: Herald, 1901).

JQA on JC: JQA to Navy Commissioners, Dec. 14, 1819; enclosure with letter JC to TJ, Aug. 27, 1821; footnote 7 to letter JC to James Madison, Sept. 18, 1821, all, ★★FO.

DH "faithful and diligent public officer": Humphreys, *The Life and Times of David Humphreys*, p. 299.

Skjoldebrand quote: ★★JLC/JBN-TC, p. 227.

JB quote about JC, "considerable service," "intelligence and zeal": JB to Pickering, May 5, 1796.

Montgomery on JC: Christine E. Sears, *American Slaves and African Masters: Algiers and the Western Sahara 1776–1820* (New York: Palgrave Macmillan, 2012), p. 81. Recommended.

Remainder of chapter: Author's analysis, except JC quote "I arrived . . . ," etc.: JC to James Madison, Sept. 18, 1821, ★★FO.

AFTERLIVES

Adamses and TJ: Overview in *Encyclopaedia Britannica* (1911). Also see www.monti cello.org.

Barlow: "to devil": Todd, *Life and Letters of Joel Barlow*, p. 146; *controversial clause in treaty*: Article 11, ★★ND, p. 178; *later life and death*: *Encyclopaedia Britannica* (1911); *his personal slaves in United States*: Peter P. Hill, *Joel Barlow: American Diplomat and Nation Builder* (Washington, DC: Potomac Books, 2012), p. 102. Recommended.

Brooks: Stevens, *An Historical and Geographical Account of Algiers*, preface.

First and Second Barbary Wars: These conflicts lie outside the scope of our main story. Allen in *Our Navy* gives a very readable account of both; also see Lane-Poole, *The Barbary Corsairs*, chaps. 20–21. For more detail on the First Barbary War, see Cathcart, *Tripoli*.

JC and Eaton, Tripoli: Allen, *Our Navy*, p. 101, chaps. 14–15, p. 265; Goodin, "The Business, Personality and Discretionary Power of American Consuls in North Africa 1797–1805," p. 632 (my interpretation).

JC career, "wandering tribe," rheumatism, pleading for role: JC to TJ, Aug. 27, 1821; JC to James Madison, Sept. 18, 1821, with enclosures and footnotes, ★★FO; ★★JLC/JBN-TC, preface; *JC marriage, children*: *The Weekly Magazine*, Philadelphia, vol. 2, p. 224, June 5, 1798; ★★JLC/JBN-TC, p. 275.

Foss: Foss, *A Journal of the Captivity and Sufferings of John Foss*, pp. 69–70.

Hassan and final days of Algiers, Exmouth and French invasion, last dey, end of corsairs: Lane-Poole, *The Barbary Corsairs*, chap. 22; Embassy of Algeria, *History, Liste des dirigeants* . . .; M. Bajot, *Annales Maritimes et Coloniales* (Paris, 1831), chap. 1; Theodore de Quatrebarbes, *Souvenirs de la Campagne d'Afrique* (Angers: Chateau, 1831).

Humphreys: Humphreys, *The Life and Times of David Humphreys*; *Yankee*: Humphreys, *The Life and Times of David Humphreys*, p. 333; *sheep*: Humphreys, *The Life and Times of David Humphreys*, chap. 15.

JC falling-out with RoB: JC to William Eaton, Nov. 9, 1799, in J. L. Cathcart and J. B. Newkirk, J. B. (ed.) *Tripoli* . . . *Letter Book* (La Porte, 1901) with a sanitized version of the confrontation (pp. 51 and 95).

RoB later life, expenses, death: Footnote to James Madison's letter to James Monroe, Sept. 6, 1819, ★★FO; Obituary in *The American Volunteer*, Feb. 19, 1824; obit in *Harrisburg Chronicle*, Feb. 26, 1824.

IS quotes, jobs sought: IS to JA, May 30, 1797, Mar. 23, 1798, and July 11, 1799; see also notes to Hannah's petition to GW, Dec. 9, 1791; *returnees left to wander*: Stevens, *An Historical and Geographical Account of Algiers*, pp. 92–93; *no financial aid*: note to Hannah's petition to GW, Dec. 9, 1791, ★★FO.